In Safe Hands

True Stories about the Men and Women of United States Customs and Border Protection

Michael H. Cunningham

Library of Congress Control Number: 2008909790
ISBN: Hardcover   978-1-4363-8141-3
              Softcover   978-1-4363-8140-6

All royalties the author receives from the sale of this book will be donated to JR Safety Crib Sheets Inc., *www.babysheets.com*.

To order additional copies of this book, contact:
Xlibris Corporation
1-888-795-4274
www.Xlibris.com
Orders@Xlibris.com
53536

CONTENTS

Dedication

To the officers of U.S. Customs and Border Protection, the members of our Armed Forces, and all the others striving to keep America safe.

Additionally, to my entire family but especially to my grandchildren: Ashley, Shannon, Jimmy, Liam, Meghan, Kaylin, Stephen, Erin, and Lauren.

PREFACE

The following stories—*forty-one* in all—are all basically true. However, I must mention the following to the reader: for privacy concerns, I have only used the first names of most of the participants. Usually this name is real, but you will not see any last names. The story "M/T *Orion*" has been fictionalized. However, it is based on a true event and follows the real story closely. In other stories I have changed the names of ships and individuals to protect their privacy. In "Treachery and Deception," I noted in the body of the text that I am rearranging some facts to protect a confidential source. Everything else in the book was written as I saw it and should be accurate.

The reason for my writing this book was simple. I spent some twenty-eight years in U.S. Customs or Customs and Border Protection,* and I loved almost every minute of it. There were only a few moments when I wished I was somewhere else besides Customs. These moments were indeed fleeting.

---

* In March of 2003, in order to form a more productive and efficient agency, Immigration and Naturalization Service (INS) and U.S. Customs were merged to form United States Customs and Border Protection. Our new title became officer, and we were no longer called inspectors. This merger was obviously a result of the events of 9/11 and was an attempt to improve the security of our nation. Although the merger has not been seamless, things are improving every day; and in the long run, the merger will prove to be a success and one of the best things to result from that tragic day.

I worked with some of the most intelligent, competent, motivated, and dedicated people in law enforcement. They gave up much of their personal life because of the needs of this country—and they are still sacrificing and will do so in the future. So I thought it would be nice to tell a few stories about them. Also about other people who are daily working to keep America safe, especially the United States Coast Guard and the Massachusetts State Police. Whenever we called out for help, these two agencies always stepped up and responded to our requests for assistance.

I have read and reread this text countless times. Hopefully, I have edited properly, and I have removed anything that would be offensive or would be useful to people who wish us harm.

My motivation for writing this book is to let the public know what a wonderful group of people they can rely on to keep America free and safe. The officers from United States Customs and Border Protection deserve no less, and I hope my efforts show to the citizens of America how wonderful these folks are. They are *in safe hands* with the men and women of Customs and Border Protection.

FORWARD

I first learned to appreciate the United States Customs and Border Protection Agency when I bought my wife a necklace for our silver wedding anniversary. I bought the necklace in London, unable to resist it but knowing its value far exceeded the amount I was allowed to import into the US. I confess there was a sneaking temptation to bury it at the bottom of the suitcase and pretend it was not there, but I sensibly did the honest thing and declared it. I was sent to a desk where two grave-faced men in uniform opened the case and stared at the necklace.

"Lot of money," one man said, fingering the receipt.

"It is a special occasion," I said.

"Couldn't buy one in the States?" the second man asked.

"Not like that," I said.

The first man peered at the platinum and diamonds. "My wife would kill for something like that," he said wistfully.

"Special occasion?" the second man asked sternly, "or special woman?"

"Very special woman," I said truthfully.

The first man touched the necklace. "Looks like cubic zirconium to me," he said derisively, "probably not worth twenty bucks."

"You're wasting our time," the second man said. The necklace's case was closed and the suitcase was zipped up. "Get outta here."

I got out of there, smiling. Discretion had been used, and though the United States Treasury might not have approved, those customs officers had shown that they were there for a far more important purpose than collecting a few bucks from honest travelers. I was impressed.

I had another stroke of luck a couple of years later when I had nothing at all to declare, though the officer who inspected my passport decided that I looked distinctly suspicious and ordered me to a line of other suspicious-looking people, all of us presumably destined for a thorough search. A more senior officer came down the line. "What are you doing here?" he demanded of me.

"I've no idea," I said truthfully.

"Got anything to declare?"

"Nothing."

"What's your job?" he asked.

"I'm a novelist."

He paused and stared at me. I thought I must have said the wrong thing and had visions of a body search in whatever dungeon they keep for offensive-looking novelists in the bowels of Logan Airport. Then, to my relief, he said, "you shouldn't be in this line," before adding, "I've written a book." And that was how I met Mike Cunningham.

That book was *Walking Point*, a memoir of Mike's service in Vietnam, and one of the best books I have read about that war. It is, and this is a compliment, a plain book. It speaks eloquently of the experience of war, but does not attempt to invest that experience with any pretentious meaning. Mike was there, and he remembers it, and he tells it as it was, and the reader comes away with an overwhelming impression of a decent man who served his country to the best of his considerable ability. Mike's experience in Vietnam is typical of most men who saw action, and the country should be proud of him and the thousands like him.

In Safe Hands continues that story, only in this book Mike Cunningham is fighting a different war against an even more elusive enemy. He is still walking point, though. Whether boarding a ship in icy seas, patrolling the pine-silent border of Canada or waiting for a swallower to disgorge poisonous parcels, Mike is fighting for us. *In Safe Hands* gives a broad and fascinating picture of the men and women who protect our borders. Most of us only encounter the United States Customs and Border Protection Agency when we arrive at airports, but this book paints a much larger picture. An officer greeting you in customs may not care about your silver-wedding present, but he or she does care about America. As Mike writes, 'this is the United States of America, the greatest country in the whole wide world, and I firmly believe all our efforts in accomplishing this mission is worth it. To take any other course of action would be a failure and weaken the fabric that holds and binds this country.' Mike is right. He is retired now, and I hope he has time for his much loved family, but he spent a lifetime fighting for the other thing he loves, his country, and we should be grateful.

Bernard Cornwell, OBE
Author of the Sharpe Books

ONE

NCIC

Today, December 29, 2005, on our flight from Iceland, we have an NCIC (National Crime Information Center) lookout from the state of Virginia. A call was made to the ORI (originating office), and they confirmed the warrant and said they would extradite.

I was roving the primary lines and, as usual, picking people out of line who needed assistance and escorting them to the head of the line. I think all the passengers appreciate this effort of ours, whether they are the recipients or not. There was a young couple with two little kids far back in the U.S. citizens' line. The father was obviously military by his demeanor, dress, and haircut (high and tight). I escorted them directly to a booth to be processed and waited for them on the other side. Once they were processed, I assisted them onto the elevator, which brought us down to the baggage floor. I directed them to the proper carousel and then left to do other assigned tasks.

As I was contemplating my next move, I noticed four inspectors processing a family at one of the secondary belts. This caught my attention because whenever you see so many inspectors together, something is up. As I looked further, I saw the family was the same one that I expedited not fifteen minutes earlier.

My initial inquiries to the inspectors shocked me. They told me the NCIC hit mentioned above was for the mother of this family. If this was true, we were going to have to arrest her, separate her from her two little kids and husband, and turn her over to the Massachusetts State Police for extradition to Virginia. Well, I thought, my on-time exit from work is going to be put on hold. I couldn't leave knowing the plight of this family. My conscience wouldn't allow it.

After questioning the wife and husband, not the entire truth came out, but we pretty much had a good insight into what was going on. Four years ago (2001), while the husband was deployed overseas with the U.S. Navy, the eight-month-pregnant wife embezzled either $7,000 or $13,000 from the company she worked for. She was caught, arrested, and prosecuted. Obviously, the judge had sympathy for this twenty-year-old young lady, pregnant with her first child and her husband overseas fighting for his country. The judge ordered her to pay $175 a month in restitution and put her on probation.

It seems the wife told her husband what happened when he was away but failed to go into all the details. If she had continued paying the court-ordered $175 a month, everything would have been OK. However, she said her mother died, they ran into personal and financial troubles, and she simply stopped payments. This led to an active warrant being issued in 2003 out of the state of Virginia for violation of probation.

The majority of international travelers have their names run through numerous databases in an attempt to screen out terrorists, drug smugglers, NCIC fugitives, etc. Thus, as the wife and husband and their two little children were coming home for the Christmas holidays from overseas, her name was routinely run. Now she was in a dire predicament.

Imagine how we felt when we understood the whole story. Did she do wrong? Absolutely, but were there extenuating circumstances? Wasn't there an alternative? We called and virtually pleaded with the Virginia authorities not to extradite, but they were adamant. We talked with the Massachusetts State Police, and they were as sympathetic as us, but they couldn't find any wiggle room either.

Consequently, the wife was going to be arrested and jailed at a local facility until the authorities from Virginia came to pick her up. As we were preparing to separate the wife from her family, we kept asking ourselves, "Isn't there any way around this?" Then the deus ex machina! One of the inspectors asked if she was breast-feeding the youngest child. The wife said yes and this is why she was even more upset. The baby wouldn't take formula, and she didn't know what would happen to the baby's health.

With this newfound information, we called Virginia and told them the baby's health was in jeopardy if we separated the mother from him. Virginia immediately concurred and cancelled the extradition process.

As we packed up all their bags, we stressed to the wife and husband to go home and straighten this matter out. They assured us they would. Because their next flight wasn't till the morning, they had to stay at a local hotel for the night. We personally escorted them to a hotel and made sure they were all set. As we were leaving, we told the wife how good we felt not having to lock her up. With tears flowing down her cheek and in between spasmodic waves of sobbing, she thanked us and wished us a merry Christmas. Her little daughter waved as she was entering the elevator, smiled, and said thank-you.

TWO

Khat

Heavy snow is predicted for today. Logan should get six inches before it is all over. Delays, confusion, and a lot of disgruntled travelers is the local forecast. Midway Airport in Chicago had a Southwest aircraft slide off the runway upon landing last night. No one on the plane was hurt, but tragically, a six-year-old boy was killed in a vehicle on the ground when hit by the plane.

Ever heard of it? According to the Partnership for a Drug-Free America, khat is a plant grown primarily in East Africa and the Arabian Peninsula. It is usually chewed and has a hallucinogenic effect. To maintain its potency, khat must be consumed fresh. It is the drug of choice for the indigenous people of East Africa, whether they reside there or here in the United States.

Our experience in the Port of Boston with khat is quite extensive. We have made seizures of this drug for many years with no abatement in sight. Usually, khat is imported from England via passengers. They are white, young (twenties), and unemployed. There are many different groups in England responsible for coordinating the export of khat to America. Here in the Port of Boston, we have experienced the majority of our smugglers originating in the northeastern part of England, specifically Newcastle. Usually the potential smuggler is approached in their hometown (Newcastle) by a "friend" who knows they are down on their luck. This friend feels them out to determine if they would be receptive to smuggling khat. If it is determined they are, this friend makes arrangements for them to be transported by car to London. Once they are in London, they meet the controller who is usually a black male. The controller sets them up for the night at a local hotel, gives them some spending money to buy beer in one of the many surrounding pubs, and makes arrangements to pick them up in the morning.

While it's bright and early, the controller picks up his smugglers and transports them to Heathrow Airport so they can make a direct flight from London to Boston. Once at the airport, the controller gives them two bags each along with a round-trip airline ticket. This is the first time they have seen these bags and don't even know what is in them.

Their instructions are clear and simple: Take the two bags each, and check them in at the ticket counter. Proceed to the boarding gate and await departure. Once they board, they enjoy a pleasant trip. After approximately a five-hour flight, they arrive in Boston, Massachusetts. As they wait to deplane, the smugglers' heart rate increases, and the palms of their hands become cold and clammy. Up to this point, everything is easy. However, now they have to confront the government officials from the United States (Customs and Border Protection). If they make it past them, everything will be OK. They will have a successful smuggling mission under their belt and will be richly rewarded for their efforts.

The smugglers join the end of the line waiting to be processed by the Immigration officials. It is a long line (or queue as the Brits say), and they are extremely nervous and fidgety. *Can't be too nervous*, they think to themselves. If they are, one of the many roving inspectors will notice and pull them out of line for inspection. Luckily for them, they are admitted into the country with no problems. They are the beneficiaries of the U.S. visa waiver program (visitors from "friendly countries" can enter the United States without the need of a visa). They now go downstairs, claim their bags, and exit the Customs Hall after turning in the Customs Declaration at the exit control point. Only one problem—an agriculture specialist. He is screening all the passengers leaving the Customs Hall and referring anyone he deems suspicious for smuggling agriculture products to the officers manning the X-ray machine.

A view of the X-ray screen shows something suspicious in a suitcase. The agriculture specialist takes a look at the screen and tells his counterpart it looks like khat. He has seen khat many times in the past. The suitcase is opened, and his suspicions are confirmed. The owner of the bag is standing there looking like a deer in headlights.

The agriculture specialist calls over the Customs and Border Protection supervisor on duty and apprises him of what is going on. The supervisor, having been down this road before, leaps into action. He knows khat smugglers usually travel in pairs and asks this guy whom he is traveling with. Where is he? The smuggler initially claims ignorance of the whole thing, but after a few sharp words from the supervisor, he tells all. His buddy already went out the Customs Hall and should be waiting for him in the lobby. Once they meet up, they were instructed to go to a hotel on McClellan Highway in East Boston. Reservations for a room were made in advance for them. Once they were in their room, they were to call back to London and tell them everything was OK. London would call their contact in Boston, and this third individual would come to the hotel to pick up the khat. The smugglers would be paid off, spend the night at the hotel, and catch a flight in the morning. Only this time things were going to be different.

The supervisor told two inspectors to put on civilian jackets and follow the smuggler out into the lobby. The smuggler was told to meet up with his buddy in order for us to identify him. After a fifteen-minute search to no avail, the inspectors and the smuggler returned to the Customs Hall. Plan A failed, now it was time to implement Plan B.

A call was made to verify if these guys truly had reservations at the hotel. It wouldn't be the first time that the bad guys gave us bad information. The call not only verified the reservations, but the desk clerk told us one of the guys had actually checked in. (This had to be the guy who got through. He must have been spooked and left the airport without his partner.) Now what? We made a quick decision—to go get this guy and the khat. An agent from Immigration and Customs Enforcement and an inspector immediately left for the hotel.

When they arrived at the hotel, they were given the room number by the clerk at the front desk and proceeded to that location. The second smuggler quickly answered a knock on the door. He stood sheepishly at the door and said, "I've been waiting for you." The agent and the inspector escorted the smuggler back to the airport, along with his two khat-laden suitcases.

After a couple of hours of processing the seizure and the individuals, we finally wrapped everything up. The total weight of the khat was just shy of two hundred pounds. Both individuals were put on the last flight of the night destined for London.

Typical fifty-to-one-hundred-pound khat seizure in two suitcases

Two of Customs and Border Protection's finest

THREE

Mung Chua Giang Sinh

T he following story is the result of a chance meeting between Joe Bodanza and me sometime in 1996. I was the shift supervisor for U.S. Customs at Logan Airport, and we were waiting for a flight to arrive from the Far East via JFK Airport in New York City. It was brought to my attention that two gentlemen wanted to come into the Customs Hall and meet the flight at the Jetway. This is obviously forbidden, and I was upset at the inspector who relayed the request to me until the inspector fully explained the circumstances. These two gentlemen were meeting four children who were coming from Vietnam and confined to wheelchairs. When I heard this, I personally escorted the two gentlemen to the Jetway—one of them being Joe Bodanza—and we have been good friends ever since.

Today, four old grizzly Vietnam veterans took a ride to Leominster, Massachusetts, to visit some Vietnamese kids, give them some Christmas gifts, and wish them a merry Christmas. Bob and I met at the Veterans Outreach Center in Kenmore Square and then drove to the Riverside MBTA Station to pick up Tom and Dave. Bob is unemployed (never really has been employed since Vietnam), is 100 percent disabled with post-traumatic stress disorder (PTSD). He was a door gunner with the 101st Airborne. Tom, retired from the post office, is also 100 percent disabled with PTSD and was a marine grunt.

9

Dave, a local college professor, is 70 percent disabled with PTSD. I myself am finishing up my thirtieth year of service with the U.S. government, am 50 percent disabled with PTSD, and was a grunt with the Americal Division.

We left the Riverside MBTA station en route to visit Joe Bodanza in Leominster. Joe, an earthly angel, is a retired advertising salesman and, for the past ten years or so, has brought severely disabled and handicapped Vietnamese kids to this country to seek medical attention. Thus, the purpose of our trip. The four of us wanted to visit Joe and his kids and to bring some joy into their lives. Actually, it was more than that. It was also extremely therapeutic for us.

We arrived in the early afternoon and were met by Thanh Nguyen. He was outside on the front lawn cooking spareribs on the barbecue, wearing a New England Patriots hooded coat. I yelled at him to come in with us, and he said he'd be right in. As we approached Joe's apartment, as usual, the door was wide open. We were greeted by Joe, Jim (another Vietnam veteran from a nearby town), Thao, Sang, and Sang's aunt whose name escapes me. We exchanged pleasantries and nervously milled around a cluttered table, which Joe used as a desk and a dinner table. Joe introduced us to everyone, and as he was finishing, Thanh bounded in from the cold with a plateful of spareribs. I have met Thanh on previous trips to Leominster and am truly impressed with his courage and determination to succeed.

Thanh, twenty-one years old, came to America from Vietnam on September 20, 2001, in an attempt to have his polio-deformed body repaired by the doctors and surgeons at the Shriners Hospital. Four years later, Thanh is still here. He is studying at a local college and wants to stay in America and study to become a doctor. He plans to return to Vietnam someday and help his countrymen with their medical problems. Thanh is from Ben Tre; and his mother, Tuyet, and two brothers, Thai and Vu, are back home. Thanh is an inspirational speaker and regaled us with stories of back home. Fishing in the Mekong River for tilapia, a thick bony fish, was a memorable story and brought a gleam to his eyes as he spoke. Thanh explained how people worked in Vietnam for $1 a day and how a family of four considered a yearly income of $300 quite acceptable. As Thanh spoke, we could only sit and shake our heads. Every once in a while a grunt or groan was emitted from one of us as we sat spellbound. Thanh hates communism, saying "They s——." He said they only take care of themselves. Bribery and corruption is everywhere. Thanh, whether he realizes it or not, has become more American than Vietnamese. I hope his dreams come true and he returns to Vietnam as a doctor.

Also in the room were Sang and his aunt from Georgia. Sang, a recent arrival from Tra Vinh, is thirteen years old and is suffering from severe spinal abnormalities. He has undergone several operations at Shriners and has a tough road ahead. The operations have helped his breathing enormously, but he is still confined to a wheelchair, and there are many more extensive medical procedures in his future.

Thao, a sweet, friendly young lady of seventeen, comes from Ben Tre and was severely burned over the majority of her body. Her injuries are indescribable and will remain private. The doctors will do all they can for her.

As we sat around and engaged in small talk, Dave and Tom suggested taking Thao and Sang's aunt to the mall. Thao smiled nervously but demurely. Joe interjected and said that it was a great idea. So off they went. The girls were bubbling over with joy. Trips out of the house were infrequent for them. Trips to the mall almost never happened.

Bob, Jim, Joe, and I remained at the apartment with Sang. Jim and I talked about our experiences. Bob and Sang engaged themselves in a SpongeBob jigsaw puzzle. Joe was on the phone making medical appointments and paying bills online. Once Joe was off the phone, he explained to us how appreciative he was for our visit. In the past ten years, Joe has brought over eighty kids from Vietnam. The vast majority have received as much medical treatment as possible and then went back home to Vietnam. (Sadly, one child died here in America while he was receiving treatment.) Joe told us about his monumental bills and how appreciative he was to Shriners for offering free medical care for all the kids.

About one hour elapsed when Dave and Tom returned from the mall with the girls. They were even more excited now than when they left. A shopping spree and a couple of hot fudge sundaes did wonders for their dispositions. Just the look on their faces did wonders for *our* dispositions.

Well, it is time to go. After a visit of about three hours, we decided we better be off. We presented Joe with a significant gift (more than what a family of four in Vietnam considered to be a good yearly income) and began to say good-bye. There was many a teary eye as we left. The girls were smiling and waving. Sang reached out his hand and shook our hands. I wanted to go, but I wanted to stay. I had to go. Joe walked us out to the lobby. Joe looked into my eyes as I left and said, "Remember, Mike, Thao needs to be adopted. She has nowhere to go back in Vietnam." My mind was racing. *Please, Joe, don't do this to me.* I left Vietnam over thirty-five years ago, but I was still there. Would it ever end? What we experienced in Vietnam will remain with us for the rest of our days. That is why we were in Leominster that cold December day. Somewhere, deep in our hearts, we are all seeking answers. Someday, with God's help, we will find them. Until then, hopefully we will find an answer to Thao's quest for adoption.

Merry Christmas to all!

Joe, me, and some of the kids at a park

FOUR

Seaport Security

Since September 11, 2001, everything has changed on this job. The airport environment has received the majority of the attention mostly because of what happened at the World Trade Center in New York City. This reaction is understandable and warranted. However, my contention and beliefs are a bit different than most others. What's new! I believe you must think like the bad guys. They know they already put a hurt on us by using airplanes. They also know we are all over the airports. Massachusetts State Police, Transportation Security Administration, Customs and Border Protection, Air Marshals, FBI, and local police—just to name some of the agencies involved in airport security. To pull off what they did four years ago is still possible but, hopefully, not probable. Besides, they already beat us in this arena. Might they try somewhere else? The Coast Guard and Customs and Border Protection are the lead agencies on the seaport. The following story illustrates how we accomplish our mission on the waterfront.

The Ship

During the month of May 2001, we had an LNG vessel unloading at a facility in Everett, Massachusetts. There was another LNG vessel anchored offshore at the Broad Sound Anchorage. (This is a body of water, about ten miles out of the Port of Boston, designated as a holding area for ships waiting to come to the dock. Ships will lie here if the dock they are going to is already occupied or if their draft is too deep to transit the harbor safely until they lighter into a barge.) This ship was going to be sitting out there at anchorage for at least a few days if not longer. The ship unloading at the dock was going to be sailing soon, but in order for the ship at anchorage to come in and unload, the shoreside storage tanks would have to be empty (at least the majority of the product would have to be used up). Otherwise, there wasn't any room for the cargo. Since this ship was arriving into the United States direct from Algeria and had an all-Algerian crew, the decision was made to board her at the Broad Sound Anchorage. This decision was correct and based on sound principles.

To board and conduct a search of a vessel at sea requires coordination and cooperation among many different state, local and federal agencies. Especially so in this case because we wanted to make an exhaustive sweep and search of this vessel looking not only for drugs but primarily for explosives and weapons of mass destruction (WMDs). Therefore, the normal participants to search a vessel—the U.S. Coast Guard and U.S. Customs (we were still called U.S. Customs at this time; it wasn't until March of 2003 when our name was changed to Customs and Border Protection)—would be augmented by the Massachusetts State Police Bomb Unit, Massachusetts State Police Dive Unit, and Massachusetts Marine Patrol.

Our plan was to board the vessel with a boarding party consisting of units from the U.S. Coast Guard, U.S. Customs, and the State Police Bomb Squad. In addition to this boarding team, the Massachusetts State Police would join in our efforts by providing several dive teams to search the entire hull of the vessel. With all these highly trained personnel, we felt quite comfortable that a complete and exhaustive search of the vessel would be conducted.

As usual, well-planned events usually go awry to some extent. Today was not an exception. As the flotilla of law enforcement vessels headed out from the Boston Coast Guard base at the foot of Hanover Street, the weather was seasonally warm and the seas flat calm. We had two 41' Coast Guard boats, and the State Police had two boats to assist their dive teams. As we were transiting Boston Harbor, everyone onboard was jockeying for a comfortable position. The boats were crowded, and there basically was standing room only. As we rounded Deer Island Light and headed up the North Channel, a slight sea swell was detected in my legs, and a visual observation of the sea surface confirmed my physical feeling. This was not a good sign. If we had a swell as we rounded Deer Island, what were the sea conditions going to be like out in Broad Sound? This was of much concern because if the swell was too bad, the divers wouldn't be able to go into the water. Thus a hull search wouldn't be accomplished. We cleared the North Channel and headed directly toward the ship. She loomed majestically dead ahead at a distance of about three miles. As I feared, the swell increased dramatically the farther we went. I knew the State Police Dive Team would do everything they could, but there were limits and the safety of the divers was paramount. The lieutenant and commander of the dive team was on scene, and no one could ask for anyone better.

As we approached the vessel, the swell was running about six to eight feet. The sea running alongside the hull of the ship looked ominous and dangerous. I knew a dive was impossible. The sea conditions were too severe and the risk too high.

The lieutenant waved and took off with his two boats and divers, heading for the ship. I held an impromptu meeting with everyone onboard my 41' and the other 41', which was lying alongside. We had already laid down all the plans and areas of responsibility when we were ashore; I just wanted to reinforce everything. Of particular concern to me were the State Police K-9 units. We were used to boarding vessels at sea, but their K-9s weren't. I wanted to make sure they were comfortable and knew what to expect.

Once I felt we were all set, I instructed the boat coxswain to bring us alongside the ship. There was an accommodation ladder extending from the main deck to three feet above the water's surface—a distance of between forty feet to fifty feet—which was going to be our access to the vessel. The 41-footers pulled alongside the accommodation ladder, and we began to disembark and scramble up the ladder. This was a tricky maneuver because of the sea swell. Your timing had to be exact when you made the jump from the Coast Guard boat to the ladder. If you missed the ladder, you could go into the water and perhaps even be crushed between the Coast Guard boat and the ship. It was in everybody's best interest to use extreme caution.

It took about fifteen minutes to get everyone onboard because there were so many of us, including the dogs. While we were continuing the boarding process, I instructed four inspectors to proceed to the captain's cabin and have him coordinate rounding up all the forty crew members to the mess deck. As I was doing this, I received a call from the dive team. He told me it was too rough to dive. If a diver was under the hull of the ship and was hit by one of these swells, he could be killed. I told him not to worry about it.

About this time, everyone was onboard, and we spread out to cover our areas of responsibility. I proceeded to climb the exterior ladders of the ship headed for the captain's cabin. As I was climbing the ladder, I looked out over the water's surface. I saw the 41' Coast Guard boats. They were circling the ship at about one hundred yards' distance. There would be a boat on either side of the ship the entire time we were to be onboard. This sight gave me a comforting feeling. Knowing they were out there and ensuring no one snuck up on us made me feel comfortable. Also, if we needed anything, they were there waiting to respond to any of our requests.

I reached the captain's cabin virtually out of breath. He cordially greeted me and warmly offered me something to drink. I respectfully declined and asked the captain if he was briefed on what we were about to do. He said, "Yes. Yes." The inspectors I sent before me fully explained to him what was expected. In fact, he had already given the order to all the crew to muster on the mess deck. "Good," I said, and I began to relax. Once we got all the crew secured on the mess deck and made sure everyone was present and accounted for, we would sweep the entire vessel looking for stowaways. The boarding team members had already received their area of responsibility to search, and once I gave the order, they would be off. The team assigned to "babysit" the crew on the mess deck called me on the radio and told me everyone was accounted for. I said fine and requested the initial search to begin. This process took approximately a half hour. Once we felt comfortable that there weren't any stowaways onboard, we initiated the systematic search of the entire vessel with drugs, explosives, and anything terrorist related as our goal. Depending on the size of the vessel and the size and skill of the boarding team, ship searches can take hours. It is exhausting and grueling work that can tire out the search teams pretty quickly. Therefore, I instructed everyone to take his or her time—be slow, safe, and methodical. Just because a crewman's cabin has been searched doesn't really mean it has been searched. Some inspectors will go into a cabin, look around for a few minutes, say it is OK, and walk out. This is not a good search. You have to go in, lift ceiling panels, crawl on your hands and knees, and really dig. Otherwise, what is the use of searching?

Three interesting things happened on this search. One, we found a few grams of hashish in an unoccupied cabin. The crew knew where to hide their stuff, if it was found, the authorities couldn't hold anyone directly responsible. If we found hash in someone's cabin, the story would be different.

The second interesting thing that happened on this boarding is also rather embarrassing for me to even mention. I had put an inspector on the mess deck to watch the sequestered crew while the rest of us were searching the ship. This is a simple operation that we have conducted on countless ships before. There has never been a problem until today. Seems the inspector guarding the crew became quite concerned with some of the crewmen's actions and behavior. A couple had homemade knives (actually they were pieces of metal ground down so they had a sharp point), and they were flipping these knives around in the mess deck, all the while glaring at the inspector. The inspector became nervous and fearful and called me on the radio. He told me he was nervous and wanted someone with him. I didn't take his words too seriously. I reacted slowly to his request for help and actually responded personally but in my own sweet time. When I arrived, even I was shocked. A few of the crew members did have knives on them and were acting in a threatening fashion. I called for a few more inspectors to respond to the mess deck. My intentions were to pat everyone down and to take away anything that was remotely dangerous. Obviously some of the crew spoke English and overheard my radio conversation because there was a bunch of chitchat among them, and then knives began to be thrown in a corner. They were dumping the evidence. When help arrived, we did pat down everyone, but all the knives had been dumped. These guys were serious punks, and we had to stay on guard with them. I bolstered the guard on the mess deck to three inspectors and relieved the original inspector and had him search with the rest of the guys. I felt bad and promised myself I wouldn't do something stupid like this again.

The last interesting item to mention about this boarding is a positive one and is directly related to the previous two items. We found hash onboard, and although it was a small amount, we knew there was more somewhere. We also knew these guys were bad apples. Then a thought came to me. Even if we couldn't find the drugs, I was going to make damn sure whoever was on this ship was going to be onboard when she sailed out of the port. In pursuit of this objective, I asked one of the inspectors to go see the captain and obtain all the passports of the crewmen. I wanted the inspector to use the ship's copying machine and copy the biographical page of each passport. On this page, there was a picture of the crewmen and all his pertinent biographical information. Jim looked quizzically at me when I made this request. I explained to him that I wanted documentary evidence of all forty crewmen onboard because when the ship sailed for foreign in a week or so, we were going to reboard the vessel and make sure all forty crewmen were onboard. We remained onboard the ship for about four hours. We searched the entire vessel with negative results; only a couple of grams of hash. After consulting with all the boarding team members at an all-hands muster, I determined the search was complete and we could leave the vessel. The State Police Bomb Squad was completely satisfied that there wasn't anything onboard, and they were happy with the search. Therefore, after a lengthy and thorough search of the vessel, we began to disembark.

The disembarkation was as tricky as the embarkation. Perhaps it was even trickier because now everyone was tired and hungry. I stood at the head of the gangway and cautioned everyone as they proceeded to leave the ship. I told them to hang on, to pay attention, and to be careful as they stepped off the gangway onto the Coast Guard boat. We made it this far without an accident and I didn't want anything to happen now. I was the last to leave.

The ship did indeed enter the Port of Boston five days later. She tied up at the facility in Everett on Friday morning, and we learned from the Boston Pilots that she was scheduled to depart the following morning at 0900 hours. Plan B was about to unfold.

At 0700 hours on Saturday, the team met at our office at the Conley Terminal in South Boston. We were about to carry out our plans that were formulated on the ship about a week ago. Armed with forty pieces of paper that had the photographs and biographical information of every crew member, we were going to reboard the ship and conduct a complete muster of the crew. The forty crew members who arrived in Boston had best be onboard and ready to sail, or else they better have a reason why they aren't there—that is, they signed off the vessel. We swung by the pilot's office to confirm the sailing time. Luckily we did this, because the pilot on duty told us the sailing of the ship was delayed until 1100 hours. At about 1000 hours, we checked on the ship's sailing time. He confirmed an 1100-hour sailing, and we decided it was time to board the ship. The drive over to Everett only took fifteen minutes. As we were driving over, we could see the tugs heading over to the ship, which confirmed a sailing was imminent. We parked our vehicle in the parking lot. I waved and said hi to the security guard and asked him how his night was. He said it was slow and then showed me the log-in sheet. This sheet is a log of everyone who either goes on or comes off the vessel. I scanned the sheet with my tired but critical eyes. As I was looking at the sheet, I said, "Look at this guy. Look at how often he left the vessel. And look at the hour of the day. And look for how short a time he was ashore." Seamen go ashore for a few different reasons: to go shopping, to go see a girl, or to go to one of the local bars. It is normal for a crew member to go ashore once or maybe twice in a twenty-four-hour period when their ship is tied up. Since the ship was in port for twenty four hours, I expected to see each crew member logged out once or twice. However, there was one crew member, the assistant cook, who left the vessel four times. Not only this, but he left in the middle of the night when he couldn't go shopping, couldn't go see a girl, and couldn't go buy a drink. Also, he only left the ship for a few minutes. I could actually visualize what he was up to. He left the ship (for the third time) at 0310 hours and returned at 0315 hours, and then he left (for the fourth time) at 0405 hours and returned at 0410 hours.

We boarded the ship and headed directly to the captain's cabin. Once we arrived, we exchanged the normal courtesies. I puttered around a bit and asked the captain if I could see the box containing all the passports. The captain readily complied but explained he was quite busy. The tugs were alongside, and they were singling up all lines. Now my attitude changed. I told the captain I didn't care about the tugs alongside or about anything else. The ship would sail when we said it could, no sooner. I told the captain we wanted to talk to this individual who had gone ashore four times (the assistant cook). I requested the captain to go find this guy and to bring him to the captain's cabin. The captain immediately called the chief mate on the radio and relayed our request. He told us the crewman would be in his cabin momentarily. After a five-minute wait, the crewman entered the captain's cabin. *So this is the guy with such bizarre traveling habits*, I thought. Because the ship was due to sail, I got right down to business. I attempted to interview the crewman and have him explain his travels. However, because he could only speak French, we had to use the captain as an interpreter. I hate using interpreters because of the time delay between your question and the subject's reply, but we had no choice. Even with the time delay, we could all tell something was wrong with this guy. He was contradicting himself constantly, and his carotid artery was bulging out of his neck. At this point, we decided to search his cabin; however, we were going to do things a little different. We were not sure of the location of this guy's cabin, and because everyone else was at their stations for leaving port, no one was available to show us. We would have to have the crewman show us his cabin in person. This procedure was out of the norm. Usually, we would not permit the crew member to be present when we searched his room. This was for safety concerns for the inspectors. If we found something illegal in the cabin, you never knew how the crew member would react. He could become violent and pose a threat to the inspectors. Today we didn't have a choice.

The inspectors escorted the crew member out of the captain's cabin to locate and search his room. I stayed behind with the captain. He was on the phone explaining to everyone the reason for the delay in sailing.

The captain was highly agitated and wanted to know from me when he could sail. I told him as soon as we were finished searching this crewman's cabin. (Our original intent on being onboard was to conduct a departure crew muster. This idea was lost in the dust of our newfound information.) An inspector's voice came crackling over the radio, "Mike, Mike, you better get down here." My heart began to race. *Oh boy*, I thought, *they have something.* I left the captain's cabin, talking on the radio, "Where are you? Where are you?" He replied, "Two decks down." I slid down two flights of stairs, turned a corner, and saw one of the inspectors in the doorway of the crew member's room. *What the hell*, I thought. As I approached the room, the other inspector was dragging the handcuffed crew member out of the cabin and into the passageway. Obviously, an explanation was forthcoming.

With the captain right on my heels, I approached the inspectors and said, "What's up?" They were holding something in their hands, which was wrapped in some kind of cellophane. As I looked at the package, they slowly folded back the wrapping, and I immediately recognized what they had found—wafers of hashish. Pay dirt!

Upon arrival at the crewman's cabin, they had the full intention of completing a thorough room search because of our suspicions. They had the crewman stand in the passageway immediately outside the room and then initiated their search. As I have said, we do not normally have a crewman in the vicinity when we are searching his room. This is a safety concern we have, but today we let our guard down. It almost cost us dearly. As one inspector was searching the main area of the cabin, the other was searching the head. When the inspector searching the room came to the wall locker bolted to the bulkhead, he started to pull out the drawers. When he pulled out the drawer containing the crew member's socks, he noticed a package and began to reach for it. As he did this, he felt someone leap on his back. Instinctively, the inspector reached over his shoulder and behind his back. His big muscular arm and hand grabbed hold of a human body. The inspector dropped his body and flipped whoever was on his back over his head. (This inspector, young and in real good shape, played center for a well-regarded local college. Therefore, he had little difficulty performing this feat.) As a result, the individual on his back, went crashing into the nearby bulkhead. Only then did the inspector see the individual and realize it was the crewman whose cabin we were searching. The inspector pulled out his handcuffs and cuffed the crew member as he lay in a listless bundle where the bulkhead and deck meet. When the inspector searching the head heard the commotion, he came running out and witnessed his partner putting the cuffs on the crew member. This is when he radioed me to come to the cabin.

Now that the scene was secure and the crew member was safely constrained (we cuffed him to a pipe in the passageway), we continued our search of the cabin. Finally, when I realized the magnitude of the situation, I told the captain he probably wasn't going to be sailing for quite a while. He was apoplectic. I told the captain I would brief him later, but he could go and make his phone calls canceling sailing for now.

Now I could give my undivided attention to what was going on. The search by the two inspectors was quite productive. In the sock drawer, the package the inspector was about to look at before the crew member jumped on his back contained four pounds of hashish. In one of the pockets of a shirt, which was hanging on a hanger in the wall locker, he also found approximately $8,000 in cash. We mockingly laughed when we found the money because during our interview in the captain's cabin, the crewman told us he only had a few dollars. This was a significant find, but we continued the search of the cabin to ensure there wasn't anything else in the room. After about fifteen minutes, we were satisfied the room was clear. We had found all the stuff.

We escorted the crew member back to the captain's cabin and secured him to a chair. Although we knew what we had was hash, we conducted a field test to confirm our findings. Now the "fun" began. It was my responsibility to make a multitude of phone calls regarding this seizure. I had to notify Customs OI (Office of Investigations) and request they respond to the vessel. OI were the "detectives" for Customs. We call them whenever a seizure is made. They respond and coordinate any other activities with other law enforcement agencies and with the U.S. Attorney's Office. After this initial call, I called my immediate supervisor to let him know what had just transpired. This was an important phone call because he was going to have to get the word out to everyone in the chain of command of what was going on. Obviously, making a significant drug-and-money seizure on an LNG in Boston Harbor was newsworthy. Before the media found out, it was mandatory we let everyone in our organization know. My third and fourth phone calls were for help. We were on scene with a bunch of unhappy and belligerent (remember the knife incident of a week ago) Algerian seamen who wanted to sail for home. We were saying no. Not only that, we had one of their countrymen in handcuffs and were preparing to take him to jail. The atmosphere was tense. I called the airport and requested they contact at least three CET (Contraband Enforcement Team) members and have them report to me on the ship as soon as possible. I also called the Coast Guard Station Point Allerton and requested they respond. Now all we could do was wait. We finally pulled off a good seizure on one of the LNGs.

Events began to unfold rapidly. OI was responding, Everett Police was on the way, CET was en route; and through the window of the captain's cabin,

I could see a beautiful gleaming white Coast Guard boat steaming in our direction, laden with Coast Guard personnel prepared to help in any way possible. We began to relax a bit. As in most drug seizures, once the seizure is made, everything else becomes anticlimactic. OI arrived and said federal prosecution was declined. Therefore, the drugs, money, and individual would be turned over to the Everett Police Department for state prosecution. CET and the Coast Guard re-searched the entire vessel with negative results. It was over. We could go home.

I would like to add a postscript to this story. About two months after the seizure was made, we had to appear in Middlesex Court in Cambridge for a hearing of admissibility of evidence. The crew member's court-appointed attorney made a feeble attempt to have the evidence (hashish) thrown out. The judge dismissed this request. However, the attorney then demanded we return the crew member's passport to him. We laughed at this because we knew he was a flight risk, but the judge ordered the crew member's passport be returned to him in jail. We complied. Some time later, the crew member made bail and left the country. I doubt if we will ever see him again.

X-ray truck inspecting an inbound sea container

Typical LNG tanker that visits Boston

FIVE

Lauren

On December 15, 2005, my daughter Marie gave birth to her seventh child, Lauren Marie Reen. As beautiful a child that you have ever seen, it was a sheer pleasure to see and hold her. The doctor detected a murmur in her heart but was not overly concerned. Murmurs are not uncommon, and scheduled tests in the days to come would probably confirm everything was normal. My daughter and son-in-law brought Lauren to the doctor's office on the following Tuesday, hoping and anticipating for the best. Unfortunately, this was not to be. The doctor was concerned enough to send my daughter and son-in-law with little Lauren to Children's Hospital Boston immediately. Here they conducted several tests and determined Lauren had ventricular septal defect (VSD) and hemitruncus. This was all foreign to us, but the pleasant and helpful nurses and doctors at Children's patiently explained what all this meant. VSD is a breach in the septum between the chambers of the hearts. In Lauren's case, it was between the right and left ventricles. Although this is a severe condition, it is not uncommon and can even heal on its own; sometimes surgery is required. The hemitruncus is a different story. This is a much more severe condition and definitely will require surgery. Hemitruncus, at least as we understand it, is a condition where Lauren's pulmonary vein is attached to the aorta instead of the right ventricle. It is complicated, and

I probably still don't fully understand and I surely don't trivialize Lauren's condition, but I compared it with plumbing. You had to disconnect one pipe and reconnect it to a different spot. Obviously it isn't that simple, especially when it concerns a little baby only a week old.

The doctors feel that Lauren can go home for now, but surgery has been scheduled for January 9. She is on medicine to strengthen her heart and to make her urinate more often. She is also on a special formula to build up her heart. So she is home for now. We are all anxious and will be until the surgery is over. We pray all will work out and our special little gift will be fine. For now, her brother and sisters are all making a huge fuss over their special Christmas gift of 2005.

SIX

Logan Runner

Today is my father's eighty-sixth birthday. I called him early this morning and wished him a happy birthday. Happily, he is in excellent health. I hope I am in as good shape when I reach eighty-six years old. Today Marie and Jimmy brought little Lauren to Children's Hospital for pre-op. Monday the ninth is the scheduled day for surgery.

I must tell you the story about the unlucky and less-than-bright "runner" at Logan Airport. From the prearrival passenger manifest, we knew we had an individual on a flight from the Caribbean who had an outstanding warrant for his arrest. Not to worry, we thought. Once the flight arrives, we will process all the passengers in the normal fashion. When we punch up this guy's name in the computer, we will get a hit for an outstanding warrant. As normal, we will then escort him down to the baggage pickup area and secure him in a search room until we verify the warrant is outstanding and the holder of the warrant will extradite. If the warrant is still active, and it should be if it is in the system, the holder must be willing to extradite. If not, we have no choice but to let the subject go. Well, it was this guy's unlucky day. The warrant was still active, and extradition was confirmed. Now all we had to do was sit on him until one of the troopers from Troop F, Logan Airport came over to pick him up.

In anticipation of the trooper's arrival, I instructed the two inspectors who were watching the guy to pat him down for officer safety. This was done with negative results. However, as the inspectors were explaining to the guy what they were about to do, I saw something in the guy's eyes I didn't like. It was a look I've seen so many times before, and it was always in the eyes of someone who was ready to try to do something dumb. Therefore, when the inspectors were finished patting him down, I told them to have him take a seat and for them to back out of the search room. I didn't want them in a small confined search room with weapons with a guy I knew was up to no good. The best thing to do was handcuff him, but if for some reason it was decided the guy wasn't going to be arrested after all, we could be held liable for a false arrest. I told both inspectors to be extremely careful with this guy. I told both of them to stand outside of the search room and monitor the guy from there. Once the State Police arrived with warrant in hand, they would arrest and handcuff him and be off to jail. Everything seemed under control, and I went off to perform some other functions. Once the State Police arrived, I would return and assist in the transfer.

Well, as usual, things didn't work out as planned. One of the inspectors guarding the guy left his post to assist another inspector with an unrelated inspection. Why did he leave the search room and go against my specific orders? I can only attribute it to inexperience and trying to appease a fellow inspector. Both of these inspectors had been on the job for a couple of years, and I thought they knew better. Whatever, this is all the bad guy needed. He saw his chance to bolt, and he took full advantage of the opportunity. When the sole inspector turned his back to the guy for a split second, he leapt off the chair and began running. He went right through the inspector who was standing in the doorway and began to run for the exit. People were being knocked down all over the place, and everyone began yelling. Passengers were yelling in fear, and inspectors were yelling in anger. All this commotion attracted my attention as I was standing at the other end of the hall. I saw the inspectors running and yelling, and then I saw the guy. He was about fifty feet from the exit door and running hard. There were at least six inspectors on his heels, but they were never going to catch him before he made it out the door. Damn! This is when I took off running. I wasn't sure what I was going to do, but I figured I better join the parade.

When I exited the Customs Hall and entered the main lobby of Terminal E, I continued running after everyone else. My run was of short duration. About one hundred feet from the Customs exit are the main exits to the street. These exits consist of a set of double sliding doors with about twenty feet in between. There is a rubber mat in front of these doors, and when you step on this mat, the doors open. In this area between the sliding doors, the subject was apprehended. It was a comical scene. At first I couldn't figure out what was going on. Finally, I sorted things out. It seems that the guy was running so fast, and because he was taking such long strides, he never stepped on the rubber mat. Therefore, the door never opened, and he went crashing into the closed doors. Upon impact, he fell on the rubber mat, resulting in the doors opening. He stood up and began to run again. Luckily, an army sergeant home on leave was entering Terminal E through these same doors at this exact time. When he saw the guy running and uniformed officers close behind, he immediately realized what was going on. This army sergeant sprung into action and tackled the fleeing felon around the knees. The inspectors were there in seconds. What resulted was comical yet effective. Everyone was trying to get their handcuffs on the guy, and in the resulting milieu, the guy had at least three sets of cuffs on him. One wrist had two cuffs on it, the other wrist had three. Luckily both wrists were bound. I wasn't quite sure how, but they were. During all the confusion and rolling around, the army sergeant even had a set of cuffs dangling from one wrist!

As the inspectors were escorting the bad guy back into the Customs Hall—to a roaring applause by all the people in the lobby who witnessed what happened—I stayed behind and removed the cuffs from the sergeant's wrist. Without his help, the guy might have gotten away. I thanked the sergeant and asked him to write down his commanding officer's name and address. I promised him I would write to his CO, commending him for his actions. We said our good-byes, and I returned to the Customs Hall. Thankfully, the State Police arrived shortly thereafter and removed our friend from our custody and brought him to jail. There he would await extradition. I had enough for the day. I talked briefly with the two inspectors who were supposed to be watching the guy. I lit into them a bit, but then I backed off when I saw they realized how lucky they were. They are both good inspectors, and there is no use humiliating and berating them once they realized what they did wrong.

When I returned to work the next day, I wrote a letter to the sergeant's commanding officer. I commended the sergeant's bravery, quick thinking, and utter disregard for his own safety. Hopefully, the sergeant will receive recognition from his command.

A few weeks later, I received a letter from the sergeant's commanding officer. He thanked me for recognizing the sergeant's actions and assured me the army would formally recognize him. I felt good. Something nice came out of a bad situation.

SEVEN

Surfing in the Wind

One Saturday morning, we were working airport cargo at Logan. We met at the CET office at Terminal E and, as usual, had our obligatory morning coffee and doughnut. From there, we went down to the main Customs office on the passenger processing floor at Terminal E. This is the location where the airlines have been instructed to drop off all the cargo manifests and copies of the air waybills of freight, which they have imported on their planes. The purpose of this is simple. Before we go out to the freight warehouses and examine cargo, we review all the air waybills and ascertain what cargo is the best to look at for drug interdiction purposes. As I look back at this process some ten to twenty years later, I chuckle at how antiquated and old-fashioned this process seems, especially compared to the way we target cargo today. But the ironic thing is, it worked. Anyhow, I was looking at all the air waybills, putting aside any which looked interesting. I was done looking at all the paperwork after about fifteen minutes and began to re-review the bills, looking for the "best of the best shipments." Since there were only two of us, we had to be highly selective. As I was looking at the bills, one really stuck out. It was a surfboard being shipped to Boston from Jamaica by an individual male. He was listed as the shipper and consignee and paid for the shipping in cash. Something is fishy about this shipment. We left Terminal

31

E by a back door and entered the ramp. We had a Customs vehicle parked here, and it was a lot easier traveling to all the cargo warehouses ramp-side rather than street-side.

The ride over to the warehouse was no longer than ten minutes. When we arrived at the back door, I gathered up the necessary tools needed to open freight and grabbed some Customs tape. This tape is fluorescent green, has U.S. Customs written all over it, and is virtually impossible to unroll. It is constantly ripping off in little pieces and is extremely frustrating to work with. When we open packages or boxes in the warehouses, this is the tape we use to reseal whatever we open.

As we entered the warehouse, I immediately began to look for the surfboard. Since the airline handled both international and domestic freight and had to keep the two separate, I knew where the surfboard should be and went directly to this area. Sure enough, I found it lying on the floor. The board was heavily wrapped in that bubbly plastic type of material and was secured with a shiny brown tape. A cursory exam indicated the board had never been looked at. This was a huge relief for me. Although on paper the surfboard shipment looked suspicious, our hopes of finding drugs could still be dashed if the shipment had already been inspected by Customs inspectors at another port.

We began to take the tape off and then unrolled the plastic covering. Once we had the board exposed, we could see it was a sailboard and not a surfboard. An initial exam for anything unusual proved negative. The board didn't seem to be too heavy, and there weren't any unusual seams or indications of alterations. The only area we couldn't examine was where the mast for the sail fit into the board. This area was about six inches by three inches and was boxed in by a heavy plastic coaming. To examine the area behind this coaming, we had to remove four screws, which held the two pieces of plastic together. I reached into our tool bag and pulled out a screwdriver. The screws readily came off, leaving the plastic unsecured to the board. With a bit of prying, both plastic pieces came off. I shined my flashlight into this now exposed area that was previously concealed by the plastic. To my excitement, I could see how the board had been sliced open and then resealed with a heavy layer of glue. I wasn't sure if this was done in the factory or if it was a homemade cut. And it was the most perfect place to make a cut because the plastic coaming concealed any tampering. It sure looked suspicious to me, but did I have enough evidence to damage the board? If I drilled holes into the board and found nothing, I was going to have a lot of explaining to do. If I drilled holes and found drugs, I was all set. I contemplated my next move for a few seconds and then decided to drill. We had enough reasons we could articulate to justify this course of action. I went out to our vehicle and set up the electric drill with the longest and thinnest bit we had. (I figured if I was wrong, I wanted to do as little damage as possible.) When I returned to the board, I had mixed feelings. I sure hoped I was right. I leveled the drill into the hole and attempted to keep the bit as horizontally to the board as possible. I pressed the button and pushed. The bit slid in easily at first, and then it became harder to push. When the drill was all the way in, I slowly withdrew the bit. As I pulled the bit out, it was full of white insulation, and the first few inches of the bit had a green leafy substance on it. I began to reinsert the bit when I realized what that green leafy substance was—marijuana. We tested the green substance with a narcotic field test kit that confirmed the substance was marijuana. As soon as we confirmed that we had a drug seizure, I called the supervisor at Terminal E. Obviously we couldn't leave this sailboard unattended in the warehouse for the remainder of the weekend, so the supervisor instructed us to transport the marijuana-laden sailboard back to the Customs office in Terminal E to secure the dope and to develop a game plan.

The following day, Sunday, CET took all the marijuana out of the sailboard and repacked the void with Styrofoam. We reassembled the coaming and repacked the board with the plastic covering. The board was returned to the cargo warehouse, and a controlled delivery was set up. This entailed having the airline cargo personnel call the consignee to tell him he could come pick up his shipment. Once he arrived and picked up the sailboard and put it in his car, the surveillance team consisting of Customs, DEA, and State Police would move in and arrest whoever picked up the shipment. This is exactly what occurred. The guy came to Logan the following week to pick up his sailboard. To his surprise, a not-so-pleasant welcoming committee greeted him. I forget exactly what happened after that. I do remember he didn't serve any time in jail and only received a suspended sentence with probation. Thus ended the sailboard escapade. We were off to bigger and better things.

EIGHT

Ecstasy in Winter Wonderland

Working the waterfront on the Boston Contraband Enforcement Team (CET) is one of the best jobs in the country. Surely it is the best job in Boston. I know other inspectors would roll their eyes hearing me say this, but everyone has their own opinion. We get to travel all over New England and participate in law enforcement activities with many other local, state, and federal agencies. These experiences are once in a lifetime, and I treasure them all. As I reflect back on some of our efforts, a feeling of warmth and pride envelops me. One of our little escapades started with a simple phone call.

I was working at the Conley Container Terminal the morning of the twentieth of December 2001. We were all pretty much in a holiday routine, getting ready for Christmas. The phone rang, and one of the inspectors in the office answered. Shortly thereafter, he was yelling at me to pick up the phone. He said someone from the regional office was calling looking for me. The caller was a program officer (PO) in the regional office in Boston. He told me he just received a phone call from an immigration inspector in Bangor, Maine. It seems this inspector was running computer checks on the crew of a ship coming into Searsport, Maine. One of the crewmen, an ordinary seaman by the name of Oliver, had hits on his name for supposedly

35

being involved with the smuggling of ecstasy. The name of the ship was *Jupiter,* and she was a bulk ship arriving direct from Rotterdam, Netherlands. The program officer asked me what I thought about this information. I told him it sounded like there was potential, but what did he want from me? He asked me if I was willing to send some guys up to Maine and search the ship upon arrival. Oh sure, I thought, a couple of days before Christmas and they are looking for volunteers to travel to Maine to search a ship. I could envision the guys climbing over each other, fighting at the chance! I told him that I would look into the possibility, but before we went anywhere, we needed to clear it with our port director. He told me that was his next phone call and, once I knew if we had any volunteers, to give him a shout. Surprisingly, I readily found at least three and perhaps four inspectors who wanted to go. However, most of them had to call home and clear it with their wives. Shortly thereafter, everything firmed up. We had four volunteers. I called the program officer and told him we were a go with four volunteers. He told me the port director had blessed the operation. He asked me if I could call up to Maine and coordinate everything. Fine, I said with a sigh of relief. Nothing is worse than taking part in an operation that you had no part in planning. If I am going to play, I want to participate in setting the ground rules.

Numerous calls ensued. I called and talked with the Immigration inspector from Bangor who initiated this whole thing and asked her to fill me in on what was going on. Basically, all she did was reconfirm everything we already were told. A bulk ship called the *Jupiter* was due to arrive at the main terminal in Searsport, Maine, sometime late on the twenty-first. The *Jupiter* was coming from the Netherlands with a load of scrap metal. Onboard was a crew member that was of interest to us for possibly being involved in ecstasy smuggling into the Port of Savannah, Georgia—interestingly the *Jupiter* was supposed to call on Savannah after Searsport. She was bubbling over with enthusiasm and was quite helpful in filling me in with the details. I thanked her and told her we would be responding. My next call was going to be to the port director in Boston, but she beat me to it. She wanted to know exactly what was going on and how I was going to handle our response. I told her the four of us were going to meet first thing in the morning and head up to Maine. We were still making calls to identify where we were going to stay for the night and where we were going to rendezvous with Customs personnel from Maine. Our plan was to travel to Maine in the morning, board and search the *Jupiter* that evening, sleep at a local hotel after the search, and then head back to Boston on the morning of the twenty-second. I stressed with the port director that these were our plans, but knowing from past experiences how things change, we were going to be flexible and prepared for anything. Besides, if we did find anything onboard, all our plans would obviously change. She was content with our plans, wished us good luck, and requested I keep her updated continuously on our status. I promised to do so, and our phone conversation ended. As I was on the phone with the port director, the inspectors were making preparations for our trip. They picked the vehicles we were planning to take and outfitted them with the tools and supplies we would need for a ship search. I also yelled at them to make sure they were filled with gas and had window washer fluid in them. They all made comments under their breath at my micromanaging, but it was all in fun. We were all excited to be going on this trip and hoped we would find something. It would be an early Christmas gift for the team. There was a lot of bantering among us. Along with everyone else, I was looking forward to getting underway in the morning. After we had finalized all the plans, it was time to go home. We were going to meet at 0500 hours on the twenty-first at Conley Terminal.

I arrived at Conley before 0500 hours and was the first one there. Shortly thereafter, the other guys arrived. We made good time, and only a wrong turn south of Portland slowed us down. We got off I-95 at Augusta and took a secondary road—Route 3—into Belfast and then north on Route 1 into Searsport. We readily found the Irving gas station but didn't stop because we were so early. Instead, we drove around the area to familiarize ourselves with the surroundings. Finally, about 4:00 PM, we pulled into the rest stop parking lot and went inside the dining area. As we were reading the menus, the rest of the crowd began to arrive. We had two Coast Guard personnel (a petty officer and an ensign) from the Marine Safety Office (MSO) in Bucksport, two Customs agents from Bangor, a K-9 team from Customs Portland, a Customs, and an Immigration inspector from Bangor. We all introduced ourselves, and everyone sat down and began to order food. I noticed the reaction of the other customers in the restaurant. They were all looking at us with darting glances. I could imagine what was going through their minds. Who were we, and what were we doing in their little town of Searsport? This was probably the largest contingent of law enforcement that they had ever seen. Then I began to think. What we are doing is quite unusual and extraordinary. Within twenty-four hours of notification of this ship's arrival, we had all got together miles from our homeports and were ready to go to work. We had never met each other before today, but we had complete trust and confidence in each other. As we awaited the arrival of our food, we engaged in idle chitchat and enjoyed each other's company. Once we finished eating, we would finalize our plans on how we would coordinate the search of the M/V *Jupiter*.

We all gathered around a couple of the tables in the restaurant and discussed our plan of attack. The restaurant personnel were obliging and considerate (they also kept our coffee cups full, which earned them a good tip). Since I was the supervisor of CET and I had perhaps the most experience in ship searches, I diplomatically took the lead. The plan was to conduct a normal ship search that we have done countless times in the past. However, this time we had information, and we would concentrate in this area. The plan was to take all the vehicles down to the pier and stand by at the dock office, which was at the near side of the pier. I wanted the inspector from Bangor to be the only inspector visible on the pier. He would call out on the radio once the *Jupiter* was all fast to the dock and we were able to board her. I was sensitive to maintaining the element of surprise. I didn't want the crew of the *Jupiter* to scan the pier with a pair of binoculars when she was still in the channel and see a gang of Customs people standing on the pier ready to board her. If there was something on board, they could throw the stuff overboard, and all our efforts were for naught. Once the ship was secured to the pier, we would all proceed from the dock office to the ship, which was a distance of about one hundred yards. The entire search party would board together and spread out to their designated areas of responsibility. I wanted to gather up the entire crew and sequester them on the mess deck. Once we verified everyone was accounted for, we could once again split up and begin the search. Everyone was assigned an area of responsibility. I attempted to pair everyone up according to their level of experience. I put someone with little experience with someone with more experience in an attempt to have nice balanced teams. This was important for two reasons: I wanted a good search to be conducted, and most importantly, I wanted everyone to be safe. There are a lot of places on a ship where you can get hurt, and I wanted to be sure nothing happened to anyone. We made sure all the individual teams had good flashlights and all our radios were on the same frequency. This sounds stupid and needless to say, but past experience proves it to be a necessary item to check. I told everyone I would be constantly moving about the ship checking on everyone to make sure everything was OK. By the looks on their faces, everyone seemed to be in concurrence and were comfortable with what I was saying. To be sure, I asked everyone if they had any questions or wanted to add anything to what I had to say. There were a few minor questions, but on the whole, we were all set to go. The ship wasn't due in for another hour. I instructed everyone to proceed down to the dock office, and I would see them all there. If necessary, I would make any last-minute alterations in plans at that time.

The drive from the rest stop to the terminal was less than a mile. As we descended the hill to the dock office, we could see off to our right the M/V *Jupiter* about two miles away. She was in mid-channel and was dead-on as indicated by her masthead lights being virtually aligned with each other and because both her green starboard and red port running lights were distinctly visible to the naked eye. The weather was getting colder by the minute, and a light, fine drizzle began to fall. Needless to say, we could think of better places to be than here. We all milled around our vehicles, and gradually a few of us decided to warm ourselves up in the dock office. By the look of things, we wouldn't be onboard for about another hour. It was going to be a long cold night. There was nothing but friendly bantering going on in the dock office. I kept going over our plans in my head. Did we have everything covered? Were all the search team members properly briefed? Finally I said enough. The inspector was down at the pier and was standing by to give us the high sign. At last the vessel was all tied up, and we could board. We all gave a sigh of relief and headed for our vehicles. As we were doing this, we cautioned each other to be careful. The light rain that was falling was freezing rapidly on the road and the dock. We didn't want any accidents, and we really didn't want anyone sliding their vehicle off the pier and into the icy, cold water of Penobscot Bay. It took only about five minutes for all of us to arrive alongside the ship. We found out it would take about another half hour for the crew to secure a gangway for us. I said, "The hell with that." The ship was low enough in the water that we would be able to climb onboard over the gunwales without a gangway. This wasn't the proper way to gain access to the ship, but time was a huge factor. I told the guys to be careful and let's go. I led the way and was the first one onboard. As I assisted a couple of inspectors who were right behind me over the gunwale, a thought flashed through my head, *We are finally onboard, and now it's time to find the drugs.*

It was real slippery trying to get onboard. One of the Bangor agents took a nasty fall trying to get on. I guess he leapt over the gunwale by putting one foot on top of the gunwale and then jumped to the deck. When he landed on the deck, he went down hard. I felt for him big-time because exactly what had happened to him has happened to me in the past—and it is not funny. Especially the older we get, these falls hurt more and more. After we were all on the vessel, we spread out on the ship to corral the crew and escort them to the mess deck. This is always a difficult procedure. The crews are always slow and lackadaisical. They don't want to be bothered and want to be left alone. Consequently, we have to do some prodding and cajoling to accomplish our mission. As the crew was drifting into the mess deck, I began to make a head count. There should be thirty-three souls onboard, and we only had eighteen so far. However, as I walked around the inner decks, more and more crew was walking toward the mess deck, and I heard our guys yelling to the crew to hurry up. I laughed at all the commotion. *What a way to make a living*, I thought. After about only fifteen minutes, we had the entire crew where they belonged. We did a head count and verified all thirty-three crewmen were there. Consequently, when we conducted our search, if we ran into anyone else onboard, they would be considered a bad guy because all thirty-three crew would stay on the mess deck while we searched. Finally, we could begin what we came here for—a ship search. As usual, I assigned an inspector to guard the crew. The Immigration inspector from Bangor had to process the crew's clearance into the country, so I asked him if he would mind keeping an eye on them and making sure everyone stays on the mess deck. To ensure safety, I asked the Customs inspector from Bangor if he would mind staying there also. They both were obliging and readily agreed. Now with the crew safely taken care of, I told all the guys to split up and go to their assigned areas. If they needed anything or had a problem, they were instructed to use their radios. I was sweating from all the exertion of climbing onboard and climbing the ladders and because the ship itself was so hot. Once the troops moved out, I began to take all my outer garments off. This was a relief and was much more comfortable. I felt satisfied with what was going on. The crew was under control, and the search teams were properly deployed. Now all we needed was a little luck. I began to walk around by myself to get a general feel of the ship. *Typical old bulk ship*, I thought. How the heck do these guys go to sea for months on end in rust buckets like this? Life back home must be pretty miserable and desolate to relegate them to a life like this. As I was lost in my thoughts and imaginations, I was startled by the blare of my radio. The inspector asked me to come to the subject's cabin on the lower deck immediately. *Oh my gosh*, I thought, *we have something.*

When we split up to start the ship search, I specifically assigned a team to search crew cabins, which included the subject's cabin. This team quite correctly began their search in the subject's cabin. "Might as well search where the highest risk is while you are fresh" is the basic logic behind this. When I arrived at the cabin, all I saw were smiles on both of their faces. My heart was thumping with excitement. An inspector immediately began talking and explained to me what was going on. When he pulled out the clothes drawer that was directly beneath the bed, he shined his flashlight into the void and saw nothing. He began to reinsert the drawer when a little voice went off in his head. This voice that he attributed to me said, "Don't just peek in, stick the flashlight and your head in and look all around." I am always preaching to the guys to go that extra step. Giving a little extra effort than normal makes seizures. With these words bouncing around in his head, he pulled the drawer back out and reshined the flashlight into the void. This time he was lying on the deck and could see all the way to the far bulkhead. That is when he saw something highly unusual. Lying against the bottom of the bulkhead at the head of the bed, he could see what looked like plastic bags with something white in the bags. He really couldn't make it out and asked the other inspector on his team to take a look. This inspector lay on his belly on the deck and shone the light into the dark empty space. He could see the bags and then thought he could identify pills. This is when they called me, and I arrived moments later. I promptly took a look and was simply astonished. At the far end of the bed, I could see at least two big plastic bags, and I could barely make out the pills. As I stood up, we all looked at each other. Talk about excitement! This is what you go to work for every day, hoping to make a big seizure. Today looked like it was going be our day. Only we didn't know how really big a day it was going to turn out to be. The three of us talked to each other and formulated a plan on how to remove the bags. It appeared if we removed a flat piece of wood at the head of the bed that measured about four feet by six inches, we might be able to gain access to the bags from the top. We hoped this was possible because it would be virtually impossible to gain access to the bags from down below. As we examined this piece of wood closely, we could see how small finish nails had been removed and then renailed. It was obvious after a close examination that this wood had been tampered with. Great, we thought, because this had to be where they gained access to insert the bags into the bulkhead. Slowly and carefully we began to remove the flat piece of wood.

For evidentiary purposes, we didn't want to destroy the wood. We were attempting to keep it as intact as possible, but our excitement in seeing what was beneath was getting the better of us. Finally, the piece of wood was removed intact, or almost so. What we saw as we looked into this area at the top of the bunk simply amazed us. All we saw was plastic bags containing pills the size of aspirins. This was a huge seizure! I had never seen ecstasy before, but based on the information we had on this guy, I could only assume these white pills were ecstasy. Slowly we began to remove the plastic bags from this area between the top of the bunk and the bulkhead.

We were careful to remove the bags without ripping the plastic because if we did, pills would be all over the place. As we were removing the bags, other members of the search team were drifting by to see what we had. They were all awestruck when they saw the drugs. After quite a while, at least a half hour, we removed the last bag of ecstasy. We counted ten bags, and each bag was about the size of a ten-pound bag of potatoes. How many pills were in each bag was a matter of pure conjecture. All we knew was that there were literally thousands and thousands. Now what? Well, we knew this was the suspect's room; and with the evidence we already had on this guy, we felt we had enough probable cause to introduce ourselves to him. However, because OI (Office of Investigations) was on scene, we conferred with the Bangor Customs agent and asked him what he thought. He was as exuberant as we were. His reply was an emphatic and resounding yes. Now that we were all in agreement with the next course of action, I had the biggest question. How the hell are we going to arrest this guy and get a set of handcuffs on him? When we were mustering the crew and calling roll on the mess deck, we were able to identify him. To put it bluntly, he was a big guy. He must have been at least six feet tall and weighed over two hundred pounds. However he was built, I don't think he had an ounce of fat on him. His chest, arms, and thighs were massive; and his waist was thin. He must have been some kind of bodybuilder, and he definitely lifted weights. I was concerned how we were going to take this guy into custody without getting someone hurt. The inevitable wisecracking ensued. Because I was the boss, I should have the privilege of arresting him, some thought. Others chimed in with their words of wisdom. All of this bantering was in fun and was just relaxing our nerves. We knew the situation was serious, but we also knew we were all in this together and we *would* arrest him. Finally, we came up with a plan. Five of us would enter the mess deck, approach the subject, and tell him to get on his feet and then handcuff him. We would use the element of surprise and shock him into submission. The rest of the guys would be standing by at the entrance to the mess deck just in case any of the remaining crew attempted to interfere. And this is exactly what happened. The subject and the rest of the crew offered no resistance whatsoever. We were relieved! As I patted down the now-handcuffed Oliver, I felt his thighs and calves; they were huge and hard as a rock. This guy could do some serious hurt to someone if he wanted to. Thankfully, it wasn't going to be us.

We brought him back to his cabin and read him his Miranda rights. He fully understood his rights, waived them, and wanted to talk to us. The special agents from Bangor brought him into an empty-accompanying cabin to interview him. Before they did so, however, we took pictures of him sitting down on a bench in his cabin with all the ecstasy piled up around him. We asked him how many pills there were, and his answer flabbergasted us—he said there were one hundred thousand pills in the bags, ten bags with ten thousand pills in each bag. What a seizure! (We would learn later that the street value for ecstasy was between $50 and $80 a tablet: 100,000 tablets x $50-$80 = $5,000,000-$8,000,000. Now we really were shocked. This seizure was worth between five and eight million dollars, and it turned out to be the largest ecstasy seizure in the history of Maine.) Once we were done with the picture taking, we escorted him into the empty cabin to interview him. The agents completed their interview within thirty minutes and were now ready to escort him off the ship and into the local jail.

Getting off the ship was even harder than getting on. Because the temperature continued to drop and the fine mist continued to fall, the decks of the *Jupiter* were a sheet of ice. You could literally skate on the deck. One inspector was walking down the main deck and fell hard on his back. He got up and continued walking, but you know it had to hurt. One of the agents also went down hard. The funny thing is, the subject was the first one to come to his aid. He reached down with his handcuffed hands and helped the agent to his feet. This was a sign of the guy's character, I thought. Here we are carting him away to jail, and he is helping us to our feet after we fall. The symbolism struck me. Eventually, we all made it off the ship and to our cars. Before I could go to bed, however, I had to make my final calls. All during the events on the ship, I was calling the port director in Boston and apprising her of what was happening. In turn, she had to call the regional office and keep them in the loop. Once my final call for the night to the port director was made, I was able to put my head down on my pillow and drift off to sleep. It didn't take long to fall asleep, but before I did, I remember thinking back on the night's events. I was immensely satisfied and proud about what had transpired.

I awoke early the following morning. After getting cleaned up and dressed, I went out on the back deck of the hotel and was struck by the panoramic view of Penobscot Bay. When we checked in last night, it was pitch-dark, and we couldn't see beyond the parking lot. This morning was our first chance to see the beauty of our surroundings. I banged on everyone's door and told them that we would go. Most were already up and were anxious to take off. While we were waiting for everyone to get ready, the rest of us went down to the hotel lobby and had a delicious continental breakfast. We sat in a little dining area that overlooked the bay and consumed dry cereals, muffins, bagels, and volumes of coffee and juice. I think the hotel lost money on us the way we consumed the chow. Before we took off for Boston, I made the obligatory call to Bangor OI to talk with Phil, the agent from the night before. He was already in the office and was in his usual chirpy mood. He asked me if we would mind swinging by Bangor before we headed south. He wanted to make sure the chain of custody and the seizure report were completed before we departed. I obviously didn't object and went back to tell the guys. They were too sleepy to comprehend and only shook their heads in confirmation.

Once we were done with our breakfast, we checked out of the hotel and headed for Bangor. The drive was only a little over an hour, but it took us time to find the office, and we finally arrived about 10:30 AM. We input the seizure information into the computer at the Bangor OI office and confirmed the chain of custody was correct. Everything was finished. By this time it was afternoon, and Phil asked us if we were hungry. We initially declined until he told us about a place right around the corner from the OI office that served the best steak subs. We acquiesced and were off to lunch. He was right on the money, the subs were delicious. As we were eating, he told us how much he appreciated us coming up and it was a real pleasure working with us. We told him the feeling was mutual. When we left home just the day before, we didn't know what we were getting into; but the important thing is, we went. Out of that, we made a huge seizure that will literally go down in the history books of Maine. When I say we, I mean all of us. Not just the Boston contingent but also everybody who participated in this most memorable event.

We finished chow and went to pay only to find out Phil had already picked up the tab. About time Phil did something for us we joked. Phil walked us to our cars, and after much handshaking and backslapping, we finally took off for the four-hour-plus car ride back to Boston. I lit up a nice fresh cigar and enjoyed the ride home.

On the way back, we had to stop off and meet the port director in a shopping mall parking lot on the North Shore. She wanted to be fully briefed on what happened in Maine, and she also wanted to convey her heartfelt thanks for a job well done. She also brought us freshly baked chocolate chip cookies. We talked for a while, but it was time to leave. I was exhausted. The port director did convey some pretty important news however. In our absence, there was a major incident at Logan Airport. An inbound flight from London was diverted to Boston because a passenger onboard tried to light a fuse that was attached to the shoes he was wearing. This incident that was eventually dubbed the "shoe bomber incident" drew national attention because it was an extremely serious event. The lives of everyone onboard the jet could have been lost if the shoe bomber had been successful. Luckily, because of a courageous flight attendant and some passengers' assistance, his efforts were thwarted.

We departed again for Boston and Conley Terminal. I had to get home and go to sleep. My adrenaline had run out, and I had hit bottom. I was exhausted.

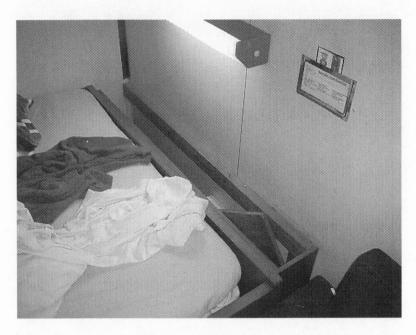

Bunk of crew member onboard bulk ship *Jupiter*

Bags of ecstasy concealed beneath headboard of bunk

Guy and I writing up seizure report for ecstasy seizure

One hundred thousand ecstasy pills—street value was
between 5 and 8 million dollars

NINE

Escort Duty

A sad event occurred at Logan Airport today. We met and escorted the body of a twenty-one-year-old young American girl off a flight from Dublin. Usually in cases where bodies are being returned to America for burial, we have a formal, polite but usually impersonal process. However, this situation was different. The family had made numerous phone calls to political and personal friends requesting special attention to this matter. Obviously, in light of the circumstances, Customs and Border Protection was receptive to the requests of the family.

We were informed by the family that the young lady traveled to Ireland on January 1, 2006, to participate in a work-study program. While there, she suddenly became ill and was rushed to the hospital where she later died. An autopsy was performed, and septicemia (blood poisoning) was the cause of death. Supposedly she was a star athlete and was quite a kid.

Her father flew over to Ireland to escort his daughter's body back home. Before the flight arrived, we met the mother and two of her aunts in the lobby and escorted them to the gate where the plane was scheduled to arrive. We arrived early enough to see the flight taxi to the gate. Previous to this time, the family was calm and appeared relax. However, as we walked down the

Jetway, the emotions and stress of the moment finally overwhelmed them. Their little girl was home, but not how they wanted.

We waited patiently on the Jetway for her father to depart from the plane. It seemed an eternity before he exited. When he finally did, the family strongly embraced, and we attempted to afford them as much privacy as possible. After an appropriate period of time, I informed everybody what we intended to do. We were going to take the family into one of our marked vehicles and follow the casket ramp side to the cargo area. The hearse from the funeral home would meet us there. The parents were pleased when we informed them that this way they would constantly be with their daughter. Once the plans were explained, an officer from CBP and a trooper from the Massachusetts State Police escorted the family to our vehicle. The casket was ready to be transported, and they followed it to the cargo area as planned.

While they were en route, I escorted the two aunts to the baggage claim area. We found all five bags after a short period and then immediately exited the Customs area. We wheeled the baggage-laden carts to the aunt's car that was parked across the street from Terminal E. The aunts were going to meet the family at the cargo area, but they surely would have become lost if they went on their own. Consequently, I had a CBP officer jump in with them and direct them to the cargo shed. When they arrived, the casket and our escort were just pulling in. The hearse was already there and was waiting patiently.

Our role in this matter was quickly winding down. We ensured the transfer of the casket from airline to the funeral director went smoothly, and then we began to leave. The family was most appreciative of all our efforts and especially the personal touch we put on it. We felt good that we could give the family just a little bit of comfort and concern at such a tragic and heart-wrenching time.

TEN

Characters: John "Dunny" Donovan

No story of U.S. Customs in Boston would be complete without mentioning two individuals—Harry McDonough and John "Dunny" Donovan. Both individuals were senior inspectors, products of the streets of South Boston, and they were intimate friends with Judge Feeney of South Boston and Speaker John McCormack of the U.S. House of Representatives.

To stay in some kind of shape and to keep my cardiovascular system pumping, I try to walk around the Castle Island loop every day. During this two-mile trek, I encounter Dunny and Harry on a daily basis. The sailing center on the southern side of Castle Island is named after Harry. On a sign in big black letters with a light blue background is the name Harry McDonough Sailing Center. As I make the left turn at Sullivan's, the hot dog and hamburger shack, I look up; and there is the omnipresent sign. Invariably a smile comes to my face, and some of Harry's antics come to mind. I am sure these stories of Harry have been exaggerated through the years, and perhaps a few are apocryphal, but I am also sure there must be a grain of truth in them somewhere. For instance, the time Harry muscled a major footwear importer out of some sneakers. The story goes something like this, depending on who is telling the story. Harry, a big muscular guy with a

51

barrel chest and loud, booming voice, also had a huge heart. He ran a boy's club in South Boston and was constantly seeking donations and gifts. Well, one day at Conley Terminal where Harry worked as a supervisory Customs inspector, a telephone call was referred to Harry. The caller was the major footwear importer. They had two full containers of sneakers at Conley that they were importing from overseas and were inquiring when U.S. Customs was going to release them. Supposedly, the containers were on the docks for some time, and the importer was confused at the delay. As the story goes, Harry explained to the importer how he ran a boy's club for poor inner-city kids and how, by the way, they were always in dire need of sneakers. He added that he was so busy with his kids that sometimes he barely found time for work. The importer, catching on right away, asked Harry if it was possible for them to donate some sneakers to this most worthy cause. Harry readily accepted, and the two containers were released that day—sans four dozen of newly imported sneakers. The number of sneakers varies with the storyteller, but the facts of the story remains pretty consistent.

Another often-quoted story of Harry was his phone call masquerades. Harry would call anyone and everyone and identify himself either as Bill Griffin, the regional commissioner of Customs at that time, or some staff member from Speaker McCormack's office. His identity would change depending on what kind of mission he was on. If something pertained to Customs, Harry would be Bill Griffin. If his call pertained to his boys in the boys' club, he would be a staff member of Speaker McCormack. If Harry was calling someone as if he was a staff member from Speaker McCormack's office, he was never reluctant to inform whomever he called how powerful the speaker's office was and how the speaker was so influential in the budget process. Invariably, Harry got whatever he needed for his boys. If it was a Customs-related matter, Harry became Bill Griffin. Harry made many personnel changes and policy decisions under the guise of Bill Griffin. Sometimes Harry would get caught at one of his games. Someone would call Mr. Griffin and verify what "he" requested. Mr. Griffin would explode and call down to Harry yelling and screaming at him, but no harm would come of it. Being an intimate friend of the speaker was even too big of an obstacle for Mr. Griffin to overcome.

I am sure there are many more "Harry" stories. Suffice it to say, Harry was indeed a colorful and charismatic individual, but more importantly, Harry was a good guy. When this guy's huge heart stopped beating, the world became a less colorful and dynamic place to be in.

As I continue my walk around Castle Island, I walk by the World War II memorial for all the South Boston boys who died. I always give them a nod and mutter a few words under my breath. If anyone is watching me, they must think I am nuts, but I gave up caring what other people think years ago. *The hell with them*, I'd say. About a good one hundred yards beyond the WWII memorial on the left-hand side and just before the start of the yacht clubs, there is a memorial for John "Dunny" Donavan and his lifelong buddy, Jack Stapleton. The sight of Dunny's name evokes so many memories. He was such a likable guy who knew everybody and had a story about someone or something constantly flowing from his mouth. He was the quintessential iconoclast and held no quarter for anyone. However, he wasn't mean spirited, just plain honest. During WWII, Dunny served on PT boats. Although he never went overseas, he was proud of his service and remained a sailor for life. He actually did a lot of sailing as a youth and for quite a few years after the war. Dunny also liked his "tea" and especially liked saddling up to the bar at Bowen's with a couple of pals to chew the fat. For me, Dunny was a great link with the past. A voracious reader, a student of history, and having lived through the Depression, Dunny was so enjoyable to talk with; and I gained valuable insights from our many conversations. Enough platitudes for the guy, I must tell a couple of stories about him.

Dunny, our little leprechaun, could do and say things to people that if anyone else did or said the same things would get in some serious trouble. Dunny never did get in trouble however. I don't know why. I think it was because he looked so innocent and so Irish. He would bat his eyes and raise his eyebrows and give that ever-familiar smile that would totally render him harmless. But beware to the unsuspecting! One day we were all working at the airport. We were processing passengers in the Customs Hall at Terminal E. The weather outside was awful, cold and snowy. As we were milling around talking with each other, an announcement came over the public-address system stating the bags off the incoming British flight would be delayed coming into the hall. Seems the cargo doors were all frozen and they couldn't open them to get the bags out. The passengers on the floor waiting for their bags gave a loud groan of displeasure at this news. One of the passengers, a woman perhaps in her early fifties but quite good-looking, came walking up to Dunny and began a conversation with him. This wasn't difficult to do because Dunny would talk to the wall. Anyhow, probably because the woman was so good-looking, other inspectors joined in on the conversation. I stood silently to the side but listened in closely. Not only was the woman good-looking, but she was also well-endowed and stressed the point by leaving the top three buttons of her blouse unbuttoned. Well, this fact did not go unnoticed by Dunny, and he let the woman know about it. She was extremely receptive to Dunny's interest and was suggestive of a few things herself. I couldn't believe this conversation. If anyone else talked to a passenger (or anyone else) this way, they would be fired. Dunny and this female passenger went on talking for a good ten to fifteen minutes. The things said were far beyond the flirtatious stage. They were clear, plain, and totally suggestive. I remember the woman telling Dunny she would love to take him up on his offer and Dunny muttering an inaudible remark. Finally, the bags off the flight began to come into the hall, and we all went back to our assigned belts. Dunny, being a senior inspector on the shift, was assigned as a rover. He was standing by my belt when this same lady approached him with her bags in tow. Dunny took her Customs Declaration Card and told her she was all set and pointed to the door. The woman then said to Dunny, "Not so quick, big boy. You don't think you're going to talk to me that way and get me all hot and bothered and then just dump me. Let's go. You're coming with me." The look on Dunny's face was absolutely hilarious. He didn't know what to do. This woman was calling Dunny's bluff, and he was totally speechless. All he could muster was a couple of indistinguishable words. Dunny just stammered and again waved in the direction of the exit. By this time, all the other inspectors saw what was going on, and everyone was roaring. Finally, Dunny had met his match. We thought we would never see this day when someone could get Dunny tongue-tied. After a few more minutes of friendly berating of Dunny and calling him a scalawag, the woman picked up her bags and left the hall. Dunny remained on the floor muttering to himself. This was the first time any of us saw someone get the best of Dunny. Finally his Irish luck had run out. We were relishing this moment because we knew it would probably be a long time in coming before we see Dunny get embarrassed again.

As I have said, Dunny loved to drink, and he knew everybody. You couldn't walk down the street with him without being constantly interrupted by passersby saying hello. One of his close friends and fellow drinker was a man named Warren. Warren was a boyhood friend of Dunny's and was in the Merchant Marine. Through the years, he had risen in rank from a seaman to mate to eventually becoming master of a coastal tanker running between Boston and New York. Warren's ship was in town docked at the Conley Terminal in South Boston. Taking advantage of some time off before sailing, Warren and Dunny went down to Bowen's to have a couple of beers and reminisce. The two of them spent the afternoon drinking; but they had to cut it short because Warren's ship was sailing at 1700 hours, and he, of course, had to be onboard. They left Bowen's about fifteen minutes before sailing, and Dunny drove Warren to the pier in his car. Dunny parked a distance from the gangway because he didn't want to get in the way of the line handlers and found a nice, safe place beside a pole with a firebox on it. The two of them got out of the car and said their farewells. Warren was off to the ship, and Dunny walked off to the side of one of the omnipresent sea containers in the container yard to relieve himself. As Dunny returned, Warren's ship was just edging away from the dock. In the background, sirens and air horns were splitting the air. The noise was getting ever louder and was mixing in with whistle of Warren's ship indicating he was leaving the dock. As Dunny was waving his last to Warren who was standing on the starboard wing of the ship, fire trucks came from all directions and surrounded the area where Dunny was standing. Warren pointed at Dunny, started to laugh, and then disappeared into the wheelhouse of his ship. Dunny was left standing there on the dock surrounded by fire trucks and firemen. The captain of one of the ladder trucks confronted Dunny and asked him what was going on. Why did he pull the alarm? Dunny was defenseless and puzzled for a second. Then he realized what happened. When he went to take a leak, Warren must have pulled the alarm and jumped on the ship—he was pulling a prank on Dunny. But how could Dunny explain this to the fire captain? Surely he couldn't inform on his buddy even though Warren did set him up. Dunny tried feebly to explain to the fire captain he didn't know who pulled the alarm and then showed him his Customs credentials as if to add some legitimacy to his cause. The fire captain wasn't overly impressed with an obviously inebriated guy who was possibly posing as a Customs inspector. The captain laid into Dunny and threatened him with severe bodily harm if he ever pulled another fire alarm. Dunny could only stand there and take it, but he knew he was going to get even with his buddy, Warren. As all this was going on, Warren's ship slipped around the corner of Berth 17 and proceeded down the channel to the open sea. However, they both knew this wasn't over. Dunny would come back with a vengeance.

There is an ironic twist to this whole story. The fire commissioner for the city of Boston, another South Boston native, was Leo Stapleton, a close friend of Dunny's. I wonder if he ever found out about this incident and what his reaction was. I don't know if Dunny ever got back at Warren, but my bet is he did.

I would like to tell one final quick story about Dunny. If you remember Barry Sadler and his *Green Beret* album, it reminds me of the song "Garet Trooper." Dunny was proud to be a veteran and constantly went out of his way to help veterans who were returning from overseas and coming through Terminal E at Logan. Dunny also had the highest amount of contempt for people who acted as if they were in the military but never were. Some inspectors loved to stand around and impress whoever would listen to them about how good a shot they were and how they could blow away the targets at the firing range. Their expertise with weapons was legendary, and the bad guys better watch out. Dunny had no patience for this shallow bantering. He would lay into the braggart and ask him if he was so great, why didn't he go into the service. Dunny used to say to the loudmouth, "Sure, it's easy to shoot a perfect score when there isn't anyone shooting back at you." Dunny didn't suffer fools lightly.

He was in his early sixties when he detected blood in his urine. A reluctant visit to the hospital resulted in the anticipated bad news—Dunny had cancer, or what he called the Big C. He kept the nurses laughing on his frequent trips to the hospital for chemotherapy. Judge Feeney often drove him to the hospital, and they became even closer than they were before. Finally, the end came. It was a sad moment when I heard the news, and somehow I felt sorry for Dunny. In spite of his humor, wit, charm, and laughter, I always felt Dunny was a lonely guy. So if you ever get up to heaven, because I know that's where he is, and you see a little leprechaun walking around using paperclips to hold up the cuffs of his pants, say hi to the guy for me; and if you have a couple extra bucks, buy the guy a drink. He deserves it.

ELEVEN

Characters: Walter Black

The *German Clipper* (fictitious name) was a small container vessel that called on the Port of Boston on a weekly basis in the 1980s and 1990s. She was about 325 feet long, had a blue hull with a white superstructure. The reason for her existence was to carry sea containers from Halifax, Nova Scotia, to Portland, Maine, to Boston, Massachusetts, and then back to Halifax to start the triangular route once again. She was engaged in what they call a feeder service. The mother ship would be on the North Atlantic route carrying containers from as many as four different ports in Europe to a like number ports on the East Coast of America. For example, the *Dusseldorf Express* would call on Halifax, New York, Baltimore, and Norfolk. She would discharge containers at all four ports and load outbound containers destined for Europe at the same time. She would not call on Boston because she only has a few Boston boxes, and it would not be economically feasible to make it a port of call. She does have Boston boxes onboard however, and this is where the *German Clipper* has a role. While the *Dusseldorf* is in Halifax, she will discharge all the Halifax boxes and the Boston boxes. The *German Clipper* will pick up the Boston-bound boxes off the *Dusseldorf* and many other mother ships that call on Halifax. Before she loads the Boston—or Portland-bound boxes, she will discharge her outbound boxes that will eventually wind up in Europe via one of the mother ships. I compare this process with a bunch of gears meshing together. As long as everything works properly, the gears run smoothly; but if a ship is delayed by weather or some other misfortune, the gears will grind together. Containers will miss their connecting ship, and delays will be caused all over.

The steamship agents for the *German Clipper* when she was in port was German Overseas. The purpose of steamship agents is to coordinate all the shoreside activities for the vessel. Pilots, tugs, line handlers, longshoremen, and ship's chandlers are just a few of the people the steamship agent must notify of the arrival of a ship. The specific steamship agents for the *German Clipper* were George and John. Both of these individuals are remarkable gentlemen. John has been in the business for his entire life. He was a U.S. Army officer and served in the Transportation Corps in Vietnam in the sixties. His job was to coordinate the sailings, arrivals, and unlading of vessels up and down the Mekong River. The transition for John from military life to civilian life was seamless. He is one of the most honest and trustworthy individuals on the docks of Boston. George was a third mate on the *American Leader*, a cargo ship, during WWII. In the fall of 1942, the *American Leader* was sunk in the South Atlantic by the German raider, the *Michel*. George was taken prisoner and remained a POW for the rest of the war. The Germans treated George and his fellow shipmates quite humanely while on the *Michel,* but eventually, they transferred him and the rest of the crew of the *American Leader* over to the Japanese on Java in Indonesia. The Japanese treated them quite severely by torturing and starving them. Many, many years later, George recalled these days with bitter memories. Finally at the end of the war, George was repatriated. He returned to the States and, like John, went into the shipping business. I worked with John and George for years and have many pleasant memories of our association.

The captain of the *German Clipper* was Walter Black. Walter was the typical German sea captain. Stern, methodical, and efficient were his trademarks. He and I became quite friendly over the years. Every time I went onboard the *Clipper*, Walter and I would sit down in his cabin and chat over a cold bottle of Beck's German beer. Only one bottle! All the times I was on the *Clipper,* I could only squeeze one bottle of beer per visit from Walter. I frequently brought Walter and his crew food, newspapers, and books. They were always pleasant and polite, and I always looked forward to the *Clipper's* weekly visits. Once I even met his family, his wife and son. They came over from their hometown of Hamburg, Germany, to sail with Walter for a couple of weeks. I still remember the days when I would be standing and waiting for the arrival of the *Clipper* on the dock at Berth 11 of Conley Terminal in South Boston. Right on time, often ice encrusted from its trip across the Gulf of Maine, she would loom in sight. She would slip out of the main shipping channel and enter the reserved channel headed for her assigned dock. Frequently, I would sail on her with one of my pilot friends and disembark at the pilot station and sail back into Boston Harbor on the pilot boat. The *German Clipper* brought me many years of happiness and fond memories. This is why the story I am about to tell is so painful for me.

The *German Clipper*, like all ships, often took on what they call ship stores. Usually this consisted of cigarettes, beer, and liquor. Because all these items were supposed to be consumed by the crew and were strictly not for resale, there weren't any taxes affixed to the items. Consequently, the prices were dirt cheap. Well, one day, a sharp Customs inspector was conducting an audit on the ship stores that went to the *Clipper* for the previous year. His findings were unbelievable. According to him, the *Clipper* took onboard an inordinate amount of cigarettes for the small crew of ten. In fact, this inspector figured out that the *Clipper* took onboard so many cigarettes that every crew member would have to be smoking a carton of cigarettes a day. And some of the crew didn't even smoke! Something had to be wrong. A second audit only confirmed the audit findings. Something indeed was terribly wrong. After a brief investigation, the terrible truth came out. The crew of the *Clipper* was smuggling the cigarettes to Canada and selling them to the longshoremen. Canada has a high tax on cigarettes, and buying the smuggled cigarettes from the *Clipper* saved them a lot of money. Likewise, the crew of the *Clipper* made a fortune, and they had been doing this for years. When I heard this news, I was devastated; the bond and trust that I had for Walter and the *German Clipper* was torn asunder. It was as if I had lost someone that I had loved for years. I never went back onboard the *Clipper*. In fact, the *German Clipper* was pulled off this route shortly thereafter and was sent to the Baltic. Walter called me several times from Germany at my home in an attempt to talk to me. I told my wife I didn't want to talk with Walter and to tell him I wasn't home. She was confused because she knew my fondness for Walter and his crew, but I couldn't tell her anything. Finally, I did talk to Walter on the phone. He apologized to me and told me he didn't have anything to do with this smuggling scheme. He asked me if I could intercede with Customs on his behalf. I emphatically told Walter no and told him not to ever call me again, our friendship was over. And that was that, I never talked with my friend Walter again.

George, the steamship agent, used to travel frequently to Germany doing research on a book he was writing about the war. On one of these trips, he visited Walter in Hamburg. Walter wasn't home anymore. He had a massive stroke and was spending his days in the care of a nursing home. When George returned home, he looked me up and told me about Walter. I was crushed. Even though I was mad at Walter for what happened, I didn't think he deserved this. From a bold and proud sea captain, he was now a poor, helpless invalid. I was depressed and melancholy, and to a certain degree, I still am. Walter was my friend, and maybe I should have been a little bit more understanding and talked with Walter. It is funny how life takes its twists and turns. I knew one thing for sure. If I had it to do over again, I would be much more considerate and understanding.

George gave me one last bit of information. The *Clipper* was still plodding the waters of the Baltic Sea. However, her owners have something in the works about sending her to the Mediterranean. As for George, I lost track of him. I know he retired and was still writing, but I don't think he ever published his book. Too bad. It would have been a good read.

Postscript: As of this writing, I have good news. George is alive and well and is working with a publisher putting the finishing touches on his book. It looks like we'll be reading his memoirs after all. George told me that on his most recent trip to Germany, he looked Walter up in the nursing home, but Walter wasn't there! He was home enjoying life. Walter's stroke was severe, but he was having a remarkable recovery, and the prognosis looks bright.

TWELVE

Characters: Captain Drummond

When one is writing about Customs and the Boston waterfront, if mention was not made of Captain Drummond, the story would be grossly incomplete. Captain Drummond was the captain of the oil tanker *Eskimo*. He would sail his ship to Boston Harbor on such a frequency that he was on a first-name basis with everyone. For years, the *Eskimo*'s shipping route was between Come By Chance, Newfoundland, and either Boston or Portland, Maine.

Once you were on the *Eskimo*, you couldn't wait to go onboard again. She was the cleanest ship I have ever been onboard (and I have been on hundreds in my career) due to Captain Drummond's high standards for cleanliness. Dining on ships is traditionally known as treading in dangerous waters. You weren't sure what the crew was serving you, and it was best to graciously decline any offers to eat. However, not so on the *Eskimo*. Dining with the captain was a pleasure, and the food was better than what was served in many of the well-known restaurants in Boston. A waiter would approach your table immaculately dressed in white and offer you a menu. From this menu, you could order anything you liked. You needn't worry what you ordered because everything was delicious. It had better be or else the entire commissary staff would suffer the wrath of Captain Drummond. After dinner, it was mandatory to be escorted by the captain for an inspection of his trophy room. Actually the room was officially called the officer's salon, but Captain Drummond unofficially made it into his trophy room. On all four bulkheads, Captain Drummond displayed all the trophies and memorabilia that he had acquired in his forty-plus years of shipping. On display were gifts from heads of states from countries most never even heard of. He also had countless plaques from all the many ports he had brought the *Eskimo* to dock. Mayors, governors, port commissioners—all bestowed gifts upon Captain Drummond and the *Eskimo* for their years of faithful and selfless service. Captain Drummond was so proud of this room and loved to show it off to anyone who was remotely interested.

Captain Drummond smoked cigarettes continuously. His fingers were permanently discolored a brownish hue from all the cigarettes he had held in his hands over the years. You can only imagine what his lungs looked like. He was originally from somewhere in Scotland but immigrated to Canada many years ago, sometime after the war, I believe. Now when he wasn't aboard the *Eskimo*, he called Peggys Cove, Nova Scotia, his home. He had a little house lady that kept an eye on things when he was away. Also at home was his pride and joy, a car. It was a light blue Jaguar that was the love of his life. When he was home, he would wheel around the back roads that surrounded Peggys Cove and be at the top of the world. He had pictures of this car all over and would talk about it all day. Captain Drummond was also an accomplished author. He wrote at least three manuscripts, all mysteries, but sadly never was able to successfully publish any of them. Often Captain Drummond and I would travel to the Legal Seafood restaurant near Park Square and enjoy a sumptuous meal. This was far too rich for my blood, but the captain insisted, and he was paying.

Often he would regale whoever would listen to him stories about his past. I was honored to listen to him and found his stories exciting and enthralling. One story I vividly remember him telling was about an incident on a ship while docked in India at the start of the war. Captain Drummond was only a seaman at the time. The ship he was on was an ammunition ship, and they were discharging their cargo at a port in India. Suddenly, Japanese planes attacked them. They strafed the docks and dropped bombs that exploded with a thunderous roar. Eventually his ship was struck by a bomb and immediately broke out in fire. All the crew valiantly fought the flames until it was obvious to even the uninitiated that it was a losing battle. While the majority of the crew were fighting the fires, Captain Drummond and a few others were attempting to pry open a bulkhead door that led below. Men were trapped down there, and their pleas for help were echoing in Captain Drummond's head. As they were futilely working on the door, the captain ordered everyone to abandon ship. The flames were too far advanced, and the ship was ready to blow at any minute. Captain Drummond told the captain that men were trapped below decks, but the captain was adamant. "Abandon ship!" Reluctantly, Captain Drummond and his fellow would-be rescuers left the vessel and began to run up the dock after the other sailors. As he ran, the thought of the helpless men below decks stayed with him. No, he said to himself, *I can't leave them, I must go back.* He turned on his heels, and followed by a couple other sailors, he ran back on the vessel. They returned to the door they had been previously attempting to open and renewed their efforts with adrenaline flowing through their veins. The trapped men were pleading to be released from their entombment. Captain Drummond and the other sailors fought feverishly to open the door but to no avail. Suddenly, by using a heavy metal rod, they flung the door open. Sailors came rushing out of the opening and immediately departed the vessel. Thanks would have to wait, the vessel was engulfed in flames, and the ammunition would blow at any second. As Captain Drummond told me this story, I could feel my heart quicken. I knew Captain Drummond, and I knew this story to be true. As he concluded the story, I realized why he was such an iconoclastic, independent son of a gun. After they were all safely off the ship, they rejoined their fellow sailors at the end of the pier. The captain was also there, and he admonished Captain Drummond for pulling off such a risky and foolhardy deed. He told Captain Drummond he would never get command of his own ship because he didn't know how to follow orders. Well, it was months later when the captain was summoned to the Admiralty in London. Was he going to have to account for the loss of his vessel? Absolutely not. He was going to become the recipient of the Victoria Cross for his gallantry and bravery in saving the lives of the trapped men on his ship. Captain Drummond and the other rescuers received nothing. I was amazed at this story, but Captain Drummond remained nonplussed. I attributed his unusual and different views on life to incidents such as this one. This was definitely a character-building experience.

Captain Drummond continued to come and go out of Boston Harbor. Every time he passed the CET office on the end of Berth 17 at Conley Terminal, he would step out on the wing of the bridge and continuously blow the ship's whistle. When we were there, we would go outside and wave. The fine captain made his final voyage about ten years ago. We all miss him, and whenever someone mentions his name, a smile comes to our faces. Knowing him, I am sure he is up in heaven entertaining whoever will listen to him with one of his most amusing stories. I say *finest kind* to one of the nicest guys I ever met.

THIRTEEN

Jamaican Marijuana

T oday is Valentine's Day, the designated day for officially loving everyone. Not too many Valentine's Days ago, when we were still U.S. Customs, we were making some good marijuana seizures off the flights from Jamaica. We approached these flights in a unique fashion and had the correspondingly outstanding seizure record. Every morning about 10:10 AM, a plane would take off from Terminal B in Boston destined for Jamaica. The same plane would return to Boston that same night and pull up to a gate at Terminal E in order for all the passengers to clear Customs and Immigration.

Our enforcement efforts started immediately after the plane took off in the morning. A couple of Customs inspectors would walk over to Terminal B and visit the airline's counter. The purpose of our visit was to review all the ticket receipts of the passengers on the plane that just departed for Jamaica. We were looking for tickets that were just recently purchased, paid in cash, and trips that were of short duration. If we found tickets that met these criteria, we deemed them to be suspicious because the majority of tickets are purchased weeks in advance, paid by credit card, and were for a stay of usually a week. However, we always had to be aware of the exceptions. For example, if someone bought their ticket the same day they traveled, maybe there was a death in the family, and they had to travel suddenly. If this was the case, the airlines offered a bereavement fare that is indicated on the ticket. If not, the suspicion was there. We had this targeting system down so tight; even the airline personnel were helping us. One morning as we arrived at the ticket counter, we were met by an airline representative. She had a ticket stub in her hand and was saying, "This is the guy you want. He'll have drugs when he comes back." We started to laugh at her exuberance and mockingly asked her why did she think so. She began to blurt out the facts in a professional and articulable fashion. Not only did the guy pay cash, purchased the ticket this morning, and was only going down to Jamaica for two days, but he had someone drive him up from Brooklyn this morning to fly out of Boston. This "someone" also paid for the ticket from a big roll of bills he had in his pants' pocket, and why fly from Logan when it would have been much easier to fly from New York. Something was up with this guy, and when we got back to our office, we would do some checks on him; and regardless of the results, we would definitely put his name down for inspection when his flight returned in two days. It was obvious the guy who paid for the ticket was controlling the traveler and they drove up to Boston because we wouldn't recognize him as a bad guy where New York might. After reviewing the rest of the ticket stubs from the flight, we found a couple more possibilities but nothing like this one. We returned to our office to do some research and to create a list of possibles for the upcoming flight.

We had so much success on the flight from Jamaica that the State Police used to come over to Terminal E and watch us process the passengers. Most of our seizures were between fifty to one hundred pounds of marijuana. The Assistant United States Attorney (AUSA) would invariably decline federal prosecution, but the district attorney would prosecute. Thus, the presence of the troopers. We worked closely with all the troopers, but on the Jamaican flight predominantly with three: Andy, Arthur "Red," and Billy. Andy was a big strapping guy from Lynn. Not only was he street-smart and knew all the wise guys, he was also extremely knowledgeable of the law and knew how to apply it. We worked many cases with Andy besides the Jamaican flight. We considered him a friend and knew we could rely on his help for anything. Sadly, Andy died a few years ago in a motorcycle accident off the job. I know it is a cliché, but the world is a sadder place without Andy around. Red is from Dorchester and has been around since they first started the State Police. There isn't anybody this side of the Berkshires Red doesn't know, and give him five minutes and he'll find out about anybody on the other side. Red is a stalwart, stand-up guy and has always been a huge help for U.S. Customs. His dry wit scares many away, but he is really a soft, caring guy. Red is still working. Billy is the third trooper who always worked closely with us. Billy was a Green Beret in Vietnam and experienced some horrible times that stayed with him when he came home. Billy was a great trooper and a warm, kind human being. Sadly, he passed away a few years ago.

Tonight is the night the Brooklyn kid is coming back. We would soon find out if the ticket agent is right. If she is, we should hire her. The flight comes into Terminal E about ten at night. About a half hour before the flight arrival, the ground crew that handles the flight arrives into the Customs Hall and presents us with the complete passenger manifest. With years of experience under our belts, we are able to read these manifests as well as most of the airlines staff. By reading certain annotations and codes on the manifest, we are able to determine that not only is this Brooklyn kid returning, but also he is with someone. Interesting, we thought. He left by himself, and now he is returning with someone. This method of operation (MO) is common among drug smugglers on the Jamaican flight. The "controller" will fly down, set up the deal, and then accompany the mule with the drugs back home. Most of the time the controller is clean. He is on the plane only to make sure the mule does what he is supposed to do. Sometimes the mule knows the controller is also on the same plane, but most of the time he doesn't. When the plane arrived at Gate 6, we set up a choke point that requires all passengers to pass through. As they did, we reviewed all their passports in order to identify our two targets. Once we identified the two guys, we fell back to the baggage carousel and waited for them to claim their bags. Both guys made believe they didn't know each other, and there wasn't any contact between them. This was good because we could link them together with documentary evidence—that is, the passenger manifest. It wasn't until almost all the bags were gone before the mule finally picked up two light blue Samsonite bags. The controller had already attempted to pass through Customs with only hand-carried baggage. We grabbed him and escorted him to a secondary search room. We wanted to search him in private, and even if he was clean, we wanted to hold him until we found out if the mule was loaded. Once we got the mule to an inspection belt, the inspection proceeded rapidly. One bag was loaded with *bami* bread. This is a type of bread indigenous to Jamaica that is imported into the States. We inspect this bread by simply sticking a long thin probe into it. The bread is soft and is easily penetrable. However, when we probed this bread, we almost broke our probes. The bread was solid as a rock! Immediately we knew we had marijuana because we have seen this method of smuggling countless times before. The bad guys will shape compressed marijuana into a circle about six inches in diameter and one-half inch thick. They then cover the marijuana with a type of thick wax. While this wax is still wet, they sprinkle something like wheat germ all over it. By looking at one of these bami breads, the casual observer would never know they were full of marijuana. This guy's bag was loaded with stinky fish wrapped in Reynolds wrap, jars of putrid-smelling vegetables, and bottles of booze—besides twelve loaves of bami bread loaded with marijuana. We dumped everything out of both bags and proceeded to examine the bags themselves. These guys were caught this time, but we know we are being constantly beaten. The total weight of this seizure was sixty pounds. The street price for marijuana at that time was $2,000 a pound. Therefore, this seizure was worth a not-too-shabby $120,000. Both individuals were hard-core and wouldn't talk. We Mirandized them, and they both said they wanted to talk with their lawyers. We couldn't do anything else but turn them over to the State Police. We have seen this scenario play out so many times in the past. The smugglers are real tough guys that night and "know their rights"; but in the morning, after a long miserable night in jail, they change their tune. Now they want to cooperate and usually say they didn't want to smuggle but were forced into it. The State Police attempts to glean as much information from them the next morning, but it usually isn't much. As we say in the business, smugglers are nothing but losers in life, and how can you expect to get anything useful out of them? The individuals we catch are always real sad cases. They are on welfare, pregnant, divorced, victims of abuse and neglect, unemployed, and unemployable. Most of us feel sad for them, but we have to do our job. The State Police arrested both the mule for possession with intent to distribute and the controller for conspiracy. This was a clean, open, and shut case; and since this was the last flight of the night, we were gone by midnight. As I was walking out, I wrote myself a note and stuffed it in my pants' pocket. I had to call Andy first thing in the morning and tell her she was right, the guy from Brooklyn was dirty.

This smuggling case was rewarding for us because we were assisted by the airlines, but we wished we could have carried it to the next level—actually delivering the marijuana to the intended recipient. These guys wouldn't play so all we could do was lock them up. When we catch someone who will cooperate, or play, we have a much more rewarding and interesting time. When a seizure is made, we honestly explain to the person their options: they can cooperate and tell us where and to whom the marijuana is destined and perhaps receive a more lenient sentence from the judge, or can remain silent and take the hit by themselves. Often the smuggler will cooperate and tell all. Usually the smuggler is told to carry the bags through Customs and, once through, take a seat in the main lobby of Terminal E and wait for a pickup.

Sometimes they are given a phone number to call once they have cleared Customs. In these cases, we follow the instructions of whoever is controlling the smuggler. We let them leave the Customs Hall with their bags full of marijuana and take a seat in the lobby to await the arrival of their controller. One thing they don't know, however, is that we have the lobby flooded with plain-clothes State Police and Customs inspectors. Once the bad guy comes to pick up their smuggler, we observe them and then watch as they exit the lobby for the parking lot. Once they get to the parking lot and throw the bags in the trunk, we commit ourselves. There are usually at least five or six of us who pounce on them; safety in numbers is more than a saying. The controller is totally surprised and usually succumbs without any resistance. To protect the smuggler, we treat them as if we never talked with one another. Cases like this are much more rewarding and fulfilling to us. Not only do we catch the mule, but also now we catch the guy behind the whole operation. We are able to recommend leniency for the mule if the situation warrants and the controller gets hit the hardest. One other big benefit we get by delivering the drugs, we seize the guy's vehicle.

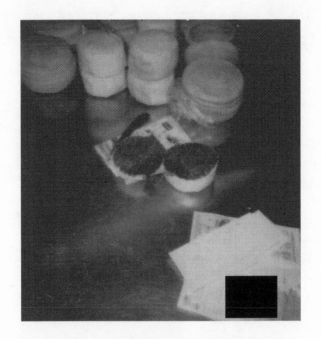

Bami from Jamaica

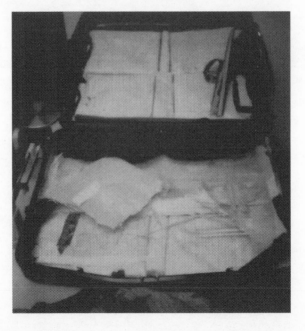

Marijuana-laden suitcase—in sides of bag

FOURTEEN

Alien Smuggling

A rumor has been going around the office for the past several days about a Chinese smuggling ring on cruise ships arriving in Halifax, Nova Scotia. Knowing one of these ships that was ostensibly involved in this smuggling was due to arrive in Boston on the twenty-fourth of September, my birthday, I planned on boarding her when she arrived either to put these rumors to rest or to substantiate them.

About 0700 hours on the twenty-fourth of September, the cruise ship *Constellation* majestically sailed into Boston Harbor. She slipped effortlessly alongside the dock at the Black Falcon Terminal, South Boston. As soon as she was all fast and the gangway was safely secured, two other Customs and Border Protection officers (CBPOs) and I boarded the ship. At the top of the gangway, we were met by one of the *Constellation*'s officers, Mr. Theodore Stephanopolos, the assistant hotel manager. Theodore was a pleasant, professional, energetic young man who was responsible for all the bookings for the passengers onboard the *Constellation*. As we met and introduced ourselves, Theodore escorted us down a passageway to a small conference room. Arrayed on the desk before us was a stack of paperwork and some Customs forms. Theodore and one of his assistants instantly began to bombard me with questions. Of major concern was the status of an elderly couple that wanted to depart the vessel early because they weren't feeling good. Theodore's assistant asked me a couple other trivial questions about Customs forms that we immediately settled. All this took me aback for a moment. The *Constellation* was traveling from New York to Boston to the Maritime provinces on a "leaf peeping" cruise. Technically, there was no need for U.S. Customs to board the *Constellation* in Boston because this was only a port of call. However, we were boarding her to check out the rumors about alien smuggling. We weren't here to process a bunch of paperwork, and I wondered what was going on. It seemed to me Theodore and his assistant were making busy work for us, and they both seemed on edge. I am not one noted for showing my cards early, so I just let things play out. Finally, I said to Theo, "Tell me about this Chinese smuggling in Halifax." The look on Theo's face was unbelievable. He looked like a calm had come over him and the weight of the world was removed from his shoulders. "Sir," he said, "I can explain that whole matter to you." I said, "Good, that is what we are here for." With that, we settled in for the anticipated explanation only to be transfixed by a lengthy story by Theo and his assistant.

Theo explained to us how the *Constellation* sailed from Le Havre, France, on September 13, 2005, for Halifax, Nova Scotia, and then New York. When they were about a day out of Halifax, his staff informed Theo that there were four Korean passengers aboard who wanted to disembark at Halifax instead of staying with the ship all the way to New York. Theo did not know what their reasons were for disembarking early, but he really didn't care. He was a busy man and had a lot of other passengers to look after. Theo told his staff to arrange the proper paperwork for Canadian Customs and Immigration and to make sure all four passengers signed a Declaration of Interruption of Cruise form. Theo didn't want any problems in the future with these four claiming they were forced off the ship. Upon arrival in Halifax, the government officials came aboard as usual, and Theo was there to greet them. He explained all was well, and the only thing out of the ordinary to report was the disembarkation of the four South Koreans. The Canadians immediately took interest in this news and asked Theo to present the four Koreans with their passports. Shortly, the four South Koreans were standing in front of the Canadian authorities with their bags dragging behind them. The Canadians were immediately suspicious of these four South Koreans and told Theo they wanted to search their staterooms. While they were doing this, other Canadian officials who were experts in passports were responding to the vessel. Upon their arrival, they inspected the passports and interviewed all four South Koreans. The result of these interviews was speedy and unequivocal—all four "South Koreans" were imposters. They were really Chinese posing as South Koreans. This news was a huge surprise to Theo, but the other news the Canadian officials gave Theo was shocking. For every individual (four) who was trying to get into Canada by using fraudulent passports, the Canadian government will issue the carrier (the *Constellation*) a fine of twenty-five thousand Canadian dollars—4 x 25,000 = Can$100,000. Theo was apoplectic. Since the boarding of passengers and the inspection of their traveling documents was Theo's area of responsibility, he would be held directly responsible for this infraction by the higher ups in his company, and as Theo explained, they would not take a hefty fine of one hundred thousand Canadian dollars lightly. Theo, in an attempt to seek mercy from the Canadians, explained that his staff examined all passports and ensured that they were valid and had *the right visas*, but they could not be held liable for a passport that was forged. Even the initial Canadian boarding team had to seek expert advice before they determined the passports were fraudulent. Theo's pleas for clemency and understanding went unheeded. Theo said the Canadians told him, "This is not of their concern" and that the carrier is liable. Theo was in a bind. The Canadians told Theo that by the time the *Constellation* was scheduled to sail, 1700 hours, they would have word back to Theo on how many of these "South Koreans" they were going to arrest and how much of a fine would be issued to the ship. As Theo was relating this entire story, he didn't realize it, but he was digging even a bigger hole for himself. If these four passengers were indeed booked for New York as Theo said, none of them had U.S. visas. They wouldn't be allowed into the United States. We would have kept all four onboard and had them leave the country the way they attempted to come in—onboard the *Constellation*. This is assuming the passports were good. If they were fraudulent, we would have done exactly what the Canadians did, but our fine would not have been anything like $25,000. More than likely, they would have claimed political asylum, and we would have eventually let them into our country. I didn't have the heart to tell Theo all this, and I didn't. He had enough problems. But as far as Theo's remark saying his crew can only check for current passports and valid visas well, if this is the case, his crew dropped the ball because none of them had a U.S. visa. Unless something else was going on. Could there be crew complicity? Could crew members be involved in this smuggling scheme in an attempt to bolster their meager incomes? I decided to stay away from this issue—at least for now. The Canadians finally gave Theo the word. All four "South Koreans" were being arrested, and the ship was being fined one hundred thousand Canadian dollars. But there was some good news. The *Constellation* could sail at her designated 1700 hours sailing time.

What Theo didn't know at the time, there was a story behind what happened to him and the *Constellation*. This was not a "cold hit" on the part of the Canadian authorities. This other part of the story began to materialize on the ninth of September with the docking of the *Jewel of the Seas* in Halifax.

Actually, the whole thing began on the first of September in Le Havre, France, when seventeen South Koreans boarded the *Jewel of the Seas*, a sister ship of the *Constellation*. These seventeen South Koreans had passage from Le Havre to Halifax and were scheduled to arrive at Halifax and disembark on the ninth of September, and that is exactly what happened. However, something happened the next day, the tenth, that tipped off the Canadian authorities that all was not right with these seventeen South Koreans. Whether it was a tip to the authorities or one of these seventeen South Koreans got in some kind of trouble, we didn't know. We did know one thing however, the Canadians were mad, embarrassed, and had egg all over their face. They allowed seventeen "South Koreans" into their country that weren't really South Korean at all—they were Chinese. That is why when Theo told the Canadian Customs and Immigration people he had four South Koreans who wanted to disembark early, they were all over the situation. The Canadians had already been duped by the *Jewel of the Seas* incident, and they weren't going to suffer this indignity and embarrassment a second time. As far as the fate of the original seventeen from the *Jewel of the Seas*, the Canadians still had no idea where they were. Supposedly they were taking a train to Montreal and then to Toronto where they were going to attempt to cross the border into the United States. The fate of these four off the *Constellation* was sealed. They were all headed off to jail.

During our discussion with Theo on the twenty-fourth, he knew there were other recent incidents with Chinese in Canada, but he wasn't privy to the magnitude of the situation. I asked Theo if anyone from U.S. Customs had interviewed him about this matter, and he said no. When I asked Theo if he would mind assisting us in putting all the facts and details of this incident together, he was eager to help. Theo was so cooperative not only because that is the type of person he is, but he figured the more cooperative he was, the quicker we could crack this case and perhaps absolve him of some of the blame that was hanging over his head. The one hundred thousand Canadian dollar fine was weighing heavily on Theo.

Coincidentally, the *Jewel of the Seas* of Royal Caribbean Cruise Lines and the *Constellation* of Celebrity Cruise Lines were somehow under the same ownership and shared the same computer software. Therefore, we had complete access to all the reservation information from both ships at our disposal. We immediately went to work, assisted by the nervously energetic Theodore. The information we found out was amazing and so readily available if someone took the time and effort to look. All thirty-three passengers—seventeen confirmed and three no shows on the *Jewel of the Seas* and four confirmed and nine no-shows on the *Constellation*—were connected and part of the same human smuggling ring. We confirmed this fact by substantiating the following information from the computerized reservation system: all tickets were bought on the same day, they were all bought from the same ticket agent, the same person bought all thirty-three tickets, and this person paid for all the tickets with the same credit card. Not only have we just broken a major human smuggling ring, we have also identified twelve more people who will probably attempt to sneak into either Canada or the United States in the not-too-distant future. Most important of all, we identified the person who was the ringleader of this entire operation. We could now go and introduce ourselves to this individual and ascertain the scope of this entire scheme. With the overwhelming documentary evidence we had in our possession, I am sure this individual will be more than cooperative.

Without Theo's help, we would still be at the starting line. He was an invaluable help, and I noted his assistance. I visited with the captain of the *Constellation* and a representative of the steamship line who happened to fly in that day from Greece. I praised Theo and sincerely conveyed my gratitude to them for all his assistance. They were most appreciative of my remarks and sentiments and promised to formally acknowledge Theo's assistance. Hopefully this might keep Theo out of some hot water because of those hefty fines from Canada. Our part was done, and the entire matter was properly relayed to our investigation division. Theo was done also. He and his pregnant girlfriend, also employed aboard the *Constellation*, were going home to Greece to marry and have their child. Theo wouldn't have to worry about passengers for at least a few months. They couldn't wait to leave on their vacation.

FIFTEEN

Northern Border Detail: Vermont

From late 1999 to the middle of 2003, Boston supplied a steady stream of inspectors to the northern New England border—Vermont, New Hampshire, and Maine. There were three major contributing factors for this major deployment of troops: Y2K, the World Trade Organization meeting in Quebec City, and the aftermath of September 11, 2001. I was intimately involved in these deployments as the supervisor of the Boston Contraband Enforcement Team and would like to briefly recount to the reader some of our experiences.

One of the areas where we focused a lot of effort was Highgate Springs, Vermont, and the surrounding border crossings: Alburg, Alburg Springs, Morse's Line, and the Pinnacle. One cold, wintry evening at Highgate Springs, we were standing around in the lobby of the main office attempting to get warm after being out in the cold for a couple of hours inspecting trunks of cars coming across the border. We were cold to the bone, and the heat was quite comforting. As we were standing there, all of a sudden, a car flew by the window at a high rate of speed heading south on Route 89. Immediately, an inspector regularly assigned to Highgate Springs picked up the phone and called Border Patrol. He described the vehicle to them, the time the car crossed the border, and then hung up. Less than an hour later, Border Patrol called and told us they found this port runner. The driver was confused and didn't know where he was. He didn't even know he crossed the border. The Border Patrol agent conducted a border inspection and released the individual. However, not before he gave the driver directions.

We constantly changed how we did business at Highgate in an attempt to keep the bad guys on their toes. Sometimes we would wait at the toll booths to pop trunks and inspect their contents. Other times we would blitz the truck lane looking for drugs, illegal aliens, or anything else. Then there were times when we would walk the line of waiting cars and pick out anyone we thought was suspicious. We would bring them to secondary and conduct a thorough exam on both the people and the car. Not only were we attempting to keep the bad guys guessing on how we operate, but I was also trying to keep things interesting for the troops. One day Jim and I were walking the line of cars that were waiting to cross the border. The weather was frightfully cold. To add to our misery, it was late afternoon and the sun was low in the sky, making it feel even colder. As we were walking along, I could see the driver of a car we were approaching start to roll down his window. As we got nearer, the driver opened up his wallet and exposed a bright, shiny gold badge. He said, "Which line is the express line?" Before I could muster up a thought, Jim said, "You're in it," and proceeded to spit out of his mouth the ever-present sunflower seeds he is always chewing on. As we walked by the guy's crestfallen face, I could barely hold in my laughter. What a funny and witty comeback by Jim, I thought, and what a nervy request by this driver who was obviously in some kind of law enforcement. Here we were, working outside in freezing temperatures hours on end and hundreds of miles from home, and this guy wanted us to show him some sympathy and expedite his passage through Customs. Not today, especially when he was probably returning from a nice vacation in Montreal while we were freezing our butts off here in Highgate and sleeping in lumpy beds in cold, noisy motels. I am sure the guy didn't know all this, but it was still nervy. At least he could have offered us a cup of hot chocolate or let us sit in his nice warm car for a couple of minutes. I would learn that this witty remark by Jim was not unusual for him. To this day, he is still leaving people speechless with some of his wry comments

To the east of Highgate Springs is a small border crossing called the Pinnacle. The hours of operation at this crossing on both sides of the border is from eight in the morning to twelve at night. Nothing can legally cross the border at this site from midnight to eight in the morning. If someone wants to cross in either direction, they must travel to Highgate Springs, a port that is open twenty-four hours a day. Even though this was the law, intelligence from the local folks told us this was not happening. Cars were frequently seen crossing over the border in the middle of the night by the local residents. The local inspectors knew this but couldn't do anything about it because of lack of manpower. They didn't have enough personnel to conduct nightly surveillances in an attempt to catch these people. Every once in a while they would set up an operation, but it was too infrequent to have any possible chance for success. Also, what was the potential here? Were these people smuggling drugs or people, or were they simply going back and forth over the border visiting friends? Because we had a lot of extra help on these northern border details, we decided to conduct as many surveillances of closed-border crossings as possible in an attempt to catch anyone illegally crossing the border. Consequently, the following story.

Jim, Craig, Dave, and I sat down one afternoon and discussed the feasibility of conducting an all-night surveillance of a border crossing with the most potential of catching someone. According to the local inspectors, the Pinnacle would be our best bet. We also liked the Pinnacle because of how it was geographically laid out. As the name implies, the station was at the crest of a high rolling hill. There was sparse vegetation on the hill, and the visibility was excellent, making it ideal for surveillance purposes. Therefore, we set up our plan of attack. We decided to set up on the Pinnacle the following night. It was a Friday night, and we figured there would be more traffic than on a mid-weeknight. Dave and Craig would move into position a little before midnight. They would pull into the border-crossing station just as the normal inspector was getting off shift. Their plan was to turn off all the lights in the station and sit there waiting for any activity. Their vehicle was parked alongside the building and was ready to move at the first sign of activity. Jim and I were going to conduct mobile surveillance. Unlike Dave and Craig who had to stay put, Jim and I could rove about in our vehicle. Even though we had this liberty, we planned on remaining mostly static on a little side dirt road about three-fourths of a mile below the station. This way we figured we could catch any "errant traveler" in a trap. If someone were heading north, we would pull in behind them and attempt to stop them. Meanwhile, Dave and Craig would head south and block their path. Cars coming from the Canadian side would be caught in our trap but in the reverse manner. Our plan was all set, Friday night we would kick off.

Both units were in place as planned just before midnight. We had a couple of potential targets, but they pulled off on side roads before they came near the border.

About 0200 hours, a car headed north at a high rate of speed. Jim and I watched him driving up the hill, and we both commented how this guy looked like he was going to attempt to cross the border. We called Dave and Craig on the radio and gave them the heads-up. Then all of a sudden, he just stopped in the middle of the road and sat there with the lights on. After about fifteen minutes, this car turned around and headed south again—false alarm. We figured it must have been kids joyriding and drinking. Maybe they stopped for a pit stop, we didn't know. That was the excitement of the night for us. After that car, there was absolutely no movement whatsoever. At about 4:00 AM, I couldn't keep my eyes open any longer. I asked Jim if he was OK because if he was, I was going to close my eyes for about fifteen minutes. I had to. We were working at a minimum sixteen hours a day, and counting travel time, it was more like eighteen hours. I couldn't keep up this pace like the younger guys, and I needed a little catnap. Jim told me he was fine and wished me pleasant dreams. I immediately went off into a deep, pleasant sleep. The vehicle bouncing down the road and the blue light on the dashboard flashing in my face rudely awakened me. I yelled at Jim and asked him where the hell he was going. He told me nowhere, he did not know where we were going. I didn't know what was going on. Jim was behind the steering wheel, the truck was bouncing around, the blue light was flashing, and he didn't know where we were going? I was wondering if I was dreaming and happened to look out the window at a clump of trees; they were motionless and didn't move relative to my position. What the hell was going on? Then we both sort of realized what was happening at the same time. After I fell asleep, Jim nodded of himself. As he was shifting around in his seat while he was asleep, his knee hit the plug going into the cigarette lighter that energized the blue light. The bright light and the whirring noise of the motor of the blue light must have startled Jim, and he jumped awake. His movement startled me, and I began to jump around. Now there were the two of us bouncing around the vehicle with the blue light flashing, thinking we were in hot pursuit of a port runner when in reality we were sitting still. After we realized what happened, we chuckled a bit but realized what happened was pretty serious. We were both exhausted and needed some serious sleep. At the first sign of dawn, we called it quits and headed back to the hotel. I promised myself to better monitor our sleep-work ratio. I sure didn't want a repeat of what happened to us last night.

East of Highgate Springs and Pinnacle are a couple more border crossings called Richford and East Richford. Jim and I had to travel to these two ports one morning to assist the local inspectors in inspecting a train that was scheduled to pass through early that afternoon. The drive out to Richford from our hotel in Winooski was quite enjoyable. The scenery of the rolling hills, ice-jammed rivers, and snow-swept fields was breathtaking. All the little quaint towns that we passed through were so Americana. After a drive of over an hour, we reached the town of Richford. We were not prepared for the sight that unfolded before our eyes, especially after all the beauty we saw coming up here. Richford seemed totally abandoned with only a few people walking around here and there. The windows of the stores on the main street were all boarded up with big sheets of plywood. It reminded us of a ghost town. We drove around for a while looking for a coffee shop but couldn't find one. Finally, we saw a group of teenage boys walking along on the sidewalk. Jim and I figured we would talk to these guys and find out what was going on around here. All four boys were between the ages of fifteen and seventeen years old. Jim and I got out of our vehicle and began to talk to them. They were not too receptive to us at all. We were both caught off guard by their recalcitrance, but being from the inner city ourselves, we figured we could handle the situation. The kids acted cocky, belligerent, and hostile to us until Jim set them straight. Jim explained to them that all we did was pull over to ask them directions to a coffee shop and eventually how to get to East Richford. For this, these kids wanted to give us a bunch of attitude. Jim did a good job humbling the kids, and they responded to Jim's toughness but at the same time gentleness. They opened up to Jim; and from being wise guys, they turned into being just a bunch of young, misguided, and forgotten kids that no one paid any attention to. None of them were still in high school, and they all were looking for jobs. They had about as much chance of finding a job in this area as me becoming president. The area we were in was called the Northeast Kingdom according to the kids. The state of Vermont sent all their welfare cases and homeless people up to this neck of the woods, they said. A couple of them were from Richford, but the others were transplants from other parts of the state. I felt so sorry for these kids. All they needed was a little break in life and they could make something out of themselves, but they wouldn't get it up here. They asked us how they could get a job with Customs and a bunch of other sincere questions. Jim and I told them that they had to get back to school and get their high school diplomas. We also told them they had to quit smoking. Every one of them was smoking the entire time we were talking. After talking for a good half hour, Jim and I had to leave. We felt like we had just made five new friends. We shook hands all around and wished the kids good luck. They responded in kind and waved as we drove away. What fate had in store for these kids, I do not know. I can only tell you one thing that tugs at my heart to this day. If they had the likes of someone like Jim up there as a teacher or as a counselor, they would all be successes. Jim and I proceeded to East Richford and worked the train as planned; however, my heart wasn't into it. My thoughts were still with those kids.

In February 2006, I was at my home in Norwood, Massachusetts, reading the morning paper while having breakfast. In the regional section, there was an article about another Vermont soldier that was killed in Iraq. As I read the story, my heart almost stopped. The young soldier was from Richford. I stared at the paper and tears came to my eyes. Could this soldier have been one of the kids Jim and I talked with years earlier? I hoped not, but of course, I would never know.

On one of our TDYs in Vermont, I was able to arrange chopper rides for some of the guys with the Vermont National Guard. The purpose of the rides was what I called area familiarization. I wanted our inspectors to see from the air what was on the ground. Besides, you don't get to go up in a chopper every day, and this might be fun for some of the guys. Craig got to go on the first trip. We drove him to the Burlington Airport to meet up with the Vermont National Guard Air Unit that was based there. After some mandatory preflight instructions by the Guard, we all walked out to the tarmac where the chopper was warming up. The chopper was what I called an LOCH (light observation chopper) that I was quite familiar with from my days in Vietnam. The LOCH was the bird of choice for our battalion commander who loved to fly around a few thousand feet in the air and bark out orders to us as we sludged through the jungle on the ground. Craig didn't have any experience in chopper flying, and I think he looked forward to this experience with much excitement but also some trepidation. Shortly before they took off, I gave Craig my personal camera and asked him to take some pictures of the "slash" for me. This is the area immediately along the border that separates the two countries of Canada and the United States maintained by the Boundary Commission. It is a swath of land about one hundred yards wide that is kept barren of any vegetation. Supposedly a no-man's-zone, it clearly defines the border and makes it virtually impossible not to know where it is. Craig assured me he would, and shortly thereafter, he was airborne for his anticipated one-to-two-hour ride. Jim and I had to wait for Craig to return so we did what some say we do best, we had lunch at one of the local restaurants. After lunch, we toured the local environs for a little bit but made sure we were back at the airport before the chopper returned. As we were walking around one of the guard's hangars, we could hear the sound of the returning chopper. Boy, was that sound familiar to me. Shortly, Craig was climbing out of the chopper with a big ear-to-ear smile on his face. Guess he liked the ride, I thought. After some small talk with the crew, we thanked them and bid them adieu. While Jim was driving out of the airport and looking for I-89, I asked Craig how the trip was. He loved it and wanted to do it again. I smiled and said we'd see, and then I asked him how many pictures of the slash did he take for me. He went silent, and his face lost all color. I asked him again, and as I did, I saw Jim looking at him in the rearview mirror. Craig was speechless. I asked him a third time in a not-so-pleasant fashion, and finally he said, "Michael, I forgot to take pictures." "What," I said, "after all I did for you in getting a ride on a chopper, and you couldn't do one simple thing that I asked of you." Actually it wasn't all that important, but it was an opportune time to crucify Craig. Jim chimed in, and both of us jumped all over Craig for quite a while. Finally Craig told us the truth. He said he was fighting airsickness the whole time, and if he tried to take some pictures, he knew he would get sick. This was a totally understandable excuse, but it was still nice ragging on him. I mockingly told Craig this was his last chopper ride. He couldn't be relied on, and I was grounding him, until the next time.

A couple of days later, we had the opportunity to take another chopper ride. I received a call at Highgate Springs from the Vermont National Guard saying they had a chopper available if we wanted to go for another ride. I explained to them that I would love to but we were busy up at Highgate and by the time we drove back down to Burlington it might be a few hours. They told me no sweat, if we still wanted to go, they would fly up and pick us up at a small regional airport just south of Highgate. How could we pass up an offer such as that? We planned on meeting at 1:00 PM, and Jim was going for the ride—sans camera. I drove the ten-minute ride from Highgate to this small regional airport. Once we arrived, we noticed an army guy out in the middle of a field setting up some kind of strobe lights. We assumed he was marking the landing zone for the chopper, and we pulled up immediately adjacent to his vehicle. Sure enough, that is what he was doing, and he said the chopper was less than ten minutes out and would be approaching from the north. Since my vehicle was close to the landing zone, I decided to move it off the field and onto a nearby dirt road. While I was transiting this meager fifty yards, I drove over something that made a loud noise and caused the vehicle to lurch. This *something* was the remains of a tree that was cut down. I got out of the vehicle and looked underneath for any sign of damage but found none. *Thank goodness*, I thought. We didn't need to be way up in Vermont with a disabled vehicle.

A few minutes later, we distinctly heard the all-too-familiar sound of the blades of a helicopter. Then we saw her descending toward us from the north. Jim was standing on the landing zone with the sergeant, and as soon as the chopper landed, Jim jumped in. Jim was now on his own chopper ride to view the slash. While Jim was gone, I went into the terminal building to see if they had a coffee machine. They didn't, but the visit was worthwhile anyhow. They had pictures all over the walls of old planes. I had time for a little reflection and thought how lucky we were being up here in Vermont. Not only were we doing a useful and important job, but also we were having a lot of fun. Jim eventually returned, and like Craig, he loved the ride. Since we really didn't have anything else planned for the rest of the day, I told Jim we were going to drive over to Champlain, New York, and visit the Customs station. Like Boston, they had a big MTXR (mobile truck X-ray), and I wanted to take this opportunity to compare how they use their truck to how we use ours. It was a much longer ride than I expected, but we finally arrived at Champlain. We left Champlain after an hour visit and headed back to our hotel in Winooski. As we were driving, I noticed a foul smell. I assumed the smell was from some of our discarded food wrappers. I told Jim that as soon as we arrived at the hotel, we had to clean out the vehicle. When we arrived at the hotel, we met some of the other guys. They said they were going down to Burlington to a nice restaurant and wanted to know if we wanted to join them. We said yes, but we would need a few minutes to change and wash up. Fifteen minutes later, we were on our way to Burlington. Now, however, the truck really stunk. It smelled like we ran over a skunk. Once again, I told Jim we were going to clean out the truck as soon as we returned to the hotel. Well, we never had the chance. As we pulled into a parking spot on the main street in Burlington, Jim noticed a film all over the windows. Even the window-washing liquid couldn't clean it. Not only did the truck stink, but also now we couldn't see out the windows. Boy, did we have a lemon. We got out of the truck and started to walk up the hill to join the others who were standing there waiting for us. All of a sudden, Rick, our canine officer, pointed at our truck and yelled out, "What's the matter with the truck?" I turned around and saw nothing but smoke and steam. "What the . . . !" Upon investigation, we found trouble, big trouble. Somehow, the metal bracket securing the bottom of the radiator to the body of the truck was pushed into the radiator itself causing a slow leak. Thus the stink we smelled must have been antifreeze burning on the engine block, and the film on the window was also antifreeze. But how could this have happened? Then it all came to me—the stump in the field when we were meeting the chopper. Oh boy, mea culpa. Well, we had to have the truck towed, and we made arrangements to rent another vehicle so everything worked out. Except for one thing, they wouldn't let me drive anymore. Jim did the majority of the driving anyhow, but now he said he was doing all the driving. They gave me my chance, and I blew it. *The heck with it*, I thought, *I don't like driving anyway.*

On another one of our trips to the northern border, Larry, Russ, Steve, and I brought the MTXR (mobile truck X-ray) up to the Vermont border for a week to blitz the inbound truck traffic. We worked primarily out of Highgate Springs but made forays over to Derby Line. It was hard work because we attempted to be unpredictable with the truck to keep the truckers guessing, but it wasn't easy because of the massive size of our truck. Our maneuverability was restricted, and truckers communicated with each other over the CB and kept each other abreast on where we were and what were we up to. We knew certain truckers were smuggling bales of hydroponic marijuana in truckloads of wood chips and peat moss. We attempted to concentrate on these special loads, but they didn't cross the border when we were there. They would wait until we moved or shut down for the day, and then they would cross. It was virtually impossible to inspect one of these trucks by hand even if the desire was there, and often it was not. We were mostly frustrated on this trip but did try to expose as many people that were interested on the potential uses of an MTXR. Customs, Immigration, Border Patrol, and the Vermont State Police all took an active interest in the potential use of an MTXR and were active participants in our endeavors. Today, most land border crossings have an MTXR assigned specifically to their station. Hopefully they are using them on a continuous basis because, although they are not the panacea to the threat of drug or weapons of mass destruction smuggling, it is indeed a giant step forward.

The "slash"—no-man's-zone between Canada and Maine

Vermont National Guard helicopter we used to patrol the border

SIXTEEN

Northern Border Detail: Maine

Boston CET (Contraband Enforcement Team) also did a lot of work in Maine between 1999 and 2003 because of Y2K, the World Trade Organization (WTO) meeting in Quebec, and 9/11. Because of all the anticipated WTO protests along the northern border, we bolstered the staff at key border crossings that we felt might be impacted. Brian, an inspector out of the Providence office, and I were sent to Jackman, Maine. We drove up to Jackman together and reminisced the whole way up. We checked into the only hotel in Jackman late in the afternoon and hurried down to the local diner to have supper before it closed. Since this was the only open eating facility in town, if we missed supper, we would be eating chips all night. After dinner, Brian and I drove around a bit; but being tired from the long drive up and anticipating an early wake-up, we hit the feathers early.

We arose early and headed directly to the port of entry. Jackman is funny in that the town is south of the border-crossing station by about twelve miles. Once you leave the town limits, you have a long lonely ride through the woods before you reach the border—that is, if the deer let you. When we left the hotel, we noticed there was a lot of sporadic low-lying fog. Consequently, we drove real slow out of town. We were lucky because we hadn't gone one mile when we came upon a herd of deer right in the middle of the road. Brian and

I, being city slickers, definitely weren't used to this. We attempted to scare them off the road by driving right up on them, but no deal—they wouldn't budge. We could see they were eating something off the surface of the road but didn't realize what it was until some time later in the day when one of the local inspectors told us it was rock salt. Eventually, the deer moved over, and we were able to sneak by and continue our trip to the border. The whole way up, we saw nothing but deer. I have often heard people jokingly say things like "There's more cattle there than people" or "There's more moose there than people." But in this case, it was true. In Jackman, Maine, there are more deer than people.

When we reached the port, we were met by a bunch of friendly inspectors. They were expecting a lot of inbound and outbound activity in Jackman over the next several days because the WTO meeting was being held in Quebec City, just north of Jackman. Additionally, there was a big protest scheduled on the American side the next day. I was involved in the meetings between the Maine State Police and the protesters regarding this protest. To many, these meetings might seem trivial and mundane; but to me, these meetings were the essence of American democracy. In Boston, when we have protests, you can expect confusion, confrontations between police and protesters, traffic snarls, and general chaos. Not so in Jackman, Maine. The protesters wanted to march on the main road from the town of Jackman to the border crossing and then back to town. The State Police saw absolutely no problem in their plans and ensured the protesters they would have plenty of police presence to ensure their safety and to direct traffic. The protesters assured the State Police that they would stick to their parade route and would actually police themselves to prevent any confusion or unnecessary delays in the flow of traffic. At the protest the next day, everything went exactly as planned. The protesters availed themselves of their constitutional rights of freedom of speech and freedom of assembly. The police presence was not confrontational but exactly the opposite. They were there to protect the constitutional rights of the citizenry of Maine. This whole episode made me proud to be an American and demonstrates how things should work between the populace and its police force. It took a trip to Jackman, Maine, for me to witness democracy in action, and it made the trip all the more worthwhile.

We had to run down to Coburn Gore, Maine, one day and had a rude awakening in geography and international politics. The distance from Jackman to Coburn Gore is maybe fifty miles in a straight line. Only problem is, this straight line takes you into Canada because there aren't any roads on the American side that connects the two towns. When traveling in Canada, it is against Canadian law to carry a firearm. Therefore, if we wanted to go to Coburn Gore via Canada, we had to disarm, which is a no-no. The other alternative was to stay in the United States and drive south on Route 201 all the way to Skowhegan and then back north on Route 27 to Coburn Gore, a trip that would take at least three hours. How would we solve this conundrum? Were we going to take an all-day trip to go fifty miles and stay in the United States, or would we take the much quicker route via Canada? Once we were done with our business in Coburn Gore, we took the long way back to Jackman that took us almost three hours.

I would like to tell one last quick story about Jackman. Between Jackman and Estcourt Station, the next border crossing about seventy-five miles to the north, lies three small border crossings used exclusively for logging trucks. These "wood ports" are manned by Customs personnel that actually live there because they are so isolated. The purposes of these crossings are to allow Canadian trucks to cross the border, load up with logs, and return to Canada. This is an arrangement that I believe is unique to the hinterlands of Maine. A couple of these ports are adjacent to Canadian paper mills, and when the inspectors wake up in the morning, their cars are covered with a couple of inches of sawdust. Doesn't sound like the place for me. It is funny, but there are a million land border-crossing stories like this one that are so different from the "normal" way of life. I remember a TDY in El Paso, Texas, when we were driving down the road along the border. Perched on top of the chain-link fence next to the road were a bunch of Mexicans or *mohados* ready to jump to the American side once we drove past them. When I asked why we didn't turn around and grab these guys, I was told that if we did, more would only jump over the fence behind us when we were busy with the first group. Only in Customs, I thought. It is indeed a unique job.

On the morning of September 11, 2001, I was home having breakfast and watching TV. The news of a plane crashing into the World Trade Center in New York City came as a shock. I initially thought what a tragic accident this was but soon realized the truth. My son Brendan called me on the phone from my brother-in-law's kennel where he worked with the news. I told him I already knew and I was watching it on the television. When the second plane crashed into the tower, I thought, *That's it, I better get to work.* As soon as I arrived, things began to happen. I received a call from the district office requesting that I get up to the Tip O'Neill building as soon as possible. There was some mention of sending troops north to bolster the land border. When I arrived uptown, everyone appeared to be in a state of shock and were all asking the question, how could something like this happen to us? I wasn't at the district office long before the Director of Field Operations (DFO) came bounding through the main door. He was talking as he was walking to no one in particular. When he saw me, he immediately began to ask questions. His main concern was how many troops I had and how fast I could get them to the northern border. I told him I had twelve inspectors standing by and we could leave within a couple of hours. He seemed amazed and pleased at my response. The DFO told me he had been in constant contact the entire morning with Headquarters in Washington. They wanted to make sure we sealed off our borders in an attempt to catch any terrorists who might be trying to flee the country. The bad guys knew the heat was going to be on in response to the attacks on the World Trade Center and they better get out of dodge while they could. When he called up north to order them to comply with Headquarters' orders, they informed him they didn't have enough manpower to do the job, thus the reason for the DFO's request. Remember, right after 9/11, all airplanes were grounded and all airports were shut down. The only practical way to get out of the country was by land. This is why it was so important to bolster the land borders as soon as possible. Leaving by sea was a possibility that was discussed but was deemed so impractical that we decided not to consider it an option. After a bit more planning and talking, it was decided we were going to split up the twelve troops between Highgate Springs, Vermont; Calais, Maine; and Houlton, Maine. Jim, Craig, and I were headed for the bitter end of Interstate 95—Houlton, Maine.

Early the next morning, the three of us were heading north at a high rate of speed. Usually you can make Portland from Boston in two hours, Bangor is another two, and Houlton two more. This is straight driving without any stops and going at a pretty good rate of speed. We actually stopped once but were going at such a clip that we still made Houlton in less than six hours. We met Bert, the area port director, and he introduced us to the rest of the folks. Bert told me he had talked with the DFO and basically we had the green light while in the Houlton area. The emphasis was on conducting outbound inspections looking for anyone remotely involved with the World Trade Center attacks, but we also had the liberty of being innovative. Bert introduced us to everyone, but of special interest were the Houlton CET inspectors because they were going to be working with us. Tim, Dan, Tom, and the three of us from Boston were going to be the point men in our enforcement actions. Knowing the importance of our mission, we began to discuss our plans shortly after we were introduced to each other. We were going to begin conducting an outbound blitz as soon as possible. We had to go into the town of Houlton and check in to a hotel, get a quick bite to eat, and then we were going to be back at the port to begin work. Tom, Tim, and Dan promised to get everything ready; and when we returned, we could get right to work.

We were back in less than an hour, and as promised, the Houlton guys had everything all set. On the outbound lanes of I-95, they had set up red cones funneling the traffic down to one lane. Adjacent to and on either side of this lane, we had a marked Customs vehicle equipped with flashing lights. Our purpose was to inspect every vehicle leaving the country and to make sure we knew who the occupants were and that they had nothing to do with the recent tragic events in New York. Also helping us were Border Patrol agents and the Maine State Police. Basically, we were conducting a roadblock on I-95 and throwing a big net over the whole port. For the rest of that day and all through the night, we searched every outbound vehicle. Other inspectors from the office would come out and relieve us periodically, but basically the whole show was ours. At about 2:00 AM, two late-model vans approached our roadblock; we waved the vehicles to a halt with our flashlights and slowly approached both sides of the vehicles. We couldn't tell how many people were inside because of the tinted windows, and because of the hour of the night, we were cautious as we approached. I noticed both vehicles were bearing New Brunswick plates, and there appeared to be many people in both vans. Craig approached the driver side of the first van and began to ask the driver some questions while the rest of us stationed ourselves to the side of the vans. In a minute, Craig walked over to me and told me the minister of New Brunswick and her staff were the occupants of the vans. With this news, I approached the van with the thought of telling them they were all set and they could proceed. Well, before I could do this, the side door of the lead van slid open and out came the minister herself. I started to apologize to the minister and explained to her what we were doing, but she would have absolutely nothing of my apology. She said it was nonsense; after what we had just been through as a country, there was no room or time for any apologies. She ordered all her people to show identification to us, and she asked me if I would like everyone out of the vans. I told her that wasn't necessary and thanked her for her cooperation. The minister was so pleasant and so sincere and seemed like such a nice lady. She told me that what had just happened in New York didn't just happen to Americans, but it was also a slap at the Canadians. She told me our countries had their differences, but we were still the closest of allies. She was insistent that if any Canadians gave us a hard time at the roadblock, she wanted to know about it. After a few minutes' delay, they were off to Canada, but she left behind a bunch of speechless inspectors. We all talked about her the rest of the night. It felt nice knowing people supported and even appreciated what we were trying to do. It made the rest of the night seem to go a lot faster. We were relieved at 6:00 AM by other inspectors and headed to our motel for a few quick hours of shut-eye. We had to be back at noon to start it all over again.

We worked some extremely long hours after 9/11 and were away from home for extended periods of time, but we also had our goof off time. We were working at the Houlton port of entry one night when Dan brought in his barbecue equipment and cooked up a whole bunch of moose burgers. Being from the city, we never had moose before; but after eating it once, we promised ourselves that we would have it again. It was simply delicious.

Another day, we went to Dan's cabin about half an hour out of town. To get there, we had to turn off a paved road and travel down an old bumpy dirt road for about twenty minutes before we came to his cabin. Located in the middle of nowhere, his property was abutted with a swift-moving stream. We sat on the embankment and ate freshly cooked steaks while we breathed in all the beauty that surrounded us. This beautiful country of northern Maine was not wasted on us city slickers. I fell in love with the country and still think of it often. Craig, Jim, and Dan took Dan's ATVs and went riding through the woods looking for animals. I stayed sitting by the stream totally enamored and overwhelmed by the beautiful scenery and the clean, crisp air. Not since Vietnam have I seen such beautiful country.

We also had to frequently drive down to Forest City and Orient to man the border. The drive down to these border crossings were breathtaking, especially when we passed through Weston. In the early evening, we had to drive with much caution because of the danger of hitting a deer or, even worse, a moose. Many inspectors did have accidents with these animals, and their vehicles suffered immensely. We learned quickly that hitting a deer or moose was not like hitting a dog back home. Often when we drove to Orient or Forest City, we would stop off at the Elm Tree Diner on the Bangor Road in downtown Houlton. Famous for their home-cooked meals, we never left that place anything but fully satisfied. The meals were great themselves, but I always had to be a pig and have a slice of pie with ice cream. Needless to say, we never lost any weight on Maine TDYs.

We even walked the slash one day between the ports of Monticello and Bridgewater. Dan, Jim, and I decided to walk the approximately five-miles distance between these ports for a couple of reasons. We wanted to get some much-needed exercise, and we also wanted to survey the area for any footpaths and trails crossing over the border. It was a beautiful day, but the five-mile jaunt turned into more like a ten-mile forced march. It was up a hill, down a hill the whole way. I don't think I saw level ground the entire trek. We were not disappointed in finding footpaths either. The whole route was rife with fresh, recently used paths that should not have been there. It was obvious there was a lot of activity in this area.

All in all, my work in Maine made me a much better inspector, and it taught me to appreciate nature all the more. Additionally, we made some lifelong friends and have had some unforgettable memories.

Outbound border stop at Houlton, Maine—hunting for the bad guys responsible for the World Trade Center attacks

SEVENTEEN

Swallowers and Packers

What are "swallowers"? For someone not in the business, the term must seem obscene or ghoulish. For someone in the business, the term *is* obscene and ghoulish. Swallowers are individuals who attempt to smuggle drugs into America (or anywhere) by ingesting them into their bodies. Once they clear Customs and Immigration and reach their final destination, they pass the drugs through their system by normal bowel movements, or so they hope. Boston has had extensive experience with swallowers. Most swallowers are extremely hard to find and are successfully admitted into the country undetected.

Once a candidate is successfully recruited, he/she must be properly trained and prepared for their trip. They actually go to a "school" and are tutored on what to say and how to act when questioned by American authorities as they attempt to enter the United States. The candidate must assume a completely new role, and they must be properly prepared. What is their job? How long have they been at this job? What school did you attend? Who are you visiting? Why? For how long? These are only a few of the questions that will be asked of them by the American Customs and Immigration officials. They must be totally prepared for all of these questions because if they are tripped up by any of them, they could be immediately turned around and sent back home. This would have devastating and even possibly deadly results. Not only wouldn't they be able to come and live in America as promised, but the possibility of one of these "eggs" in their stomachs leaking its contents into their system is dramatically increased. The results would lead to a swift and terrible death. Therefore, proper tutoring of the candidates is compulsory, and they had best learn their lessons well. Once this role-playing tutoring is complete, the candidates are introduced to the methodology of swallowing.

What they swallow is called by different names, but the most common names are "eggs," "balloons," and "pellets." These eggs, balloons, and pellets are actually tightly compressed heroin weighing between eight and ten grams. The heroin is wrapped in saran wrap, taped tightly with black electrical tape, and then stuffed into a child's balloon with its end tied off with usually a dental floss type of string. The usual amount of eggs swallowed varies, but the number 100 is the norm. Therefore, on one trip, a swallower can bring into the country two pounds of almost pure heroin. Once this is stepped on and diluted to the usual street purity of six to eight percent, one swallower can be responsible for at least ten pounds of heroin being introduced on the streets of America.

To assist the candidate in the swallowing of these eggs, they are given drugs to relax them (both during the swallowing process and for their entire trip), and they are also given some kind of local concoction that helps them swallow the eggs. Supposedly, they coat the eggs in a bowl of this concoction that allows them to swallow the eggs easier. Also, they are given extensive antiacid medicine that totally neutralizes the acids in their stomachs. This is imperative because if the stomach's acid is not neutralized, it will eat at the cover of the eggs and expose the heroin to the lining of the stomach. If this happens, death is virtually assured.

Once this training is complete, they are issued their travel documents—a ticket and false passport. However, not everyone makes it to this stage. Many drop out because they cannot pass the "final exam" given to them by their instructors. Either they cannot remember all the facts and biographical information they are required to remember, or they cannot pass the physical process of swallowing the eggs. For those who do make it this far, they are at the final stage. They receive a round-trip ticket to America and a passport. So once all the training is completed and all the traveling documents are issued, the day they have all been working toward has finally arrived.

The swallowing process is done as close to flight time as possible to minimize the risk of one of the balloons leaking. The event is conducted in privacy with only the swallower and two handlers present. One hundred balloons swallowed is not an inordinate amount and takes a couple of hours to complete if all goes well. Sometimes the candidates, after all the training and preparation, chicken out at the last second. Obviously, this is extremely frowned upon by the handlers. Hopefully, the weeding-out process prevents this but not always. Once the swallower is finished, he is whisked off to the airport. To arrive in Boston, the smuggler will have to take a plane to a city in Europe and then connect to Boston. Time is of the essence, and they don't want to be needlessly waiting around in airports waiting for a connecting flight. Also, the swallower has to watch what and how much they eat. Although they have been given medicine to neutralize the stomach acids and to prevent them from having a bowel movement, no one can be sure how each individual reacts to the medicine. Eating the wrong food could counter-react with the medicine and cause an early bowel movement that would pose grave concerns for the swallower. This exact case has happened before, and we actually caught an individual with two eggs in his travel bag. When questioned, the passenger told us he couldn't hold it anymore and accidentally passed the eggs. When we questioned him why he didn't throw these eggs away so he wouldn't get caught, he told us he was responsible for a certain amount of eggs; and if he didn't deliver all of them, he would be in real trouble. Well, he didn't deliver any of them, so he must have been in real trouble with his handlers; and he knew he was in real trouble with us. If all goes as planned and if the airline connections are made on time, the swallower should be at his point of destination—Boston—within twenty-four hours of first swallowing the balloons. Now all he had to do was get through Customs and Immigration, and he would be a success story. It would be up to us to stop him.

When we had someone we thought was a swallower, we had a couple of different routes to take. We could present the evidence to him, explain to him that we thought he had drugs in his stomach, tell him we wanted to take him to a local hospital for an X-ray of his stomach; but in order to do this, we needed him to sign a consent form. If he would sign, we would be off to the hospital. If he wouldn't give consent, we would still be off to the hospital for an MBM (monitored bowel movement) but would have to go through a couple more steps before we did this. The whole process is a bit more involved than what I described, but basically, this is the procedure.

Whatever, in this case, it was not problematic. The gentleman traveler insisted he didn't have any drugs inside of him and, yes, he would gladly sign a consent form to go to the hospital for an X-ray. He was adamant that he didn't have any drugs in him, and he would prove it by having an X-ray. We knew he was dirty, but at this point, some of us began questioning ourselves.

The guy was so believable by his actions, but his story still stunk to high heavens. I told everyone I knew how they felt, but we had to handle the situation as if we were going in front of a judge applying for a search warrant. The facts indicated we had to take this guy to the hospital for an X-ray. If we didn't, no one would question or challenge us, but we would be guilty of at least misfeasance for not doing our job. So we drove on. The passenger gladly signed the form, and we prepared him for the ride to the hospital. We taped his pant legs closed at the ankles so he couldn't pass any balloons and kick them out, but we didn't handcuff him. We felt there were enough of us and only one of him that safety was not a concern. We also didn't want to needlessly aggravate the situation. As we were taping his legs, he asked us about liability and whom he could sue for our outrageous actions. The more skittish among us became even more so.

As we escorted the gentleman out the back door of Terminal E to the ramp where our vehicle was parked, I had an inspector call the hospital to tell them we were en route with a detainee for an abdominal X-ray. They had been through this procedure numerous times in the past, so this was more of a courtesy call than anything else. The drive to the hospital took less than fifteen minutes.

As we pulled up to the emergency room, I thought to myself, *This is it. The moment of truth.* We went through the normal check-in process, and then we were directed to a changing room area. The nurse attending to us said that once our passenger changed into a nightie, we should escort him down to radiology; there was an X-ray technician awaiting our arrival. It took us no more than ten minutes to have the passenger change, and we then took custody of all his personal articles. A short walk down one of the hospital's bright, shiny, picture-bedecked corridors brought us to radiology. A diminutive young nurse who immediately took charge of the situation met us. She told us where we had to stand and then gave her undivided attention to her patient. From what we could tell, she took two pictures of our guy as he lay on his back on the table. What was on, or not on, these two X-ray films held the fate of our passenger. The whole process took only ten minutes, but the reading of the X-ray prints would take longer; the radiologist was somewhere in the hospital but couldn't be found. Finally he arrived and immediately went to work. Although we are not allowed to inject any opinions or comments regarding the X-rays, no one said we couldn't peek over the doctor's shoulder. The doctor took the prints and snapped them in place in one of the glass-encased boxes mounted on the wall. He flicked a switch that illuminated the box, and thus the X-ray. Looking over his shoulder, I could readily identify objects that looked like balloons in the passenger's intestines. I looked closer to ensure what I thought I saw was for real. A closer examination was unbelievable. The guy was loaded! My heart was pounding, I was so excited. *Thank gosh*, I said to myself. Then the doctor spoke up to confirm my own beliefs. He said the guy had "foreign articles in his alimentary canal" and he would have to be admitted to the hospital.

When I walked into the room where the passenger was waiting, I was wondering what I was going to say to him. How was I going to break the news? I had a copy of one of the X-rays in my hand, and as I entered his room, I put it behind my back. I walked up to him and asked him if he now wanted to change his story. He looked at me, and in the same convincing way he did at the airport, he explained to me that he wasn't carrying any drugs. I then showed him the X-ray picture that showed eggs throughout his system. He looked at me and asked me whose picture this was. When I explained to him that it was his, he went crazy. He denied everything and accused us of setting him up. Now I almost went crazy. I took a couple of deep breaths and then went into my liturgy. I explained to him that I didn't care what he said anymore because everything out of his mouth was nothing but lies. I also explained to him how he was now admitted to the hospital and was under direct medical supervision until he was released from the hospital. We would obviously remain because he was still in our custody, but all medical decisions were up to the doctors.

From radiology, our passenger was wheeled down to a private room in the emergency room section. We would spend the next twenty-four to forty-eight hours in this room monitoring our patient as he passed all the balloons. To facilitate this process, the nurses administered a liquid orally called "go litely". This was supposed to loosen his intestinal muscles so the balloons could flow out of him. And did it work! Our friend would lie in bed drinking this stuff, and all of a sudden, he would jump up and run to this hospital chair that had a hole cut in the middle of it. Beneath this hole was a plastic bedpan to catch whatever came out. As soon as he reached the chair, he would let loose. It sounded like Niagara Falls and pellets bouncing off a plastic roof all at the same time. When he was done, what a mess! It was up to us to take the contents and wash it out at the sink. The first round resulted in a resounding twelve eggs with a total weight of ninety-eight grams. We settled in for a long haul, knowing from experience we would be there for a long time. At this juncture, it was up to me to figure out a schedule that would give us twenty-four-hours-a-day coverage for at least the next two days. As I was doing this, our friend asked if he could talk with me. I knew what was coming because it always wound up like this. Our friend knew it was all over, and there wasn't anymore he could do. His bravado and cocky spirit had left him. Now he was humble, penitent, and meek as a house cat. He apologized to me for being so uncooperative and then pleaded with me for mercy. I told him there wasn't much I could do for him, but there was much he could do for himself—cooperate with the investigators when they arrived. If he helped the investigators catch whoever was behind this drug transaction, they could make recommendations to the judge on his behalf, and his sentence could be appreciably reduced. He promised to cooperate, and I told him it was all up to him.

We spent the next two days in the hospital with our friend with brief respites at home. He continued to pass the balloons at a steady pace for the first twenty-four hours but then dramatically slowed down. After twenty-four hours in the hospital, we had seventy-eight balloons weighing 674 grams. We asked our friend how many he swallowed, and he told us he honestly couldn't remember. Regardless, the attending physician ordered another X-ray to see how many were left inside of him. The X-ray showed at least another thirty balloons left, and some of them were still in the transverse colon, which meant we had a way to go. At this rate, we would have over two pounds of almost pure heroin in our possession. This was a good seizure, but we were paying the price for it. We had to stay in the same room with our friend the whole time, and boy, did it stink. Some of the guys started to wear masks, and even then the smell was obnoxious. Every time he passed a balloon, we had to don rubber gloves and wash them clean. Our friend was getting weak and was constantly cold. The medical staff fed him by intravenous and provided him with numerous blankets. He couldn't believe how nice everyone was to him, and I truly believe by the end of the whole ordeal he had become remorseful. Finally, on the morning of the third day, we thought we were done. We had 108 balloons with a total weight of 975 grams—over two pounds and just shy of a kilogram. We had to have one more X-ray to make sure he was clean, and then we were done. We could go home. However, this was not to be. The X-ray showed there were still three balloons left, and they were in the descending colon. Hopefully, they would be out soon. Finally after a few more hours, he passed the last three, and we had a clean X-ray. It was over, at least for us. We had 111 balloons with a weight of 1,005 grams.

Our friend did cooperate fully with our special agents, and a successful controlled delivery was effected in Chicago. We were able to arrest some more bad guys, and we were able to put another organization out of business. Sadly, we knew another organization would spring up just as suddenly. As for our friend, even though he cooperated fully, he was still looking at twelve years in jail as compared to a possible thirty years. His cooperation got him eighteen years shaved off his sentence, and hopefully he gets out a little earlier on account of good behavior. As usual, this whole thing was sad from start to finish. We only hoped that through our efforts, we kept some bad stuff from hitting the streets and thereby might have saved a few lives.

I haven't mentioned "packers" up to this point in order to prevent confusion with the term "swallowers." Packers are simply individuals who pack contraband in a cavity of their body—either vaginally or anally. The mission of the passenger is exactly the same as the swallower, to introduce contraband into the United States. The means is the only difference. We detect packers exactly like we detect swallowers, through the use of X-rays. For some reason, packers cannot or will not swallow the drugs but are willing to pack it in their bodies.

The last item I would like to discuss is, is it worth all the bother? Is finding dope in swallowers' or packers' stomachs, intestines, or body cavities worth all the problems? Are the lawsuits and the risk of exposure to possibly deadly diseases worth it? Is the apathy of the system insurmountable and not worth attempting to overcome? Is all the expense to the government in an effort to seize possibly two pounds of heroin worth it? Where does the cost/benefit factor intersect and no longer make our efforts worthwhile and cost-effective? Is this a low return for a high investment, not only in dollar sense but in the human safety factor sense also? Does the big seizure/ big problem, little seizure/ little problem, or no seizure/ no problem philosophy of some come into play here?

My reply to all these questions is pure *hogwash*. Yes, it is worth all our efforts in spite all the problems we encounter and all the obstacles we must overcome. What is the alternative? Should we let this stuff come in and further endanger our kids? I say no! We must fight on and discharge the responsibilities of our positions in a professional and admirable fashion. This is not a mere cliché on my part. I sincerely and firmly believe we must fight on and uphold the law of the land. This is our country, our value system, our constitution, and our children that we are fighting for. Yes, we have problems. Yes, we have a bureaucracy that is befuddling at times, but so what? Overcome! We in leadership positions must learn to lead and to inspire and motivate the troops and to set exemplary examples. Anything else is inexcusable. This is the United States of America, the greatest country in the whole wide world, and I firmly believe all our efforts in accomplishing this mission is worth it. To take any other course of action would be a failure and would weaken the fabric that holds and binds this country together. I am confident that if we work together as a team in spite of our differences, we will win this battle and will strengthen America in the process.

EIGHTEEN

Brazilian Smuggling

T here isn't a week that goes by at Logan Airport that we don't receive a call from either the TSA (Transportation Security Administration) or the Massachusetts State Police regarding suspicious people in one of the terminals. We respond to every one of these calls, and invariably, the people turn out to be illegal South Americans. We administratively process these people by allowing the ones that were planning on leaving the country by plane to do so (self-deportation) and serving a notice to appear (NTA) to the others. In the last few years, the rise in illegal South Americans in the Boston area has dramatically increased.

My first experience with illegal Brazilians goes back to the fall of 2004. I was temporarily assigned to Bangor, Maine, as the acting port director. Bangor's area of responsibility covered a large geographical area including much of the coastline of Down East Maine to include Bar Harbor. Coincidentally, my son was living with his family in Ellsworth, Maine, which is midway between Bangor and Bar Harbor. He is in the United States Coast Guard and was stationed in Southwest Harbor on the Aids to Navigation team. Therefore, I was able to see my son, his wife, and my two grandchildren, Ashley and Liam, quite often while I was stationed there. It was during one of these visits with my son and his family when I received a phone call from John, the Customs inspector stationed at Bar Harbor. John told me there was a problem with one of the cruise ships, the *Crystal Symphony*, that was in the harbor on a port of call. A couple of the crew, both South Americans, went ashore earlier in the day and never returned to the ship. The ship was now ready to sail, and the steamship agent gave John a courtesy phone call about the missing crew members. John, knowing the law, told the steamship agent they couldn't sail until we boarded her and ascertained the circumstances of the missing crew members. Needless to say, the cruise line wanted to sail to stay on schedule and weren't too receptive to John when he told them not to sail. John, feeling the heat, immediately called me for assistance. I commended John for making a quick decision and assured him he was exactly correct in what he had done. I asked John to call Phil (the same agent who worked with us on the ecstasy case), the Customs special agent that worked this area, and ask him if he was available to respond. Shortly after I hung up with John, my cell phone began ringing. It was John again, and he told me Phil was responding, and John suggested we all meet at the ferry terminal in Bar Harbor. From there, we could go together to the town pier and ride out to the anchored vessel on one of the *Crystal Symphony*'s liberty launches. I concurred with John's suggestions and asked him to coordinate and convey our plans to both Phil and the *Crystal Symphony*. I told John I would be leaving immediately and would see him in about thirty minutes. Phil was leaving from Bangor and probably wouldn't arrive for at least one hour.

John, Phil, and I met as planned at the ferry terminal at approximately 7:00 PM. We drove together the five-minute ride to the town pier and were met by several crew members off the *Crystal Symphony*. They had a boat standing by and were ready to transport us to the ship right away. During the fifteen-minute boat ride out to the anchored ship, the three of us discussed our plans. We decided to interview the ship's officers who were directly in command of the two deserting crew members and then interview some of their friends and close associates. After the interviews, we planned on conducting a thorough cabin search to see if we could find any suspicious information. We were finalizing our plans as we pulled alongside the ship. As we left the boat and climbed aboard the *Crystal Symphony*, dusk had arrived, and the temperature had dropped considerably from earlier in the day.

We were escorted directly to a conference room by one of the ship's officers, and on the way, we told him who we wanted to talk to. He was cooperative and promised to make those arrangements immediately. It was soon thereafter when the desired people began to enter the conference room. We interviewed each one privately but really didn't come up with anything significant. The two missing crew members appeared to be pleasant enough, and they didn't give any indication to anyone that they were contemplating jumping ship. Well, this was a dead end, we thought. But we still wanted to search the shared cabin in the hope of finding something there. One of the officers escorted us to their cabin, and as John and I entered, Phil stayed outside in the passageway and continued talking with a few members of the crew. The cabin was quite barren, but John and I began our search as planned. It was not long before John spoke up in his native Maine twang, "Well, well, what do we have here?" I was on my hands and knees searching under the desk and looked up to see John holding a piece of paper. I stood up, and John showed me what he was holding. It was a sheet of paper that had a heading of Map Quest. The body of the paper gave directions to a street address in Atlanta, Georgia. John found this paper under one of the mattresses, and it appeared new, but we weren't certain if it belonged to our deserters. I suggested to John that we keep searching to see if we find anything else of any significance. I returned to the area I was searching and noticed the trash bucket was full. I dumped the contents on the deck and began to examine each piece of trash. After I was done looking at each piece, I would put it back into the bucket. When I was about halfway done, I came across a postal receipt from Halifax, Canada (the *Crystal Symphony*'s previous port of call). I examined this receipt closely. The receipt showed that a twenty-pound package was mailed from Halifax the previous day to an address in Atlanta, Georgia—the same address on the Map Quest—and the shipper was one of our deserters. Now we had something! The deserters obviously were planning on jumping when they arrived in the States, and in preparation, they mailed their personal belongings in Halifax. We continued to search the cabin but didn't find anything else. Although the interviews didn't provide any information, finding the Map Quest letter and the postal receipt were significant. Once we went back to the ferry terminal, we could sign onto our computers and put all the information together and see exactly what we had. We thanked the crew for all their cooperation and assistance and told them we were done and were ready to leave the vessel. Again, we were escorted to the launch and jumped in for the ride to shore.

Once we arrived at the ferry terminal, we sorted out all the facts. It was obvious to us that these two crew members were planning this desertion once they arrived in the States. The mailed package from Halifax told us this, and it also told us where these two were probably headed. The same address on the Map Quest search only confirmed our beliefs. One other piece of information sealed the case for us. John ran some checks on the Atlanta address that indicated five South Americans had used this address on their entry documents in the previous two years. All five were overstays (still in the country when they should have already left), and two of them had the same last name as one of our deserters. It all came together now. But what could we do about it? In Maine, nothing, but Phil called his counterparts in Atlanta and filled them in on the details. They concurred with our findings and promised to pay this address a visit in a week or two—they wanted to give our deserters time to get there.

NINETEEN

The United States Coast Guard

T he United States Coast Guard has been around since the beginning of this nation. It originally started out as the Revenue Service. The modern-day Coast Guard has been through many changes before she reached the structure of today. She has been bounced around from one department to another, but today, she is an integral part of the Department of Homeland Security (DHS). When the Coast Guard was in the Treasury Department or the Transportation Department, her identity was somewhat masked. Today, under the Department of Homeland Security, her identity has been enhanced. She is playing a significant and vital role in the protection of our country against any potential terrorist attacks while maintaining her more traditional roles of lifesaving, aids to navigation, fishery and drug enforcement, pollution control, and vessel inspection. Having a force between thirty thousand and thirty-five thousand active duty personnel, smaller than the New York City Police Department, the only thing I fear is that the Coast Guard will be overwhelmed by all the responsibilities placed on her.

The Coast Guard is manned by some of the best-trained, highly motivated, and conscientious people I have ever worked with. In my over thirty years in working with the Coast Guard, they have never been in such a high state of readiness as they are today. United States Customs and Border Protection (CBP) relies on the Coast Guard not only for transportation on the water but also as a highly skilled workforce to complement us in our antiterrorist activities. Vessel searches and container examinations are two critical endeavors that we work on together daily. Intelligence sharing is also of vital concern. Working together and complementing each other in these areas have made us both better agencies and has actually increased the security of our nation. Believing as I do that the threat of a terrorist attack in the maritime environment is probable and imminent, this close working relationship between the Coast Guard and CBP is of utmost importance.

Over the last few decades, the face of the Coast Guard has changed remarkably. The old 30' and 40' search-and-rescue boats were replaced with the 41' boat and the self-righting 44'. The 41' and 44' are being replaced today with the 47'. The old but reliable 65' harbor tugs are still chugging along even though they are at the advanced age of fifty years old (goes to show what a good preventive maintenance program can do to stretch out the life of a boat). The 87- and 110-footers have replaced the 82' *Point* class and the 95' *Cape* class respectively. The old 133' and 180' buoy tenders have also been replaced by the ultra modern (but not as pretty) 175- and 225-footers. The old, old 327' *Secretary* class cutters have been replaced for some time by the 210-, 270-, and 378-foot cutters. All these vessels and their crews are playing a pivotal role in protecting and securing today's America. Except for the 378-footers, CBP in the New England area has utilized all these marine resources and their assigned personnel in conducting maritime law enforcement operations. The following stories, I hope, illustrate the role we are all playing in the pursuit to keep America safe and secure from any potential enemies and in responding to the ever-present threat of drug and people smuggling on our waters.

In the mid to late 1990s, we had a lot of interaction with the Coast Guard in conducting joint boardings of ships and boats at sea. Because of the tightening of the fishery laws, many fishermen were having trouble catching enough fish to meet their financial responsibilities. Some trips were actually *costing* them money. Consequently, some boats were looking for other means besides fishing to pay their expenses—that is, drug smuggling. Knowing this, Customs and Coast Guard thought it would be prudent to increase our maritime presence and concentrate on conducting three-to-five-day random patrols and board and search as many boats as possible. Even if we didn't find anything during all these boardings, we thought we would discourage any illegal activity in our area of responsibility by having such a highly visible law enforcement presence.

Three of us were assigned to the 82-foot Coast Guard cutter *Point Barrows* to conduct one of these three-to-five-day patrols. The Point Barrows—home ported out of Montauk Point, Long Island—picked us up one morning at the

Woods Hole Coast Guard Station. The weather was less than cooperative, and the forecast was for more of the same—cool temperatures, cloudy skies, and a constant mist in the air. The first thing I always did when I joined a vessel was to size up the crew, especially the senior petty officers. I attempted to ascertain what their attitude was toward our mission. I say this because back then I always experienced two different viewpoints from senior petty officers. Some enjoyed law enforcement (LE) work and looked forward to working with us; others showed outright disdain toward both the mission and us. They thought the Coast Guard's role was search and rescue and not LE. If they wanted to be cops, they would have joined a police department, they often said. When I sized up the crew of the Point Barrows, I was met with a mixed reaction. A few of the crew seemed excited about conducting LE. However, my read on the rest of the crew was not so rosy. They seemed upset, and I overheard a couple of them say out loud that they should be tied up and resting instead of boring holes in the sea. *Oh boy*, I thought, *this is great*. Not only is the weather going to be lousy, but it appeared we also had an unhappy crew to deal with. In addition to all this, we were informed that all the bunks were full because they had a couple of reservists onboard, and we would have to bunk out on the mess deck. Bad weather, an unhappy crew, and now no sleeping area for us—I couldn't wait to see what was for chow.

We left the dock just before noon and headed east. Before we sailed, I conferred with the master chief, and he and I formed some tentative plans. We thought we would transit Nantucket Sound and head out into open water, searching for any boats to board as we traveled. Once we were in the open Atlantic, we were going to head south and stay to the east of Nantucket Island. Once we reached the shipping lanes to New York that are south of Nantucket, we would head west and stay offshore of Nantucket and Martha's Vineyard. Once we reached the Elizabeth Islands, we would turn north and head up to Buzzards Bay, transit the Cape Cod Canal, and enter Cape Cod Bay. Basically, we were steaming in a big-box pattern. We planned on keeping our speed at a fuel-efficient ten knots and would be constantly monitoring the radar, looking for any potential targets that we could board. Well, as the saying goes, the best-laid plans of mice and men oft gang aglee.

We hadn't been underway for long before the visibility really began to drop. Eventually, the fog became so thick we could just make out the bow of our own boat. The master chief reduced speed even slower than the original ten knots and ordered the foghorn to be sounded. He also ordered someone to stay on the radar and not to lift his head off the eyepiece. A tense feeling pervaded the bridge of the Point Barrow, everyone paying close attention to every little detail. Every two minutes, the air was split by the prolonged blast of the foghorn. I tried to anticipate the blast and prepared myself for the ear-splitting sound, but I always unwillingly jumped at the sound and scared everyone else accordingly. Everyone on the bridge talked in hushed tones when there was any talk, and all commands were short and to the point.

Suddenly, the sailor with his head stuck in the radar called out, "Contact, starboard bow and closing fast." The master chief jumped over to the radar set and took a look for himself. "Where the hell is this guy going, and what the hell is his rush?" the master chief said. He ordered the sailor to keep a close eye on this approaching boat, and he ordered the foghorn to be sounded more frequently. I looked out the window to starboard in the direction of the approaching vessel, and I might as well have had my eyes closed. The visibility was close to zero. The sailor at the radar set called out in an understandably anxious voice that the boat was still heading directly at us and hadn't slowed down at all. The master chief slowed our vessel to bare steerageway, personally grabbed the foghorn handle, and started blasting away. He yelled to the sailor at the radar set, "Where is he?" The sailor yelled out that the boat was inside the one-mile ring headed right at us. Things were now really jumping on the bridge. All along, someone was trying to hail this invisible boat on Channel 16 to no avail. Now this sailor on the radio was changing to all possible frequencies trying to hail this boat. Still nothing! The master chief inquired "Where is he, where is he?" to no one in particular. The sailor called out that he didn't know because he was lost in the clutter in the center of the radar screen. *Holy smoke,* I thought, *this guy is within reaching distance.* I physically grabbed the railing along the chart table and hung on, possible collision was imminent. No one talked or moved. The foghorn went silent, the radio chatter ceased, and the sailor at the radar stopped calling out bearings. Everyone on the bridge just stood motionless and looked out into the floating gray void, anticipating a sudden flash of a boat and then a wrenching crash. Fifteen seconds passed, then thirty seconds, and then an entire minute. What was going on, I thought. Then the radar operator called out, "Distance is increasing off the port quarter, Master Chief." A mental image flashed across my brain. The boat had crossed our path and was continuing on, and we hadn't even seen or heard her. It was a mystery ship!

The tension on the bridge broke a bit, but everyone was still in a state of shock. That boat couldn't have cleared us by more than a boat length, and the stupid bastard probably didn't even know we were there. He probably was headed back to port from the fishing grounds, had the boat on autopilot with no one on the radar and probably not even on the bridge, and he didn't even realize how close he came to a catastrophe. Ignorance is bliss, they say. However, we did know how close we came to a catastrophic collision, and we didn't like it; but what could we do? We weren't about to chase after the guy, that is for sure. The master chief broke the silence by speaking up. He asked his XPO (executive petty officer) and everyone in general what they thought. Everyone just shook their heads and muttered. The XPO wanted to know how that guy missed us because she came so close. Finally the master chief took control of the conversation and advised us all of a change of plans. The visibility was obviously too bad to conduct a maritime enforcement operation, and it was even too bad to be underway if it wasn't absolutely necessary. Therefore, he ordered a change of plans and a change of course. He wanted to snuggle in close to Martha's Vineyard about two hundred yards offshore where there was still good water. We would stay there for the night and hope the fog lifted by morning. If it did, we would resume our law enforcement efforts, but until then, he planned on getting a good night's rest in the lee of Martha's Vineyard. After what we had all just been through, no one was about to disagree. We just felt lucky to be alive.

I awoke early, about 6:00 AM (I never actually fell asleep, all I did was nod off all night long), and went out on deck. The fog was as thick as ever, and it was miserably cold. I went back inside and had a cup of the ever-present coffee they had onboard and whiled away the time talking with some crew members. (I think they were awake. At least they were moving their lips.) This is how we spent the rest of the morning until about 10:00 AM. The fog had lifted considerably by then, and we had about one mile of pretty good visibility, enough that we could get underway and attempt to conduct some law enforcement operations.

We proceeded in an easterly direction, planning on transiting Nantucket Sound. Once we reached the open ocean, we decided to head north toward Provincetown to see if there were any boats in that area we could board. Although weather and sea conditions had improved dramatically, it was still lousy weather. We hadn't seen the sun in a few days; and everything was cold, damp, and dreary.

We were off the tip of Cape Cod, in the vicinity of Provincetown, by early evening. Visibility would increase and then decrease just as rapidly all day long. We were keeping a watchful eye out with the radar, but as of yet, we didn't have any contacts. Finally, about 6:00 PM, we had a solid contact about five miles away. We immediately notified the boarding team to start preliminary preparations for a boarding, and the master chief headed the Point Barrows in the direction of this unidentified object. Slowly the distance decreased between us, and after about thirty minutes, visual contact was made. It was a fishing boat, looked to be about a seventy-five-feet dragger, but she wasn't fishing. She was slowly plodding through the water, heading in the general direction of the Cape Cod Canal.

We made frequent attempts to hail this boat on the radio without success. After at least five minutes of trying, we heard a slow, dry, dull voice reply. He didn't even identify himself and asked us what we wanted. We identified ourselves and explained our intentions. We told the captain of this fishing vessel that we were going to send a boarding party over to him in a Zodiac, and we requested he proceed at maneuvering speed (as slow as possible) and make a lee for our boarding team (meet the seas at about a forty-five-degree angle, thus creating relatively calm waters on one side of his vessel). But before we did this, we required some information from him: name of vessel, homeport, destination, and number of people onboard. Asking the captain for this information seemed to be causing an extreme burden on him. He was slow to respond, and we had to repeat our request numerous times. This guy can't be that stupid, we thought, and we knew he wasn't. He was just giving us a hard time in the hope he would frustrate us and we would go away. Well, he was wrong. We were just as tenacious as he was feigning stupidity, and we were going to board his boat! Eventually, we had all the necessary preliminary information and radioed it back to our sector communications. We wanted them to run all the checks on the name of the fishing vessel. If there was any information on this boat, we surely wanted to know about it before we went onboard. We were in no mood to walk into a hornet's nest. Sector radioed back to us that all his checks were negative. We thanked Sector and proceeded to get the boarding team underway. Depending on the amount of personnel available, our boarding teams for fishing vessels usually consisted of six people—three from Coast Guard and three from Customs. The boarding officer (BO) was from Coast Guard; four others and I were usually sufficient for a safe and efficient boarding and searching of a fishing vessel. Sometimes the issue of who was the lead agency would come up during the planning stage. I always maintained that it was a joint boarding with joint responsibility, but I always was receptive if the Coast Guard wanted to do the boarding under the guise of Customs authority. Our policies, procedures, and practices were a bit more law enforcement oriented than the Coast Guard's, and this allowed more flexibility if we worked under Customs law. However, I was always sensitive to prevent the perception that Customs was coming onboard to run the show and we were the boss and people would do what we told them to do. It is always more productive and creates a safer and more efficient work atmosphere if everyone feels they are part of the operation and are contributing to its successful outcome.

Once we were all ready, we jumped into the Zodiac that was lying alongside the 82'. There were the six of us on the boarding team and the boat coxswain. A sailor on deck cast off the painter that was our umbilical cord to the Point Barrows, and we were off. The ride over to the fishing vessel was unpleasant at best. We were tired, wet, and cold, and the sea conditions were not helping our plight whatsoever. There was about a four-to-six-foot swell running, and the coxswain of our Zodiac had to pay close attention to what he was doing. The distance from the Point Barrow to the fishing vessel we were boarding was only about seventy-five yards, so we came alongside fairly quick and without much difficulty. However, when we were alongside, the difficulties began. The captain hadn't made a lee as requested, so we really began to take a beating. To compound the worsening situation, no one was on deck to take our line. We kept running with the fishing vessel, banging into her and taking water over the bow. As if things couldn't get any worse, the bilge pumps on the fishing vessel came on and discharged the oily sludge in the bilges over the side-smack in the middle of our Zodiac. We had a $5,000 radio that took a direct hit from some of the oily wastewater and was ruined. Was pumping the bilges a coincidence, or was it one more significant event indicating how much of a moron this captain was? I chose the latter option. Finally, a crew member came out on deck and caught our bowline. He secured it to a cleat on the fishing vessel, and we began to disembark from the Zodiac. I remained onboard to the last because I wanted to make sure everyone made it. Once everyone was onboard, I dragged my miserable self up and over the railing of the fishing vessel. Finally, we were all safely onboard.

As my feet hit the deck, I saw the Coast Guard and my guys gathering the crew of the fishing vessel onto the stern. Good, I thought. Exactly as planned. We sweep the vessel, escort the crew out into the open area of the stern; and once everyone is accounted for, we gather IDs from the crew members and run their names through our sector communications. Doing it this way, we know exactly what and who we have in front of us. If there are any bad guys, we will know about it quickly and will take extra precaution; and if there are any crew with drug convictions, we will concentrate on their living area. As I was watching the crew move aft, I noticed the Coast Guard boarding officer talking with what appeared to be the captain. They were just aft of the bridge, and by the captain's gesturing and waving his arms, it appeared to me to be less of a discussion and more of a lecturing by the captain. I decided to inquire. When I was walking up behind the Coast Guard boarding officer, I could see the anger in the captain's face. When I came within hearing distance, I *knew* the captain was mad. He was using every four-letter word in the book, and it was all directed at this poor Coast Guard guy. The captain said he had had it with the Coast Guard, and all they were good for was harassing the poor, honest fisherman (obviously this guy was never in trouble while at sea when the Coast Guard would respond and risk their lives regardless of the weather or sea conditions). The captain kept blabbering on, and the Coast Guard guy couldn't get a word in. Finally, I had enough. I gently pushed the Coast Guard guy aside and looked directly into the captain's eyes. I asked him, "Captain, do you know who we are?" He replied, "Yeah, you're the freaking Coast Guard." (Edited) As I pulled out my Customs credentials and raised them eye level to the captain, I said, "No, Captain, we're United States Customs." When I said this, I could see the color drain from the captain's face. He stammered, "Customs, what are you guys doing out here?" The tone of his voice had dramatically changed, and his aggressive persona suddenly disappeared. He actually tried to be civil. I explained to the captain that we were going to search his vessel for contraband. If we didn't find any, we would be quickly off his vessel and he could resume doing whatever he was doing before we came on scene. The captain was now a totally different person. I think he was trying to intimidate the young Coast Guard petty officer, and he did a good job of it. However, when I came along and got in his face, he quickly realized he had met his match. I say this in a most respectful manner of the Coast Guard boarding officer. He was a young relatively inexperienced man who came up against an old ornery fisherman who overwhelmed him. I also say this with respect to the captain. Yes, he was trying to intimidate the Coast Guard guy because all he wanted to do was fish and try to make a living. He didn't want any interference from some bureaucrat who wouldn't help him pay his bills. Especially if he wasn't doing anything wrong. My presence just leveled the playing field.

While all this was going on between the captain, the boarding officer, and me, the rest of the guys were searching the boat and running the names of the crew. The boat was clean; we only found some papers used for smoking marijuana. If we dug deeper, we probably would have found some personal-use marijuana, but that is not what we are looking for. We are looking for loads. Running the names of the crewmen resulted in an outstanding warrant for one of the crew. A North Shore police department issued a warrant for his arrest for an assault and battery charge. It was an old warrant; the crew member said he had already gone to court on it, and it might not have been cleared out of the court system yet. We told him to address the matter once he got back in, and he promised he would.

We had been onboard for a little over an hour, but now we were done. The boarding officer and I went to tell the captain we were finished and were leaving his boat. As we did this, the rest of the boarding team assembled aft by the Zodiac. The captain was on the bridge and greeted us differently this time. He was rather apologetic and polite. He thanked us and said he was anxious to get back to work. Honestly, I didn't blame him. Fishing was a hectic business at the best of times, and these were the worst of times. The pressure on a captain had to be immense.

In furthering our attempts to increase the visibility of law enforcement in our area of responsibility (AOR), we often conducted what we called saturation boardings. What this comprised of was exactly what it says; we saturated a particular area for a particular period of time with as many resources that were available. Usually, we would put the Coast Guard cutter *White Heath* about twenty-five miles offshore in the middle of Massachusetts Bay. Farther inshore, we would stage the cutter *Pendant*, usually about ten to fifteen miles offshore. From the small boat stations at Gloucester, Boston, and Point Allerton, the 41-footers would get underway. The *White Heath*, a slow, cumbersome 133' buoy tender, and the *Pendant*, a 65' harbor tug might seem to be odd vessels to use in a law enforcement operation. The purpose of using these two vessels was to act as staging platforms for the 41-footers. These were the boats that would do the actual boardings, and during periods of inactivity, they would come alongside either the *Pendant* or the *White Heath* for rest, chow, and crew changes.

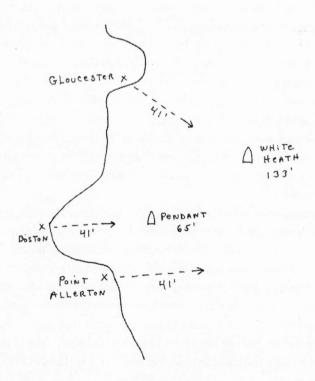

We thought that this was a good foundation to conduct LE from and attempted to put the theory into action as much as possible. One thing is for sure, the word got out fast, and there wasn't a fisherman in the area that didn't know we were there. Consequently, we would shift our operational area frequently to keep everyone on their toes.

One such shift is when we moved our efforts down to the Narragansett Bay—Block Island—Montauk Point area. Participating in this event was a 65' with the officer in charge (OIC) being the one and only Chief Jack Downey and a 55' out of Bristol, Rhode Island, with Chief Jim Annis as the OIC. We patrolled these waters jointly for two days without any success. The weather was horrible with heavy fog, and the seas were running a good six-foot swell. The conditions definitely were not conducive for boarding operations, and Chief Downey suggested we pull into Block Island until things settled down a bit. Once we arrived in the harbor of Block Island and tied up for the night, Chief Downey gave us a tour of the island via a government vehicle that was stationed on the island. During this tour by the chief, I realized how comical and yet how professional this guy was. He could find humor in just about anything, but when it got down to business, he was knowledgeable and professional. During the next almost twenty years, the Coast Guard would assign Chief Downey to all their trouble spots in New England. From Jonesport, Maine, to Chatham, Massachusetts, to Nantucket to Point Judith, he would roam. Everywhere he visited would benefit from his presence, and he would always leave a place in better condition than when he arrived. Presently, Master Chief Downey has command of the 82' out of Woods Hole, the *Hammerhead*. He is on his sunset cruise and is scheduled to retire this summer ('06). Chief Annis was another professional and good seaman. He didn't have the humor of Chief Downey, but he was pleasant company in spite of his dearth of humor. He is retired from the Coast Guard; and the last I heard, he was a police officer with the Bristol, Rhode Island, Police Department.

We let the seas settle down for the night, and the following morning, we got underway again. Both boats headed for the Montauk Point area, running abeam of each other at a distance of a mile. Although the seas had settled down, the fog was omnipresent. We had a good contact and the 55-footer took up the chase. Chief Annis kept the engines wide open and began to close the distance. I was on the 55' with the chief, and I was amazed he kept chasing this boat because we couldn't see fifty yards in front of us. I guess he was frustrated in not finding any boats to board and was pushing the envelope a bit. Finally, he called off the attack. He was hoping things cleared up as we were going along, but they didn't. Now we had to find Chief Downey and the 65-footer. After steaming around for a couple of hours, we connected with the 65' and lay to at a distance of about twenty yards. By yelling across the water, we all concurred that maybe we better go home. It was getting dangerous being out there when you didn't have to be, and besides, there wasn't anything to board anyhow. Slowly we steamed back to Bristol on the 55'. Chief Downey was going to take his 65' and tie up at the Massachusetts Maritime Academy.

An important aspect of the Coast Guard is their Air Wing, both fixed-wing aircraft and choppers. Over the years, we have worked extensively with both. In early 2001, Boston CET (Contraband Enforcement Team) with the close cooperation of Lieutenant Paul Roone, who was stationed at the Law Enforcement Office at the Coast Guard District Office in Boston, developed a strategy that would allow a joint team of Customs inspectors and Coast Guard personnel to respond to any maritime incident anywhere in New England within a couple of hours of notification. We dubbed these deployed personnel "jump teams," and the use of the Coast Guard Air Wing allowed us to respond in such a quick fashion. To prepare for any such eventuality, Lieutenant Roone coordinated Coast Guard chopper rides for Customs personnel to train on. We would set up a mock situation and plan on how we would respond to this "incident." Chopper rides up and down the coast helped us accomplish our training exercises. In today's environment where a quick response to an incident could result in prevention or at least a mitigation of a catastrophe, the jump team concept could be the answer, especially if the scene is in a remote area where Customs and Coast Guard personnel are not normally stationed. I am confident that if the jump team is ever called upon, it will respond in an outstanding fashion.

Shortly after September 11, 2001, we did have the opportunity to work with the Coast Guard Air Wing. The first arrival of an LNG (liquefied natural gas) tanker into the Port of Boston since the World Trade Center attack was about to occur. For obvious reasons, every agency, even remotely involved with maritime security, was concerned with this situation none more so than the captain of the port (COTP), Captain Brian Salerno, of the United States Coast Guard. A meeting was scheduled for the day before the scheduled arrival of the LNG at the Coast Guard base at the foot of Hanover Street in the North End. Every federal, state, and city agency with any interest at all was invited to attend and to participate at this meeting. Captain Salerno and his able staff got the meeting off exactly on time. Everyone was aware of the potential for a disaster if there was an accident or terrorist attack against the LNG. Additionally, Captain Salerno was under pressure from the mayors of some of the surrounding towns such as Boston to stop the LNGs from entering the harbor altogether. If the LNGs just disappeared, the safety problem would be solved, but how about the thousands of homes and businesses that relied on this source of energy to heat their homes and facilities? This is the problem that confronted us all that morning. The LNGs were coming, there was no stopping them, but how could we make their arrivals as safe as possible. Well, as in all such meetings, everyone had to have their say. Eventually a plan began to unfold that was spearheaded by the Coast Guard, U.S. Navy, Customs, State Police, and many of the surrounding local police departments.

Essentially, here is the plan that we settled on. We were going to keep the LNG offshore and have her anchor in Broad Sound. While she sat there, a security zone provided by the Coast Guard would completely surround her. We had a 270-foot medium-endurance cutter stationed permanently at the mouth of the North Channel providing an overall security blanket and had a 110' *Island* class cutter with a 41' search-and-rescue boat in the immediate area of the LNG providing an inner security blanket. Security warnings were constantly broadcast over the maritime channels, warning other boats to stay away from the LNG. Once the LNG was safely secured in place, the boarding team would spring into action. This team was comprised of members of a Coast Guard LEDET (law enforcement detachment) out of Virginia that was onboard the USS *Firebolt*. (When I first heard someone mention the *Firebolt*, I thought they said the "fireboat." I wondered to myself why were we getting a fireboat involved in all this.)

This team consisted of approximately a dozen Coast Guard personnel highly trained in the maritime field (i.e., our jump team). They were brought up to Boston on the *Firebolt* specifically to address the LNG issue. The Coast Guard's Boston Harbor Defense Unit was also supplying personnel and boats, and lastly, Customs was supplying ten members of CET to round out the team. The Coast Guard, State Police, and marine units from local police departments would provide escort once the LNG transited the harbor, and the State Police Dive Team was going to dive on the LNG facility in Everett to ensure there weren't any explosive devices attached to any of the pilings. We all met after the main meeting and firmed up our plans. After the windy and often nonsensical conversation of the prior meeting, it was enjoyable talking with a bunch of professionals that was focused in on the mission. All the plans were tentatively approved by everyone involved, but as usual, we all stressed to be prepared for the inevitable changes. As I left the meeting, I established my point of contact to be with Eric Lepley and Dave Considine of the Coast Guard Harbor Defense Unit.

Initially, we were preparing to board the LNG in the late morning; but as anticipated, things changed and the early afternoon was the next projected time frame set for the boarding. We all met at the Coast Guard base in Boston and stood around having coffee and talking. I was impressed by the guys from the LEDET. They appeared to be well trained, well led, and highly motivated. As we were talking, we got the word that we could get underway. The Coast Guard cutter *Grand Isle*, on scene at Broad Sound, radioed in that the LNG was anchored, secured, and ready for boarding.

We were quite the sight leaving Boston Harbor. The USS *Firebolt* was the first to leave, followed by the Coast Guard cutter *Thunder Bay* out of Rockland, Maine, and then a flotilla of Coast Guard, State Police, local police, and environmental police small boats. The ride out to Broad Sound took a little less than an hour, and when we were approaching the NC buoy at the beginning of the North Channel, we could plainly see the massive hulk of the LNG with the *Grand Isle* and a Coast Guard 41-footer circling her. Boarding the LNG was going to be an experience for those who have never done it before and even for some of us who have. All total there were at least twenty-five of us on the boarding team, and it would take awhile for all of us to get onboard.

In our preplanning, we decided to have members of all three distinct units (LEDET, Harbor Defense, and CET) on the initial wave of boardings, followed closely by the rest of the team members. As expected, the climb wasn't easy. We went from the *Thunder Bay* over to the LNG in a Zodiac. The coxswain snuggled the bow up to the Jacob's ladder, and one by one, we began the long climb up. After climbing about thirty feet, the crew of the LNG had the accommodation ladder arranged so we could step off the Jacob's ladder onto it. Climbing the accommodation ladder was a lot easier than the Jacob's ladder, but the problem was it couldn't reach all the way to the water. Slowly but surely we all made it onboard. As planned, we dispersed and began to search our assigned areas of the ship. Search teams were comprised of individuals from all three disparate groups. We wanted to foster a feeling of cooperation and unity and not of competition. BM1 Eric Lepley of the Harbor Defense Unit and I went to the captain's cabin and introduced ourselves and explained to the captain our intentions. He was most cooperative and ensured us of the ship's total compliance with our requests.

The individual teams maintained constant radio contact with Eric, and all was going well. The crew was mustered on the mess deck, and all

were present and accounted for. An initial sweep of the vessel indicated no
stowaways or obvious discrepancies, and now we would conduct an in-depth
search. About an hour into the search, I received a call from one of the search
teams requesting my presence to one of the empty crew cabins on the fourth
level. Eric accompanied me to see what was up. When we arrived, one of the
CET members briefed us on what was going on. We have a tool that we use
extensively to test for the presence of explosives. As the teams are searching
the ship, they will swipe areas of interest with a two-by-two-inch swab that
picks up the minutest particles that are present. These swabs are immediately
secured in sterile envelopes until we test them. Usually when the ship is at
the dock, we bring the tool onboard with us. However, because we didn't
want to risk lugging the heavy and bulky machine up the side of the LNG,
we left it onboard the *Thunder Bay*. The inspectors would periodically leave
the LNG and run over to the *Thunder Bay* and test the swabs in the machine.
Well, on one of these runs, Guy had a positive test for explosives on one of
the swabs. We wrote on every envelope the location of the swipe so it was
readily identifiable the location of the vessel we were concerned with. And
the cabin we were standing in was the location of the swipe. What to do? We
were under tight time constraints for this ship search because if we weren't
done in a certain period of time, the ship would miss the tide and have to
lie at anchor for another twelve hours. This would necessitate using up a lot
more man-hours on the part of every law enforcement agency concerned
because now they would have to reschedule everything. But I couldn't clear
the LNG for transit, knowing we had a positive test for explosives. This is
exactly why we were out at Broad Sound, to detect any threat or danger while
the vessel was offshore and far away from the heavily populated metropolitan
area and not tied up to a pier in the inner city among millions of people.
Well, I decided we couldn't be concerned with anything but what we had
in front of us, and I was determined to get to the bottom of it. Therefore,
I called for the captain and requested he come to this cabin immediately.
When the captain arrived, he was as confused and dumbfounded as us when
I told him we had a positive test for explosives from this cabin. The captain
ordered his chief mate to the room, and as we were waiting, we discussed
with the captain how we were going to search the room. The deck appeared
to be disturbed with a lump in the middle, and even the captain admitted
something was unusual. We were wondering how best we could pull up the
deck when the chief mate arrived. The captain, chief mate, and the steamship
agent for the ship stood among us and discussed the problem. Then the light
came on in the chief's head. Not more than a month ago, the ship had to

update its pyrotechnics onboard per SOLAS (Safety of Life at Sea) regulations. They used this particular cabin to perform that function, and some of the pyrotechnics had spilled. As coincidental as it was, I believed the whole story and was satisfied the apparent threat was totally innocuous. However, it did prove one thing, we could have faith in our technology. She proved herself under real-life conditions.

As the clock continued to click, I checked with all the teams and asked them for a SITREP (situation report). All teams were finished and were satisfied with the search. We could get off the vessel and let her transit the harbor. We had less than fifteen minutes to spare. Talk about working under pressure.

As we left the interior of the vessel and came out on deck, we were surprised to see how dark it had become and so suddenly. Actually it wasn't so suddenly at all. We were preoccupied with the search and weren't paying any attention to the local atmospheric conditions. A thick dark grey cloud cover had enveloped the whole area, making it darker than normally expected. Nonetheless, it was an eerie feeling when we were leaving the vessel. I don't know why, but a feeling of gloom overwhelmed me. Steve and I were the last ones to leave the vessel. As we were riding in the Zodiac back to the *Thunder Bay*, a Coast Guard and State Police chopper were hovering overhead. They had their powerful spotlights on, and the whole area was illuminated in this artificial lighting. This only reinforced my feeling of gloom, and the whole atmosphere seemed surrealistic. I was deep in my thoughts when I heard Steve's voice yelling in my ear. "Isn't this cool. Who the f—back home would believe we're doing s—like this, huh? Tell me!" I looked in Steve's face and saw his ear-to-ear smile and all his white teeth aglow in the artificial lighting. "Shut the hell up," I said as we took solid water over the bow of the Zodiac and got completely soaked. "You're nuts," I said. He kept smiling and laughing. I realized why Steve was so happy however. He really believed in the mission as I and wasn't afraid to show his exuberance. He was right though. It was an unbelievable scene that night in Broad Sound. Choppers overhead, navy gunboat alongside, Coast Guard cutters vigilantly on the prowl, LNG weighing anchor, and countless blue lights flashing from all the law enforcement boats in the area. As I was hanging on for my life on the Zodiac as we went airborne over a huge swell, I laughed to myself and agreed with Steve. Who would ever believe?

When we got back to the Coast Guard base on board the *Thunder Bay*, we noticed the *Firebolt* was already tied up. In fact, when we were disembarking, I noticed a large group of the LEDET guys in civilian clothes walking up the pier toward Hanover Street. When I asked them where they were going, they told me they were going for a cup of hot chocolate and asked if I wanted to accompany them. I laughed and declined; I was exhausted and wanted a hot shower and some nap time. I'd leave the nightlife to the young guys. My days for that were long over.

I have a sad footnote to tell about the USS *Firebolt*. After this operation, they were sent back to Virginia and eventually deployed to the Persian Gulf in the Far East. While stationed there, the *Firebolt* saw a lot of action, and during one of these actions, a couple of the Coast Guard guys in the LEDET were killed. I often wondered if my feeling of gloom that night was a premonition. Whatever. All I can say is that it was an honor working with these guys. I hope our country realizes how much these guys are giving in an attempt to keep us safe from a terrorist attack.

Speaking of the *Grand Isle* reminds me of the time when Jim and Patrick went on a three-day patrol on this boat. Luckily, they had fine weather during the entire patrol and had the opportunity to board quite a few fishing vessels. Jim is a strong, strapping young man in his late twenties, and he is a former football star at Brockton High School and Northeastern University and has an appetite that could break the bank. Luckily, the cook on board the *Grand Isle*, Sean, loved to cook and loved even more to watch the crew eat his fine cooking. Well, Sean did a lot of watching of Jim when he was onboard the *Grand Isle*. Jim ate and ate and ate. To this day, I am stopped by people in the Coast Guard and am asked about this guy on the *Grand Isle* who had a voracious appetite.

Off the coast of the Cape in the Nauset Beach area, Jim, Pat, and some of the crew of the *Grand Isle* boarded a fishing vessel. During the search, Jim found some personal-use heroin hidden underneath the mattress of one of the crew members' bunk. We went easy on this guy regarding a fine because he told us he knew a lot about the drug trade on the Cape, and he promised to cooperate with one of the local police departments. The last time we checked, he was working with the local police but nothing of substance yet.

Jim is still with Customs and has become a supervisor at the airport. Patrick chose to seek another line of employment. I was sad to see him leave because Patrick was a bright, energetic, and loyal guy. If he had any faults, it was that he couldn't keep his mouth shut. Patrick would even argue with this statement by saying, "Oh, I know how to keep my mouth shut, I just choose not to." As the Irish say, Patrick is the salt of the earth. And one final story about the *Grand Isle* and her crew is mandatory.

On the morning of September 11, 2001, the commanding officer of the *Grand Isle*, Lieutenant Paul Baker, was at his home in Gloucester playing with his children. The TV was on in the other room, and as Paul was playing with his kids, he heard something come over the TV about a special bulletin. Paul walked into the room where the TV was, curious to see what the bulletin was about. When he saw an airplane had hit the tower at the World Trade Center and then another plane, he knew this was no accident. America was under attack. Instinctively, Paul knew he had to get to his boat. That is where he belonged. He asked his wife if she was OK in watching the kids, and when she agreed, Paul was off to the boat. As Paul pulled into the parking lot alongside the *Grand Isle*, he noticed a lot of activity on the *Grand Isle* and adjacent pier. As Paul approached his boat, he saw his entire crew onboard, and they were getting the *Grand Isle* ready for sea! Initially, Paul was confused because the entire crew except for the usual watch standers had the day off. What was going on? he thought. The executive officer (XO) met Paul at the gangway and briefed him on what was going on. When the crew of the *Grand Isle* heard about the attacks in New York City, they all felt the same as Paul and immediately reported to the boat. The XO had called Paul's house to fill him in, and Paul's wife told him he was already headed to the boat. Assuming Paul would want to get underway, the XO ordered the crew to prepare for sea. As Paul crossed over the gangway, his heart was pounding, and he had a huge smile on his face. Boy, was he proud of these guys.

Within ten minutes of coming aboard the *Grand Isle*, Paul had his vessel underway and headed for sea. Where he was going, he wasn't sure; all he knew was that at a time like this, he belonged on the *Grand Isle* and the *Grand Isle* belonged at sea. He called the radio watch room in Boston and advised them of his status; he was underway in Massachusetts Bay awaiting orders. Shortly thereafter, Boston called on the radio requesting how long it would take Paul to get the *Grand Isle* underway for a trip to New York Harbor. Having just returned from a patrol the other day, Paul's practice was to replenish, restock, and refuel before anyone went home for a much-deserved rest. Therefore, the *Grand Isle* was ready to proceed to New York Harbor immediately. With adrenaline pumping through his system, Paul informed Boston he was underway, headed for New York. Boston was incredulous with Paul's reply but much relieved.

Paul had a quick muster with the entire crew and briefed them on what was going on. They were heading for New York at best possible speed, and when they got there, they would receive further orders. The entire crew was ready for battle. The excitement onboard was palatable. The *Grand Isle* softly vibrated as she headed south and streaked through the calm seas. While still a good distance from the Cape Cod Canal, Paul radioed the Corps of Engineers—run Control Center and requested emergency clearance through the canal. Control Center acknowledged Paul's request and told him they would have the canal wide open for his passage. Paul also told Control Center he would not reduce speed through the canal because of the situation. The dispatcher at Control Center advised Paul to make any speed necessary and wished him Godspeed.

And this is how Paul and his crew onboard the *Grand Isle* responded to the emergency of 9/11. Fine Americans indeed.

Coast Guard cutter *White Heath*

Bales of marijuana on dock at Coast Guard base, Boston

TWENTY

Paul Hogan: My Hero

T oday is Evacuation Day in the city of Boston. Two hundred and thirty years ago today, we kicked the British out of Boston and sent them packing to Nova Scotia. The passing of time has diminished this historic event to the pages of history. However, today is also St. Patrick's Day. The passing of time will never diminish the importance of this event, at least not to the average Bostonian. I cannot think of a better day to write about a good Irish-American lad by the name of Paul Hogan than today. Paul is a Customs and Border Protection supervisor. However, in the story I am about to tell, he was a Customs inspector.

Fred, Paul, and I were traveling down Route 24 one evening headed for New Bedford. We were going to meet Dave and Steve from the New Bedford office and then proceed to Brayton Point to search a coal ship. The three of us were chatting away when we noticed the car in front of us begin to swerve in and out of the passing lane. Freddie was driving, and he slowed down to distance himself from this car. All of a sudden, the car in front of us took a hard left turn and smashed into the median barrier. Without slowing down, the car bounced off the barrier, reversed direction 180 degrees, and sped off to our right. We watched helplessly as the car drove off the highway and literally went airborne as it flew into the woods at the edge of the road. Paul and I were yelling at Fred to pull our car off to the side of the road onto the breakdown lane. We wanted to get out and run back to see if anyone was hurt. Fred eventually pulled the car over. As Paul and I started to jump out of the car, I told Fred to get on the radio and call for help. Fred asked me where we were, and I told him to figure it out. I told him to drive up to the next exit and use that as a reference point.

Paul and I ran as fast as we could back to where the car went off the road, a distance of probably one hundred yards. We were the only ones to see what happened, and consequently we were the only ones responding. As we reached the site where the car left the road, Paul and I slid down the embankment and entered the woods. We still couldn't see the car, but we knew where it was because of all the broken twigs and crushed brush. About twenty-five yards in, we came upon the car. As we approached, I remember seeing steam and smoke coming from the engine area and vividly recall the cries for help and the moans of agony. *Oh my gosh*, I thought, *people are really hurt.* Amazingly, a couple of people had already extricated themselves from the wreck and were heading in the direction of the road. Paul went to the right side of the car, and I went to the left. As I fought through the brush and came up to the left rear door, I was met by the most horrific sight—there was a body trapped underneath the car. I knew we were going to need help, and as I was assisting a third victim away from the vehicle, I yelled to Paul that I was going to go back to the car and tell Fred to hurry up on the emergency vehicles. Thankfully, Fred was there with our vehicle as soon as I came out of the woods. By this time, other vehicles saw what was going on and had pulled over to assist. I told Fred to please hurry up the emergency vehicles because people were trapped. Fred told me we must be in a dead zone, and he wasn't able to get through to anyone. I was shocked at his response. I yelled at Fred to drive out of the area until the radio worked and call for some much-needed help.

I turned around and headed back down the embankment when I heard a loud pop and then saw a bright glow coming from the direction of the vehicle. *Oh no, the car is on fire, and the person is still trapped.* When I got back to the car, the entire front of the car was ablaze. Surely we were going to lose this person trapped under the car. *Where's Paul?* I thought. Then I saw Paul moving around in the backseat. I yelled at Paul to get the hell out of the vehicle before the whole thing blew up. Paul told me to shut up and help him get the guy out of the car. I was confused for a while but then saw what was going on. The person that I thought was trapped under the car was actually lying half in and half out the backdoor. He was in obvious shock, and when attempting to get out of the car, he must have got his foot caught on something. This is what Paul was doing in the backseat, trying to free this guy's foot. Before I could even help, Paul had the guy free and was pulling him out of the car. Without any exaggeration whatsoever, within thirty seconds after Paul was out of the car and carrying the guy up the embankment, the entire car was engulfed in a roaring fire.

When we reached the top of the embankment, a State Police cruiser was pulling up with fire trucks right behind. They got there as soon as possible, but it would have been too late for this guy. We started to help the injured, but shortly, there were plenty of EMTs on site; so our services were no longer needed. We sort of just waved at everyone, got in our car, and took off. We still had a ship to search.

To this day, I cannot believe what Paul did. He saved this man's life. When the time came to step up to the plate, Paul was there. I was proud of him then, and I still am today. I have only one regret regarding this whole incident. The following week, the powers-to-be heard about this incident and told me to write a report about what happened. I complied with this request but responded rather halfheartedly, assuming it was just another government report. Little did I know it was for some national award that Paul could have been nominated for. Well, my report didn't help him get this award, so I hope this little story helps make a few amends. Knowing there are people like Paul in this world instantly brings a smile to my face, and what better day to have a smile than today. Happy St. Patrick's Day to all.

TWENTY ONE

Welcome Home, Soldier

Major Robert McNamee of Hudson, New Hampshire, came home today after being deployed overseas with the U.S. Army for the past eighteen months—the last twelve months in Afghanistan. I know because as I reported to work this morning, I overheard his wife and two beautiful little daughters as they were inquiring about the arrival time of his flight. Caroline, the officer on duty at the Customs and Border Protection (CBP) desk, was advising Mrs. McNamee what time the flight was due and where she should wait to meet her husband. The little girls were waving American flags and were wearing T-shirts with a picture of a soldier on the front. It didn't take a genius to realize they were there to meet a loved one coming home from overseas. Being the sentimental type and remembering the type of welcome-home I received when I came home from Vietnam many years ago, I inquired of Mrs. McNamee where her husband was coming from. When she told me Afghanistan, I knew what I was going to do. Since the flight was still over an hour away, I told her to go get a cup of coffee and come back in one hour. When she came back, I was going to have a surprise for them.

Mrs. McNamee and the kids showed up at the CBP desk before the hour was up. I knew they were excited, and I explained to them what I was going to do. Instead of waiting in the main lobby, I was going to bring them topside so they could see the plane arrive. As we were looking out the window awaiting the arrival of the flight, Mrs. McNamee briefly told me the history of her marriage and the separation they endured because her husband was in the army. Whatever one's opinion is of our foreign policy, your heart has to go out for the men and women who wear our country's uniform. After only a few minutes more, I saw the tail of the plane coming around the corner. When I pointed this out to Mrs. McNamee and the kids, they became even more excited. Daddy was finally home. We walked down the Jetway to meet the major as soon as he deplaned. I was standing by with a camera to take some pictures of this wonderful moment. And then he was there. Much embracing, hugging, and kissing ensued with a tear shed by many—by the major, Mrs. McNamee, some passengers, and me. What I enjoyed so much was the way the other passengers treated the major. Many walked right up to him, shook his hand, and thanked him for serving his country. I was pleased to see how people genuinely appreciated what people like the major was doing.

We had to wait an inordinate period for his bags to arrive, but finally they did. We packed them on a cart, and with one of the little girls riding atop the bags and the other atop the major's shoulders, we proceeded out the exit. As we left, passengers and inspectors were saying welcome-home to the major and thanking him for all he has done. I had a huge frog in my throat. When I escorted the major and his family out of the Customs Hall, I turned and shook the major's hand and once again said, "Welcome home." We departed, but as I started to re-enter the Customs Hall, I heard a resounding noise coming from the main lobby. I turned and witnessed passengers in the entire main lobby of Terminal E at Logan Airport giving the major and his family a thunderous applause.

TWENTY TWO

Treachery and Deception

I n the early eighties, maritime smuggling seemed to be rampant in the northeast. Oil rig supply vessels were constantly being seized with tons of marijuana onboard. However, the story I am about to tell is quite different from all the rest and is full of deceit, treachery, deception, and double-crossing.

One day in the early eighties as I was drilling with my unit in the Coast Guard Reserve at Group Boston, I took a walk along the piers after I ate lunch. There were a couple of old Coast Guard cutters, the 327-foot *Secretary* class, tied up at the base awaiting to be scrapped. Being a history nut, I just had to see these ships up close and in person before they disappeared off the face of the earth. (I know the fate of three of these WWII greyhounds. The *Bibb* and the *Duane* were towed down south off the coast of Florida and sunk to be used as artificial reefs. The *Ingham* is a memorial in Charleston, South Carolina.) As I was walking slowly along the side of one of the ships, along came a woman who I assumed worked on the base. I thought she was doing exactly what I was doing, and I mentioned to her how beautiful these ships were compared to the modern—day cutters. Their lines were so graceful and just seemed to flow compared to all the right angles on the newer cutters. She acknowledged what I had to say but didn't seem to have the same enthusiasm that I had. Her mind was on something else. As she started to talk to me, her eyes darted all over the place. "You work for Customs, right?" she said. Who the heck was this woman who knew all about me? What did she want? I forgot about the *Secretary* class cutters, and I immediately went on the defensive. "Yeah, I do," I said to this beautiful young lady. "Why?" Although I went on guard, there was something about this woman that didn't convey danger or trouble, but just the opposite. She looked like she was in trouble and under a lot of duress. She apologized for bothering me but asked me if I could see someone who wanted to meet me and, if so, when and where. [To be totally honest with the reader, I must tell you I am rearranging some facts here to protect the individual who was revealing some information to me about drug smuggling. To this day, only that person and I know who each other are.] Anyhow, whether it was smart to talk with this individual or not, I did. And the information I received took the breath away from me. According to this individual, a well-known businessman on the South Shore was smuggling cocaine by boat into a local harbor. He also told us what dock they were using. The source even told me the date and time of the next delivery. Now I was skeptical. How the hell could the source know not only the date but also the exact time when it was still over a week away? I became leery of him and began to doubt the validity of the story until the source told me how the exact time could be calculated. The pier that the drug boat pulled into was accessible by only one shallow, narrow channel. The boat had a draft that only allowed her to transit this channel at high water. Since the source knew that the rich businessman always came in under the cover of darkness, he was able to compute the high tide with the cover of darkness and figure out the exact date and time the boat would arrive. After hearing this explained to me, the skepticism flowed out of me, and I became a believer again. But now what was I going to do? Yes, I did work for Customs; but I was only a clerk at the time, and I had no authority or responsibility in matters such as this. Well, I wasn't going to trouble the source with all this, so I just asked him for a contact phone number where we could reach him at in the future. "Leave the rest to us," I confidently informed him.

Well, what I did was simple. The following Monday I was with Rick, at that time, Boston's only K-9 dog handler. I explained to Rick in generalities what happened over the weekend, and I asked him whom I could talk with to give this information. Rick thought for a second and then told me he knew exactly whom I should talk with. He referred me to a Customs patrol officer who had years of maritime experience and was a trusted and loyal friend of his. *Great*, I thought, *when can I see him?* Rick asked me what my schedule was and then told me he would coordinate the meeting and set up a tentative time for 10:00 AM tomorrow. I was relieved and looked forward to passing along this information to Rick's friend.

Well, when I met Charlie, Rick's friend, the following morning, things went south pretty quick. Charlie wanted to know the source's name, address, what kind of business he was in, contact phone number, etc. I explained to Charlie that the source wanted to remain anonymous, his identity known only to me. Charlie became furious. He demanded to know the identity of the source and told me nothing would develop until he had this information. Well, I told Charlie that I was sorry, but I gave the source my word and I wasn't about to go back on that; so I guess the entire issue was dead. Charlie was fuming and began to explain to me how things worked in Customs. I was fast becoming turned off to Charlie's remonstrations and seriously considered telling him to go jump into a deep, dark lake (if not worse). Well, I kept my mouth shut and continued to listen to Charlie's haranguing. When he was done, the silence was deafening. I guess Charlie assumed his lecture would convince me to give him the source's name and phone number, but when I again refused, he was totally frustrated. We continued to drink our coffee in silence when Charlie suddenly spoke. He told me that he would talk to his bosses about this information, but he couldn't guarantee me anything unless he knew the source's name. I told Charlie I fully understood his position, and I only hoped he understood mine. After a few more minutes, Charlie left. Where we stood, I really didn't know.

A couple of days later, Charlie called me at the Customs Mail Division, South Postal Annex in Boston. He told me they were going to run with this, but I had to keep him posted on a daily basis. He didn't like this arrangement, and I know he was totally peeved with me, but he also knew he didn't have any alternative. Charlie instructed me to call the informant, get an update on what was going on, and to call him back. I did as instructed and talked with the source. He told me everything was the same; the off-load was to be a week from this Sunday at 2:00 AM. He also confirmed that the cocaine was to be hidden under coils of rope in the lazarette (a compartment in the aft part of the vessel used to store rope and buoys). The amount of cocaine, he was not sure; but from previous shipments, he estimated fifty pounds or more. After I hung up, I immediately called Charlie and filled him in. Charlie seemed satisfied and gave me his work and home phone numbers. He seemed excited when he heard how much dope was involved. Charlie told me he would have all the troops lined up to respond to the boat's arrival and asked me to maintain contact with the source. I think I only talked with the source once, maybe twice, during the next week. Both times he told me everything remained the same. My last contact with the source was Friday night of the weekend when the load was coming in. He seemed excited but mostly satisfied that finally something was going to happen to these guys. They had been bringing dope into this country for some time, and now the gig was up.

I went to bed Saturday night thinking that when I woke up Sunday morning, the whole thing would be over with. Well, a little before 3:00 AM, my phone rang. I ran to the kitchen, picked up the phone, and whispered hello. On the other end I heard the low, muffled voice of the source. He told me the boat was in, they were off-loading, and no law enforcement was there. He seemed frightened, agitated, and totally confused. He wanted to know what was going on. Little did he know, but I had no clue. Charlie told me he had it covered, and that was all I knew. I told the source not to worry, everything was OK. Immediately I called Charlie at his house. The phone rang several times before Charlie answered. I hurriedly told Charlie I just received a call from the source, and he told me the boat was in and none of us were there to greet him. Charlie seemed confused, and as unbelievable as it may sound, Charlie asked me if tonight was supposed to be the night of the off-load. I was speechless. I told Charlie he had to be kidding me. He knew full well tonight was the night, and he was supposed to have people there. Charlie uttered a few expletives and told me he would immediately call a couple of his guys, and they would be there in no time. I hung up the phone in complete and utter disbelief. After all I had been through the last couple of weeks only for things to end up like this.

It wasn't until the next week when I was told the entire story. Charlie had screwed up big-time. For some unexplainable reason, he didn't convey the information to the two Customs patrol officers correctly. They had no idea the boat was coming in that night. When Charlie called them Sunday morning, they were surprised. They responded immediately, but when they arrived at the pier, all they found were workers standing around drinking beer and laughing. The captain was standing on the wing of the bridge and welcomed the two patrol officers. He inquired if he could help them and then asked them if they would like to come onboard and search his boat. Perhaps we wanted to look in the lazarette, the captain asked.

With that comment from the captain about looking in the lazarette, it was obvious the word got out that Customs knew what was going on. But how? Additionally, it wouldn't have mattered if we were at the pier and boarded the boat as soon as she pulled in. The dope was off-loaded at a pier as they transited the Cape Cod Canal. This whole operation began as a gimme and turned into a complete boondoggle. There is only one thing about this whole affair that I was happy about—I never revealed the name of the source. Could you imagine if I did?

TWENTY THREE

Cocaine Conundrum

Today is my granddaughter Ashley's twelfth birthday. She is such a sweetheart, and we all love her so much.

We were sitting around the CET office at the airport late one morning planning our activities for the day when I received a phone call from an airline ticket agent. She told me there was a suspicious passenger at the counter and if we could come down and talk with the individual. I said sure and told her we would meet her in the bag room just behind the ticket counter. I said this because I didn't want to confront the passenger until I talked with the ticket agent, and I wanted to talk with her in private. This call meant something to me because we had been talking with the airlines and asking them to call us if they had any problems or questions. Finally, someone from the airlines called.

Three of us from CET exited Terminal E out the back door onto the ramp and walked down to the corner of the building where the baggage area was, a distance of about one hundred yards. As I walked into the baggage area, I noticed an open suitcase lying on the floor with numerous airline employees standing around. I also noticed a package lying in the suitcase that from past experience looked to me to be a "football" of cocaine. *Oh boy, we have something*, I said to myself.

As I engaged in conversation with the airline personnel, they told me they had opened the bag for security reasons; and when they did, they found this package. They told me the gentleman had already boarded the aircraft, and the plane had already pulled away from Gate 3 and was on the taxiway awaiting clearance from the control tower for takeoff to Detroit. Boy, the situation was completely different than when I talked with the ticket agent not more than five minutes ago. I thought I was coming here to talk with a suspicious individual, but instead I had an opened domestic bag with what appeared to be cocaine to me, and the individual wasn't even here anymore. As usual, what do we do now?

U.S. Customs has broad search authority of necessity because we are protecting the nation's borders. However, when it comes to domestic matters, we are restricted in what we are able to search just like any other police department—to a point. And this is where we dwell into legalese. The United States Code says that as a United States Customs inspector, if there is evidence of a drug transaction in my presence, I *shall*, not may, take immediate action. Well, wasn't this exactly the case? I didn't instruct or cajole or hint to the airline personnel to open this bag. They opened it entirely on their own for what they said was security reasons. When I came on scene, there was evidence of a drug transaction in my presence; and therefore, I felt I was obligated to take action.

I told one of my guys to go get a drug test kit and pronto. I told another to call on the radio for a K-9 unit. As this was happening, I asked who had a pen probe. Fortunately, one of the guys had one in his shirt pocket. This probe appeared to be a pen, but when you pressed the top button, a long thin probe emerged that allowed you to probe and sample packages inconspicuously. When the inspector returned with the drug test kit and not having heard anything from the K-9 unit, I decided to take action. We probed the package that was sitting in the bag and tested the contents in the drug kit. We received a positive reaction indicating the presence of cocaine. I inquired from the airline manager the location of the plane that the individual who owned this bag was on. He told me it was still sitting on the taxiway awaiting clearance for takeoff. I had to think fast about what I wanted to do. I could call the plane back to the terminal, causing a major disruption in service, and then grab this guy; or I could let the plane proceed to Detroit and call our agents out there to pick him up. I knew we could grab this guy here in Boston and could only hope that we would grab him in Detroit. I made a request to the airline manager to have the plane return to the gate. Surprisingly, the manager was extremely receptive to my request, and I think he was even hoping I made this decision. I think they wanted to see the guy get grabbed and wanted to see a successful culmination of this whole thing.

I instructed two of my guys to stay with the suitcase while the rest of us went up to the Jetway to await the return of the aircraft. As we were waiting, I asked the airline where this guy was seated on the aircraft. The ticket agent told me the seat number, which was about a third of the way down the aisle and on the right-hand side. I asked her, since she could identify the passenger, if she would mind joining us when we boarded the aircraft to grab this guy. She readily agreed. About this time, we could hear the loud whining noise of the jet engines of the returning aircraft. We all crouched down so the suspect passenger couldn't see us if he was looking out a window of the aircraft. We wanted the element of surprise and didn't want him waiting for us. As soon as the aircraft stopped, the Jetway was rolled up to the door, and the attendant banged on the door with the palm of his hand to indicate to the flight attendant it was OK to open the door. When the door sprung open, we boarded the aircraft. Three of us from CET, accompanied by the ticket agent, went on the plane and walked briskly up the aisle. I had a description of the guy and knew he was sitting on an aisle seat, so it was relatively easy to pick him out. When I thought I had him, I stopped and looked at the ticket agent. She nodded to signal "yes, indeed this was him."

I told the suspect passenger to stand up. As he did, I grabbed his arm and moved him into the aisle. One of the other CET members patted him down to ensure he didn't have any weapons. Once we were comfortable that he was clean, I asked him if he had anything else with him besides the sweater and newspaper he had on his lap. He said no, so we started to escort him down the aisle off the plane. This is when a passenger on the other side of the aisle spoke up and told us our guy was lying to us. He had a jacket in the overhead, according to this observant anonymous passenger. I walked back to the overhead compartment and opened it to find a lonesome jacket sitting there. I picked up the jacket and asked our guy if this was his. He said it was. He had forgotten all about it in the confusion. I thanked the passenger for telling us about the jacket, and we once again proceeded off the aircraft headed for our office.

While walking the now-handcuffed suspect back to the office, I radioed our sector communications and requested he contact the Customs special agent on duty and have him meet us at the airport CET office. Protocol mandated that whenever we have a drug seizure, arrest, or any other significant event, we must contact the duty agent, and they act as the liaison officer when dealing with other agencies such as DEA or the U.S. Attorney's Office. A good analogy would be the inspectors are like street patrolmen and the agents are like detectives in a local police department. When we arrived at the CET office, the two inspectors babysitting the suitcase with the cocaine were just arriving also. Now we had to wait for the agent.

Within the hour, Bill, a Customs special agent that I had worked with numerous times, arrived at the CET office. I escorted Bill into a private room and briefed him on the circumstances of the seizure. Bill started shaking his head and began to mutter to himself. Once I was finished briefing Bill, he looked at me and said something like, "This is one for the books." What Bill said was what we were all feeling. This was an unusual seizure. Without getting into all the legalese of the situation, I will tell you that search authority must be established before a seizure can be effected. Otherwise, the seizure is called "fruit from the poisonous tree." In other words, if the search was not legal, you cannot present the seizure as evidence in court. No evidence means no trial. The question before us was simple, was this search legal? An even better question was, was this even a search? We never opened the suitcase or asked anyone to open it for us. When we came on scene, the suitcase was opened and the cocaine was in plain sight. Well, as Bill said, this was one for the books. A call was made to the Assistant United States Attorney's Office. Counsel was fully briefed on the circumstances of the seizure, and we asked for legal guidance. Counsel asked numerous questions of us before she made her decision. She felt that the circumstances of this case could be defended in court, but the time and effort was not worth it. She advised us to seize the cocaine and money, but it would be best to let our subject go. If he wanted to protest the seizure, he could file a tort claim in court. None of us thought this would be a serious option to be pursued by the subject. Who in his right mind would claim ownership of a kilo of cocaine and request its return?

When we let the guy go, he was so brazen as to ask us for a receipt for the kilo of cocaine. When we declined to give him one, he asked how he was going to explain to his handlers the missing cocaine. We told him that was his problem, but we did offer him a solution. We told him to tell the owners of the cocaine to come down and see us; we would love to talk with them. I often wondered how he did explain the missing cocaine. Obviously, he was just a courier being paid to transport this stuff. How could he go back to his handlers and say the feds seized their cocaine but didn't arrest him. Would they believe him and simply accept the loss? I doubt it. In one way, he lucked out in not being arrested, but he might have suffered even a worse fate.

Cocaine in bag

TWENTY FOUR

Outbounds

U nited States law has established strict requirements for transporting money in and out of the country. You can import or export as much money as you want, but if the amount is over $10,000, reporting is required. Failure to comply with the law results in significant fines and even total forfeiture of all monies, depending on whether the violator can substantiate the source and legality of the funds in question. The primary purpose of our currency reporting laws are to curtail the flow of money gained by illegal means—that is, drug smuggling. However, many others are caught in the legal web besides the intended targets. Additionally, when exporting cars, titles and Shipper's Export Declarations (SEDs) must be filed in a timely manner.

We were waiting in the boarding area at the bottom of the stairs just before the Jetway for the passengers to board. Once they began to come down, we would pull people aside, inform them of the currency reporting requirements, and then ask them how much money they were carrying. The vast majority would be way below the $10,000 threshold. Often we would ask them if they had over $10,000. Invariably they would say, "I wish."

As I was standing there, I noticed a passenger that seemed startled and concerned when he saw us. I called him over and began to talk with him. I explained to him what our purpose was and asked him the currency question.

He laughed and said he wasn't carrying over $10,000, but I didn't like his mannerisms. His mouth seemed dry, he kept licking his lips, he was awful nervous, and he wouldn't make eye contact with me. When I tried to establish his reason for visiting the United States, he couldn't give me a legitimate answer. His occupation back home seemed doubtful also. He claimed to be an accountant but didn't know the difference between a debtor and creditor and didn't know what GNP meant. As I riffled through his passport, I counted three trips in the last eight months that he made to America. When I questioned him about all his travels, he couldn't give a proper answer. I suspected him to be a possible heroin courier when he was coming to America and possibly a money courier when leaving. He was really nervous, and I believed he had money on him. When I checked how much he had on him, it was only a few hundred dollars. When I asked him how much he had in his checked bags, he said he didn't have any money there.

I didn't believe him, but pulling his bags out of the belly of the plane would cause heartburn for the airline, especially because he came from Philly. His bags were loaded first and would be the hardest to get at. Paul, another inspector on CET, was watching my entire inspection; and I asked him what he thought. Paul agreed with me but also said getting his bags out of the plane would cause holy hell with the airline. I was convinced he had money in his checked bags and told Paul I was going for it. Paul rolled his eyes and wished me luck.

When I told an airline representative that was processing the flight that I wanted this guy's checked bags, the expected reaction occurred. The station manager came to talk with me and explained the ramifications of my request. The airplane would be delayed; people would miss their connections in Europe, they would have to be put up in hotels. My request was simply cost prohibitive. *What about enforcing the law?* I thought as the station manager rambled on. When he was finished, I told him the quicker he got the bags, the quicker we could do our inspection, and the quicker the plane could leave. Eventually he realized there was no more sense of pleading; he would have to get the bags. But he tried one more tactic. To let the plane go with the bags, and he promised he would have the bags returned to Boston on the next flight, untouched by the owner. I was angry and insulted. Here we are, attempting to enforce the laws of America, and the airline couldn't give a hoot. All they care about is being on time! I told the manager enough was enough and I wanted the bags.

As we were standing around waiting for Swissair to retrieve this gentleman's bags, Paul smiled and said he hoped I was right. Otherwise,

I might be reassigned to Madawaska, Maine, in the morning. This was an obvious overstatement by Paul, but it is for sure a lot of people wouldn't be happy with us pulling the bags and not finding anything. After fifteen minutes had elapsed, Swissair delivered the passenger's three bags to us on the Jetway. My moment of truth! I grabbed a bag, opened it, and started to examine its contents. Other CET members began to inspect the other two bags. We wanted to hurry in case I was wrong. I removed the gentleman's top layer of clothing, pants and shirts, and then I saw a Pampers diaper box. *What the heck is he doing with Pampers*, I thought. Obviously, this was it. When I opened the Pampers box, all I saw was diapers. I removed the top layer of diapers, and then I saw the money. Was I relieved! Blocks of $100 bills fell to the floor. Everyone there stared in disbelief. Paul had a huge smile on his face. The station manager walked away in a huff, and our passenger stood silently with a blank expression on his face. All in all, there was over $50,000 in the Pampers box. Needless to say, our passenger lost the entire $50,000; and an investigation was opened with possible criminal charges pending.

Tap

During another outbound inspection for money, Jim made a good seizure. We were working a flight destined for the Azores and then to Lisbon, Portugal. The money on this flight is not drug or terrorist related but is usually money earned by legal means. It is money earned under the table. If they haven't reported this money to the IRS as income but then report it to us when leaving the country, they know they will be paid a visit by an IRS agent because a copy of the currency reporting form is forwarded to the IRS by Customs. They could get into a lot of trouble for tax evasion and could be fined heavily or even sentenced to jail. Consequently, they are secretive when taking money illegally out of the country and go to extremes in hiding it.

We were all busy interviewing passengers that were about to board the flight when I noticed Jim motioning for this family to step out of line. It was a father, mother, and young daughter about thirteen years of age. I was surprised to see Jim pull these people aside because they seemed totally innocuous to me, but maybe Jim saw something that I didn't. As Jim was interviewing this family, I finished my inspection and walked over to where Jim was and listened in to what he was saying. Jim is a seasoned inspector, one of the best, and conducts meticulous inspections and interviews. If something gets by him, the passenger is good.

Jim asked the wife and husband how much money they were carrying. They both feigned they couldn't speak or understand English that well and asked the daughter to translate. The reply was a tentative "about $8,000." Jim hammered at this and wanted to know how much. Was it less or more than $10,000? The couple began to look scared and nervous and furtively looked at each other. Jim told the daughter to tell her parents it was not illegal to carry more than $10,000, but if they were, they had to fill out a form. After much talking among themselves and obvious hand-wringing, the daughter said they had exactly $13,000. "Fine," Jim said, "but now you have to fill out this form." Jim presented them with the currency reporting form and told them what blocks they had to fill out and just to ask him if they had any questions.

After much confusion and a lot of questions, it appeared they were done filling out the form. Jim and I were talking as they were writing, and we already came to the same conclusion; once they were done declaring the exact amount of money that they had, we were going to count and verify the amount. When the mother handed the currency form to us, we read the amount declared, $13,000. "OK," Jim said, "where's the money?" The look on the mother's face revealed something was terribly wrong. She literally turned white. All the color was completely gone from her face. The mother, father, and daughter started talking rapidly together and seemed to be perplexed. Jim was losing his patience and told the daughter to tell her parents to put all their money on the counter to be counted, all $13,000. The daughter started to equivocate by saying, "We think it is about $13,000." Jim curtly replied, "Look it, I'm done playing games. I want to know exactly how much you have, and I want you to place it on the counter, now." Again, there was much bantering among the three of them, and the mother kept looking nervously at Jim. Again Jim said, "OK, I've had it. If you can't tell me how much you have, we'll go back to our office and count it there." This is when the mother distinctly said, "$124,500." I almost fell over. Obviously she didn't know English well enough to say how much she had. Did she mean $12,450? That was close to $13,000, and that was probably what she meant, but the daughter confirmed the figure. She repeated to us, "$124,500." I chuckled and told Jim I couldn't believe how he knew who to grab. I wouldn't have stopped this family in a million years because it was obvious they were just a hard-working family going back to the old country for a visit. Jim stopped them and made a huge seizure.

Jim asked the daughter where the money was, and the daughter said the majority was on the mother. When Jim told the girl to tell the mother to put all the money on the counter, the girl told us we didn't understand. The money was really on her—in her shoulder pads, girdle, bra, etc. *Oh boy*, I thought, *this is a good one*. I told Jim we would have to escort the family back to the office for two reasons: Because of the location of the money, we would have to find a couple of female inspectors to search the mother, and this would have to be done in the privacy of a ladies' search room. Secondly, because of the amount of money they didn't declare, we would have to call the duty agent, and they would want to respond to interview the family. Possible criminal proceedings could be started because of the severity of the case.

Returning to the CET office, we were met by two female inspectors from passenger processing. I briefed them on what was going on, and they took the mother to the ladies' room across the hall from the CET office. They returned with $114,500. "I thought you said $124,500," I said to the daughter. She reached into her purse and pulled out a block of one-hundred-dollar bills. "Ten thousand dollars," she said.

I was still having a problem comprehending all this. The $124,500 was a lot of money, and to be carrying that much around so loosely was just baffling to me. After a Customs agent arrived and interviewed all three members of the family, we were convinced the money was not illegal. The family had recently sold a couple pieces of property, and it appeared there was some money passed between the buyer and seller that went unreported, but the money definitely wasn't from selling dope. Ironically, they were bringing the money to the Azores to build a retirement house. Well, their plans would have to be put on hold for a while. They would definitely be fined by Customs for not properly reporting this money, probably 10 percent or $12,450, but no other legal action would be taken. However, if their story did not check out after an investigation by the agents, they could forfeit all the monies.

This is one of those cases where you had to do your job, but it didn't feel too good. Busting a drug smuggler or money courier, as in the previous stories, was richly rewarding and satisfying. Taking the money from this family, knowing they were hard workers all their lives and were planning their retirement dream house, was less than satisfying. They made a mistake and would have to pay for it, but we all hoped they wouldn't have to pay too severely. When Customs processed the final disposition of the money, I knew I would recommend leniency because of mitigating circumstances.

Once we were done processing the seizure and taking all the money, we explained to the family who they had to contact in Customs to begin the appeal process. They thanked us, and after all they had been through, they shook our hands as they departed for home. Their planned trip back to the old country would have to be put on hold for a while.

Cars for Northwest Africa

As I said in the beginning of this chapter, requiring the shipper of a vehicle to present to Customs and Border Protection (CBP) the title of the vehicle and three copies of the Shipper's Export Declaration (SED) at least three days before the anticipated exportation of the vehicle tightly controls the exportation of vehicles. Creating this time period allows CBP to run all checks on the vehicle and even inspect the vehicle if desired. However, even with these laws in place, we have to stay on our toes because people are always looking for a way to circumvent the law.

One day as an inspector was routinely running all the SEDs through our computer databases, he received a hit on the name of one of the shippers. The shipper was attempting to export two vehicles, a 2005 Lexus SUV and a 2005 BMW SUV, to Northwest Africa. The hit or record on the shipper was for being a known associate of heroin smugglers and allegedly being a money launderer. *Well, this is easy*, we thought. The sea container containing these cars was on the same dock at Conley Terminal in South Boston as our CET office. It was sitting there awaiting arrival of the ship that would take it overseas. We could easily pop the container and inspect the cars, and if the record was correct, we should find money hidden in the vehicles. Well, easier said than done.

The following morning, three other CET inspectors and I located the container containing the two SUVs. When we opened the container doors, sure enough, there were the two SUVs. They were brand-new, sparkling clean, and didn't have anything in them. We are used to inspecting vehicles that are loaded with personal effects that make the inspection quite difficult. However, in this case, the SUVs were empty; and the inspection would be easy. We thoroughly went over these vehicles. We used all our modern high-tech tools to assist us in the inspection but to no avail. If the record on this guy was correct, there had to be money concealed within these vehicles somewhere, but we couldn't find it. The only thing we didn't do was to start disassembling the vehicles, but if we did this, we had better find something or else someone's head was going to be on the chopping block—like mine.

Then it came to me. "Guys," I said, "we found it!" They all looked at me quizzically and thought for sure I had lost it. Then I explained. "Don't you see, the vehicles are the money." What I went on to explain to them was that the shipper was indeed laundering money, but in a nontraditional fashion. Instead of exporting cash, he was using the dirty money to buy these extremely expensive vehicles and launder the money in this manner. He was accomplishing his goal of getting the dirty money out of the country by using expensive durable goods. Once he got these goods overseas, he could sell them and receive the much-sought-after cash or keep the vehicles for his own use. He had the option. However, this time he was caught. We could now detain the shipment and refer the whole matter over to our agents, and they would open an investigation on the shipper. If he couldn't prove how he acquired the money to purchase these vehicles, we could seize the vehicles as proceeds from illicit drug transactions. We would have to do some investigation, but it was worth it. The value of the two vehicles was estimated to be $100,000. Not bad for a morning's work on the docks of Boston.

Cars for the Middle East

Another car story is just as intriguing. One of the major responsibilities of the inspectors on the outbound team is to examine outbound freight, ensuring all the laws and regulations are complied with. One day while pursuing this goal, an inspector was reviewing the dock receipts for cargo scheduled to be exported later that week. One of the dock receipts indicated a forty-foot sea container full of "personal effects" was being exported to Lebanon. Since Lebanon was a hot country for us, the inspector scheduled a tailgate exam for this container. A tailgate exam means we open the doors of the container and climb in as far as we can, looking for anything illegal or even out of the ordinary. If we are not satisfied with the results of a tailgate exam, we can totally strip the container of its contents at a nearby warehouse. This can be a timely and costly procedure and is not done unless we can sufficiently warrant this course of action.

Later in the day, CET inspectors conducted a tailgate exam on this container. Not only did they find the expected personal effects, but they also found an unmanifested automobile. As I mentioned in the introduction of this section, when automobiles are exported, titles and SEDs must be submitted to Customs at least three days before exportation. The paperwork relating to this shipment didn't contain any title or SED. To an inspector who has spent any amount of time on the seaport doing outbound exams, this would indicate the shipper was trying to sneak a car out of the country. However, we didn't want to rush to any hasty judgment. I have seen too many times in the past where we assumed something only to find out we were wrong—that is, the paperwork was filed properly but U.S. Customs misplaced or lost it. Therefore, we did our homework. Our endeavors indicated two things: first, no, the shipper hadn't submitted the required title and SED as required, and second, a query of the shipper in our databases indicated he wasn't the nicest guy in the world. He had a history of allegedly exporting cars illegally, and he was also a known player in the drug running business. We could have done a couple of things here. We could have immediately seized the vehicle for improper exportation. At the most, the shipper would have received a minimal penalty, a slap on the wrist, because we knew he would have claimed there was a misunderstanding between him and his broker and the paperwork was inadvertently not filed. But there was a second option. We could document the exportation and see what developed. We knew this guy was a wise guy and was involved in exporting cars illegally, so we decided to give him some rope and see if he would hang himself. Time was on our side.

That Friday, we witnessed the container with the car being loaded onto the MSC ship. Now it was a waiting game. Paul had already set up a log. He had run the VIN (vehicle identification number) of this car initially, and it was not reported stolen. He planned on running the VIN on a weekly basis for the next couple of months to see if the status of the vehicle changed. Week after week, Paul ran the VIN with negative results. We began to question ourselves and wondered if we had been outsmarted. I think it was the beginning of the third month when Paul ran his routine check on the VIN. But this time, the results were less than routine.

The car had been reported stolen a few days previously to the Brockton Police Department, the town where the shipper lived. We contacted the agents, and Customs opened an informal investigation. A trip down to the Brockton Police Station revealed some interesting information. The man who filed the stolen vehicle report was the same guy who shipped the car overseas. The signatures on both the police report and the shipping documents were the same. Our perseverance paid off. We had him cold!

A couple of our agents, armed with this information, paid our friend a visit one night. Initially, he denied everything and said he was being set up. After a little attitude adjustment, he confessed to the whole scheme. He said that he waited until he received word from his cousin overseas that the car arrived safely before he filed the stolen vehicle report. He thought it was impossible to be caught. His plan was to make money by selling the car, a highly sought-after commodity in the Mideast, bringing him thousands of dollars and by receiving a check from the insurance company. Well, things didn't work out this way. The agents advised him that he was looking at years in jail for fraud and a few other charges they were working on with the Assistant United States Attorney (AUSA). All of a sudden, this cocky, swaggering hustler who "thought it was impossible to be caught" was now looking at some serious hard time. Unless he wanted to cut a deal.

The deal was that if he gave us good, hard information about drug smuggling and we made some seizures from his information, we would cut him some slack. We knew he was involved in drugs, and he knew who else was involved. All we wanted was some information. Well, he flipped immediately. He provided U.S. Customs with enough information that several heroin importations were seized that perhaps might not have been made without his information. Because of his cooperation, he was spared jail time. The moral to this story, at least to me, is perseverance pays. If we had made a quick, easy seizure, the results would have been negligible. By being patient, we successfully kept some heroin off the streets and shut down this guy's operation. This is one battle that we won.

TWENTY FIVE

Boston Mail Division

When I joined U.S. Customs on January 29, 1979 (my mother's birthday, b. 1917), I was assigned to the file room on the second floor of the Customs House and worked there for the entire year as a file clerk. After that, from December of 1979 to July of 1983, I was assigned to the mail division at South Postal Annex in Boston. The purpose of the Customs Mail Division is to receive and clear all international mail destined for the New England area. This was a daunting task but proved to be an extremely rewarding, enriching, and gratifying experience. Before I tell my story, I must explain the processing and handling of the international mail. We had several large conveyor belts that we used to cull out the dutiable mail from the nondutiable. If the package was dutiable, we pulled it off the belt and dumped it into a nearby hamper. If the mail was nondutiable (and the vast majority was), we would simply stamp the package with a "free of duty" stamp and release it back into the postal system for delivery. Additionally, because letters, magazines, newspapers, and all other printed matter were free of duty, we instructed the mail handlers not to even bother dumping the bags onto the belt. They could simply release this type of mail directly into the domestic flow. Succinctly, this type of mail was "blessed" by Customs, and we didn't want to waste our limited amount of manpower processing it. This system worked fine for years and helped expedite the flow of international mail, but we soon learned there were pitfalls and loopholes in the system.

On a typical day, Larry, the mail handler, would dump the bags of mail into a chute on one end of the belt. Joe, a mail clerk, and I were stationed at the other end. Once I stamped the mail, Joe would grab the package and flip it into one of the many hampers he had positioned nearby. These hampers were designated by geographical locations and helped separate the mail for faster delivery. Larry, Joe, and I were engaged in our typical small talk as we were working; and Larry must have became too engrossed in the conversation because he took a sack full of rolled-up newspapers and dumped them on the belt. As soon as he did it, he started to apologize and attempted to retrieve as many newspapers as possible and stick them back in the sack. Joe and I started to help the embarrassed Larry, and as I grabbed one of the newspapers, I noticed it seemed rather heavy and was stiffer than normal. I looked at the postage stamps and saw the paper was mailed from the Netherlands. Wondering what was causing the paper to feel so heavy, I took my knife out of my pocket and cut open the outer wrapping. I then began to unfold the paper one page at a time. When I was about midway through the paper, I turned to the next page and was shocked at what I saw. From the top of the page to the bottom and from one side to the other, wrapped in a clear soft plastic was a dark gooey substance that I thought might possibly be hashish. I had seen this stuff before in the army, so I had a little familiarity with it. I was standing there looking at this stuff when Joe and Larry walked over to see what was going on. When I showed it to them, they were amazed. Larry came up with a terrific idea. He suggested that we look through the sack and see if there were any more similar newspapers. Sure enough, we found four more that contained a similar amount of hashish. I brought all five newspapers back to the Customs office and showed them to Jim O'Leary, the acting supervisor of the mail division. Jim said we better call the Customs patrol officers because this stuff was out of our league.

Within the hour, Bob, Rick, and another member of the Boston MET (Mobile Enforcement Team, the predecessor of CET) arrived at South Postal. As soon as they saw the stuff, they knew it was hashish. To be certain, we broke off a bit and tested it using a standard drug test kit. The reaction was immediately positive. We took the hashish out of the newspapers and weighed all five at the same time. We had a bit over one pound. Bob, a supervisor, signed the chain of custody for the hashish and took the entire bundle into his custody. He told me they were going to do some research on the addressee, and if possible, they would do some controlled deliveries. Whatever the result, Bob promised to call me and tell me the final disposition. With that they were off.

We learned a good lesson from this experience. Printed matter, newspapers, magazines, although not dutiable, was not as low-risk as we thought. The bad guys learned our system and exploited it to the fullest. We would have to change the way we do business in the future, that is for sure. This leads to the next story.

Now that we knew printed matter was being used to smuggle contraband into the country, we focused our attention in this area. What we found was shocking. We dumped and inspected printed matter mail from Germany, France, Great Britain, Denmark, Sweden, Netherlands, and Spain—mail mostly from Northern Europe. Immediately we noticed the sacks from Sweden, Netherlands, and Denmark—what we started to call the blue-sack countries because of the color of the sacks—all contained contraband, either pornography or hashish. The hashish mostly came from the Netherlands and was usually of small quantities, a few ounces. The mail from Sweden and Denmark contained hard pornography, child pornography by even the most liberal standards. Some sacks contained up to five shipments of this stuff. Luckily, two great individuals, Dave and Ernie, bolstered the staff of the mail division about this time. In addition, Jim, a postal inspector, and Fred, a Customs agent, were assigned to cover this recently discovered problem. With all this new life, we were able to inspect the mails with a renewed vigor and had a huge success. In the first year of our effort, we had over five hundred seizures at the Boston Mail Division of either drugs or child pornography. Jim and Fred were kept busy with the U.S. Attorney's Office in conducting controlled deliveries and making arrests and prosecutions. They even had to enlist other agents in their office to assist them.

The smugglers attempted all different ways to get their contraband into the country. The pornography was usually hidden in the inside pages of a regular magazine. Sometimes they would cut out a square shape of the inside pages, and the child pornographic magazine would be inserted into this void in an attempt to avoid detection. However, all mail from these three countries was scrutinized intensely, and I don't believe much got by us. Drugs, mostly hashish, was hidden in jars of peanut butter, candles, soles of shoes, just about anywhere that was possible. Heroin seizures, although not as frequent as hashish, were also made. The most unique heroin seizure I recall was in a plaster of paris wall plaque. During shipment, the plaque was broken in numerous places, revealing its illegal contents hidden inside. We were kept extremely busy conducting our enforcement efforts, and for a few years in a row, Boston made more seizures than any other mail division in the country. This was quite a feat since Boston was considered one of the smaller mail divisions and received far less mail than the others. In fact, our stellar performance earned us a visit one day by the regional commissioner of Customs. He said that he had heard so much about us he had to pay us a visit. One day, accompanied by the district director, he walked into our office and paid us his personal compliments for a job well done. I guess the boss wasn't known for personally paying visits to the troops in the field and paying his respects, so we could take his visit as an extra special event. In fact, his visit was quite enjoyable, and in spite of everything I had heard about the guy, I enjoyed his company and enjoyed our conversation. The commissioner was on destroyers in WWII, and when he saw some of my ship pictures on the walls, he maneuvered the conversation from mail division seizures to sea stories. We engaged in nautical talk over a cup of coffee for a good hour—to the chagrin of the district director—and I enjoyed the talk immensely. More importantly, I think Mr. Griffin did also. He was just a normal guy, and his trip back to the old days when he was aboard ships seemed to be quite relaxing and pleasant for him. Though Mr. Griffin had his critics, he treated me fair. In fact, in the months ahead, Mr. Griffin promoted me to the position of Customs inspector; and my career opportunities increased dramatically. I started to make a lot more money, and the job became even more interesting. And as they say, you don't bite the hand that feeds you.

The only other interesting thing I can think of about the mail division is the time we held up all the mail from Cuba, incurring the personal wrath of Fidel himself. We had, and still do, an embargo on Cuba for years, but with a Foreign Assets Control (FAC) license, printed matter from Cuba was allowed into the country. The problem was, the license had expired and no one had renewed it. We detected this problem when we were engaged in our printed matter enforcement action and started to detain the Cuban mail. At one time, we had a few forty-foot container loads on hold. The *New York Times* even wrote a big article about how U.S. Customs was holding up the mails. Finally, someone in an office a lot higher than mine made the decision that we could release the Cuban mail. The international crisis was de-escalated; and Dave, Ernie, and I could go back to our prosaic pursuits of inspecting the mails.

TWENTY SIX

Ramsland/Valhalla

I n the late 1980s, there was a lot of maritime drug smuggling. Fishing vessels resorted to this illegal activity because they couldn't make ends meet by fishing. Oil rig supply vessels, no longer needed in the Gulf of Mexico because the oil rigs were shutting down, also were diverted to drug smuggling. Here in the Port of Boston, we had several significant marijuana seizures in the maritime arena during this time frame. However, the most memorable and perhaps the most written about is the *Ramsland*. I am not about to attempt to give a blow-by-blow description regarding the *Ramsland/ Valhalla* connection, but I will relate the small part that I was involved in.

As the story goes, the *Valhalla* sailed out of the Port of Gloucester one bright, shining day headed for Ireland. Onboard, she was laden with guns and explosives destined for the IRA (Irish Republican Army). Unbeknown to those onboard the *Valhalla*, the U.S. government was fully aware of their illegal intentions and had already arranged a welcoming committee for them once they reached the coast of Ireland. In fact, the *Valhalla*'s every movement was being tracked by satellite. Her fate was sealed from the beginning. As the *Valhalla* closed the coast of Western Ireland, she was met by another vessel and the transfer of the weapons and explosives was made on the high seas. Once the transfer was complete, the *Valhalla* headed for home while the

Irish vessel headed for a nearby port to unload her precious cargo. Instead the Irish authorities met her; and the cargo, crew, and vessel were all seized. The *Valhalla* continued to sail on into oblivion. No one knew where she had disappeared to until a couple of Customs patrol officers on routine patrol spotted her tied up at Pier 7 in South Boston. Naturally, her crew was gone, but this wasn't a problem. As in the destination and purpose of the *Valhalla's* most recent trip, U.S. authorities knew who all the players were, and it was just a matter of time before they were all apprehended. But how do the activities of the *Valhalla* tie in with the seizure of the *Ramsland* and her cargo of marijuana? Again, as the story goes, the marijuana onboard the *Ramsland* was payment for the weapons that were seized off the *Valhalla*. Even though the gun running operation was thwarted, payment was still due, and it came in the form of thirty-four tons of marijuana.

My involvement with the *Ramsland* began one afternoon when I was asked if I would be the boarding officer for a ship arrival that night. The ship's name was the *Ramsland*, and I was told our agents were also going to be there when the ship arrived at the Coast Guard base at 1800 hours. You didn't have to be overly bright to figure out something was up with this ship because the Customs agents do not routinely board ships, and ships do not normally dock at the Coast Guard base. I took the job assignment and figured I would find out what was going on when I arrived at the Coast Guard base.

As I usually do, I arrived an hour early for my assignment and took the free time to stroll around the Coast Guard base. The weather was fine, but I noticed a touch of fog in the air. As I was wondering if the fog offshore was thicker and consequently might delay the arrival of the *Ramsland*, the Customs agents arrived, led by Chris, the special agent in charge (SAC). Chris and I knew each other pretty well from working different cases together, and I think we had mutual respect. He was a bear of a man with a loud, booming voice that was never afraid to tell everyone within hearing distance his thoughts and opinions. We all said hello to each other and then quickly got down to business. Chris did most of the talking and explained to us that the *Ramsland* was on time and should be docking right around 1800 hours. Our guys on the *Ramsland* said everything was fine and the Coast Guard was escorting them. I piped up and asked Chris what he was talking about. I was in the dark and didn't have a clue what was going on. Chris apologized and went into a lengthy explanation. In his usual eloquent and expletive fashion, Chris told me the *Ramsland* was a drug ship, she was loaded with marijuana. This marijuana was the payment for the guns that were supposed to be delivered to the IRA by the *Valhalla*. Like the *Valhalla*, we were tracking the *Ramsland* since she left the Canary Islands over a week ago. Her arrival was no surprise to us, but to make sure everything went smoothly, the Coast Guard and some agents met her at sea by Graves Light and were escorting her into the Coast Guard base. Now I started to get the picture. Now I knew this wasn't going to be a normal boarding. I knew a little about the *Valhalla*, but the connection with the *Ramsland* and the payment in marijuana was all news to me.

As Chris continued his briefing, someone called out that he thought he saw the *Ramsland* off in the distance. I looked off into the fog-shrouded darkness and could barely make out a shape that was darker than its surroundings. As I continued to look, she became more distinguishable and defined. Within fifteen minutes, the entire vessel was visible to the naked eye. She was about 350 feet in length, with black hull and white superstructure, and appeared to me to be an old cargo vessel or what they call a tramp steamer. It was not long before the *Ramsland* was alongside the dock and the crew was throwing over heaving lines for us to pull ashore. Attached to these heaving lines were thick, wet, greasy mooring lines that were extremely hard to handle. As we were attempting to loop the eye of the mooring lines over the nearby bollards, amid a lot of cursing and yelling, a bunch of sailors from a nearby-docked Coast Guard ship came to our assistance. Finally, after a lot of sweat and confusion, the *Ramsland* was secured to the dock at the Boston Coast Guard base. Before we boarded her, Chris asked me to conduct a normal Customs boarding. He wanted me to have the captain fill out all the necessary paperwork like any other vessel coming from foreign would. Even though Chris knew this ship was dirty, he wanted everything to be as legal-like as possible and didn't want to afford the crew any chances of slipping through the cracks. As we were boarding, Chris told me there should be five British subjects onboard and they were coming from the Canary Islands with a load of crushed stones.

As I was boarding, I looked around the ship and saw the deplorable shape she was in. I wouldn't want to be sailing the North Atlantic on her, I thought. When I met the crew, I was surprised how cheery and welcoming they were. I expected a bunch of intimidating ruffians with knives between their teeth, patches over their eyes, and rings dangling from their ears. On the contrary, they were polite, professional, and quite inquisitive about Boston. According to them, they had signed on to the *Ramsland* as a one-trip contract. Supposedly someone in the Boston area had bought the *Ramsland*, and this crew was only the delivery crew. They already had their airplane tickets with British Airways and were scheduled for a flight in a couple of days. All this was fine with me, and I wasn't about to tell them the U.S. government might rearrange their plans for them. I figured Chris could perform this function eloquently enough. Well, as events unfolded over the next few hours, the crew realized something was up. When they caught wind that we thought the *Ramsland* was a drug ship and they were implicated in the whole affair, the crew became distraught. They claimed to know nothing about marijuana smuggling and were simply a crew delivering a ship and trying to make a living. I wasn't sure if I could believe them or not. They seemed to be telling the truth, but they could be good actors also. Anyway, it wasn't any of my business. Chris and his office was running the show and calling the shots. I was there to do the boarding and assist in any way asked.

After quite a few hours, everything was settled. The crew, all five British subjects, was being arrested and taken to jail. The *Ramsland* would stay tied up at the Coast Guard base for the night, and the Coast Guard would provide security. In the morning, Chris would decide how we were going to unload all the little rocks from the two holds of the ship. Hopefully, somewhere among the tons of rocks we were going to find the mother load. Chris asked me, as a member of CET, if we could offer him and his office assistance. I replied in the affirmative, and we both agreed we would be talking with each other in the morning. We shook hands and went our different ways. As I drove home, I reflected on the night's events. I was extremely excited and couldn't wait until the morning. Hopefully we were going to find a big load.

As anticipated, one of the agents called CET first thing in the morning and filled us in on what was going on with the *Ramsland*. They were making arrangements to have one of the local tug companies tow the *Ramsland* from the Coast Guard base in Boston to a remote, secluded, empty pier on the other side of the harbor in East Boston. Once the *Ramsland* was secured, they asked if we could have our K-9 drug dog, Harvey, run over the ship and see if he alerted to the odor of drugs. We told them not to worry, we would be there. A tentative time of two in the afternoon was set, but if there were any changes, they would call us on the radio. Even though the agents knew there was dope on the *Ramsland*, they wanted to do everything exactly right just in case. You never know what to expect in this business.

Rick and I showed up on time; and as we pulled into the old, decrepit pier, we could see the tugs gently pushing the *Ramsland* the remaining ten feet or so to the pier. Once in place, we all assisted in tying her up and placing a makeshift gangway so we could get the dog and ourselves onboard. Before Rick brought Harvey onboard, he took him for a walk so he could relieve himself. The dog works best on an empty bladder according to Rick. As soon as Rick and Harvey climbed the gangway, they went to work. Harvey sniffed and sniffed without any indications he smelled anything. Harvey is an aggressive dog, and if he smells the odor of drugs, he will vigorously scratch the area where the smell is coming from. Rick gently lifted Harvey from the deck and placed him into the forward cargo hold onto a huge pile of crushed rocks. Carefully Rick began to work Harvey along the starboard side of the hold. Suddenly, Harvey began to scratch and claw at the pile of rocks. Rick had to use all the force he could muster to pull Harvey away. Once he settled Harvey down, Rick and I physically examined the area he alerted to. All we found were some dirty, greasy sheets of plastic. What's up with this, I thought. Then Rick explained to me what he thought was going on. The plastic was probably used at one time to cover the drugs, and the odor was still on the plastic. Thus, Harvey alerted even though there actually wasn't drugs there. Made sense to me, and the agents were quite pleased with the results. Now all we had to do was unload the tons and tons of crushed rock to find the dope. We didn't know if the drugs were intermingled with the rocks, at the bottom, or wherever. The only way we were going to find out was to get to work.

Arrangements were already made with a local contractor to off-load all the rocks. He had an old-fashioned steam shovel he was going to use, and as Rick and I were leaving the *Ramsland* to put Harvey back in Rick's truck, they were already positioning the scoop over the aft hold. I had no idea how long the off-loading process would take, but I thought it was safe to assume that it would be days. Kevin, a Boston agent, was primarily in charge of getting all the rocks off. There was a lot of bantering between Kevin, Rick, and me. We told Kevin they finally found a job that he could handle. Kevin was most appreciative of our humor and expressed his sentiment in quite a few rich, salty expletives. Since there was absolutely nothing else we could do, we told Kevin we were leaving to work airport cargo but if he needed us, then to please call us. Kevin expressed his thanks and told us it would probably be a couple of days before anyone knew anything. In the meantime, Kevin had to establish a schedule to ensure an agent was on site at all times. We didn't want to lose the case because of a chain-of-custody issue.

Over the next couple of days, we would drop by and check on the progress of the unloading. It was indeed a long, slow process; and after a couple of days into it, there still wasn't any dope. The agents insisted there was tons of marijuana onboard, and it was at the bottom of the rock pile. The information supposedly was coming from a CI (confidential informant) and was deemed extremely credible, but I wasn't about to ask. I think it was about three days after they started to discharge that things became interesting. The bottom of the hold was exposed in spots and still no dope. We attempted to look at the blueprints of the ship to see if we were missing any hidden spots, but our findings were inconclusive at best. But Dave, a Customs agent, made an astute observation. At one of the spots we were standing on in the middle of the hold, there was supposed to be a manhole cover that allowed access to the double bottoms. (Double bottom means the vessel has two hulls, an inner and outer hull. This method of construction serves two purpose—it is a safety feature and is an area where fuel and water tanks are located.) After looking all around and actually using a broom to sweep the deck clean, we still couldn't find the manhole. We went back to the blueprints to double-check, and sure enough there was supposed to be a manhole exactly where we were standing. We were perplexed until someone noticed the difference in the deck material. In some places it was wood, and in others it looked to be of concrete. Upon close scrutiny, it was obvious the decking on the bottom of the hold had been patched. Armed with this knowledge, we plotted out exactly where the manhole cover should be. Not surprisingly, the area over the manhole cover was concrete. Dave, swinging a large heavy sledgehammer, took a couple of powerful swings to the concrete. Cracks immediately developed, and soon we were able to pick up chunks and throw them aside. Shortly, part of the manhole cover appeared through the dust. We cleared the entire area around the manhole cover and were confronted with twelve thick nuts about an inch in diameter holding the cover down. After much running around looking for something to remove the nuts, someone finally returned from the engine room toting a bright, shining wrench. With a lot of grunting, sweating, and swearing, we began to remove the nuts. They were on real tight, and it was a job removing them, but eventually we got them all off. Dave took a thick, heavy screwdriver, inserted it under the cover, and pried it up enough so he was able to get his hand underneath. Once he got a good hold, we pried up the other side, and together we lifted the cover off the manhole. We were met with the foulest, most acrid smell possible. However, as we shone our flashlights into the void, our beams illuminated rectangular sacks about three feet long, one and a half feet wide, and one and a half feet thick. We finally found what we were looking for. Dave reached into the hold and, with much difficulty, pulled one of the sacks out and laid it on the deck. Oily water was oozing out of the greasy sack as Dave pulled out his knife and cut a slit along the top. This exposed what we were looking for—marijuana. After days of removing crushed rocks and fretting over the possibility nothing was here, we were finally rewarded. Believe me, there were a lot of smiles and a lot of backslapping down there in that hold. There was a feeling of elation and satisfaction among all of us. But now the fun was only beginning; we had to unload all the bales out of the double bottoms. Actually, we only acted as checkers and counters. The agents hired some day laborers, and they did all the work. All the bales of marijuana were off-loaded into two forty-foot containers that we situated on the dock alongside the vessel. The total weight of all the marihuana was an amazing thirty-four tons! If you did the math, 34 tons x 2,000 pounds = 68,000 pounds x $2,000 = $136,000,000. The street value of this seizure—assuming marijuana was selling for $2,000 a pound at the time, which it was—was humbling indeed even to the most hardened among us. Once the *Ramsland* was completely off-loaded (we checked and rechecked to make absolutely sure), both forty-foot containers were escorted off the dock and secured at an undisclosed site. We had to keep the marijuana as evidence for court proceedings, but as soon as the judge was satisfied as to the evidence, we would dispose of the marijuana by burning it in a local incinerator. And believe me, this couldn't be soon enough. Having all this marijuana hanging around could only cause problems.

Well, as I said in the beginning, my role in this *Ramsland/Valhalla* affair was quite limited but exciting nonetheless. I know there were lengthy court proceedings in which the five British subjects onboard the *Ramsland* were charged with drug smuggling. However, the U.S. Attorney's Office couldn't convince a jury of this, and all five defendants were found not guilty and were sent back home to England. They claimed they were hired to sail the *Ramsland* from the Canary Islands to Boston, and they had no knowledge whatsoever of the cargo. The *Ramsland* was already loaded when they went onboard, and they thought the crushed rocks in the holds were acting as ballast. They were told someone in Boston had bought the vessel, and this was just a repositioning voyage. This was not a ridiculous assumption on their part, and obviously the jury agreed because they came back with a "not guilty" finding. In my opinion, the crew must have been suspicious of what was going on, but you can't convict someone for not being inquisitive.

While all this was going on, the *Ramsland* was secured at a local Boston commercial pier awaiting final disposition of the trial. We spent a lot of money winterizing the vessel and for storage fees; but we had no choice, the vessel was in our custody, and we had to maintain it. A marine surveyor hired by Customs valued the *Ramsland* at over a million dollars so it was well worth taking good care of. After the trial was over, we were able to auction off the *Ramsland* on the open market in an attempt to recoup some of our expenses. Unbelievable as it may sound, we were only able to fetch $25,000 for the Ramsland. Our cost for storage was way over this amount, and we wound up losing money. I found out that the reason why we could only get $25,000 for the ship is because the engines were ruined. It seems the guys we paid to winterize the vessel did a lousy job and didn't properly protect the engines from the ravages of a New England winter. We were big losers all around in this affair, and the best thing to do was to let the *Ramsland* go and cut our losses. The only fruitful result we had was the seizure of the marijuana, and this wasn't too shabby after all.

Manhole cover providing access to double bottoms *(Ramsland)*

Bales of marijuana discovered *(Ramsland)*

Tramp steamer *Ramsland*

TWENTY SEVEN

Diplomatic Diplomacy

Ninety-four years ago today, the HMS *Titanic* struck an iceberg and began her descent into the icy depths of the North Atlantic.

Yesterday morning, as soon as I arrived at work, things began to happen. We received a call from our IAP (Immigration Advisory Program) officer in Amsterdam that a passenger destined for Boston was highly suspicious to him. The only problem was, this passenger was carrying a diplomatic visa. The newest officer on the job knows you do not mess with diplomats. The easiest and fastest way to be transferred to some remote one-person post somewhere in never-never land is to mess with a diplomat. However, the officer articulated his suspicions, and there was a preponderance of evidence indicating something was up with this guy. We had no alternative but to introduce ourselves to this gentleman when he arrived in Boston. However, before the flight arrived, I wanted everyone to do their homework and see if they could dig up any information indicating any wrongdoing. Our research connected this diplomat in question with some other individuals who were recently arrested by Customs and Border Protection (CBP) in other U.S. cities for visa fraud. In addition to this, we had documentary evidence indicating numerous U.S. visas appeared to have been obtained illegally and were being used to facilitate the entry into this country of illegal aliens. Consequently, we notified JTTF (Joint Terrorist Task Force) and State Department security and advised them of our findings. Once they were apprised, they expressed great interest and informed us that they wished to respond when the flight arrived. Through years of experience, I have found it is best to inform everyone of the potential of a situation and let them act accordingly. It is called professional courtesy, and all agencies reap benefits from this policy. Now that we were prepared for the arrival of this ostensible diplomat, all we had to do is await the arrival of the aircraft.

At about 1700 hours on the thirteenth of April 2006, the flight rolled up to the gate at Terminal E at Logan Airport. As the passengers deplaned, officers stood nearby and observed the passengers as they lined up to begin the formal process of applying for admission into the United States. Our target, Mr. Hello, was readily identified through pictures that we had previously obtained. He was dressed in a new blue suit that he did not appear comfortable in, was wearing a tie that was ridiculously short, and was extremely fidgety and nervous. We allowed him to be processed in a normal fashion and then followed him down below to the baggage area. Once he claimed his single bag and began to walk toward the exit, we made our stop. At all times, we were keenly aware that Mr. Hello was carrying a diplomatic visa and that we were traveling in uncharted waters. Mr. Hello was escorted to the baggage secondary area, and some initial questioning was conducted. After a few minutes, it was obvious our conversation wasn't going anywhere. Therefore, in light that Mr. Hello was carrying an A-2 or diplomatic visa, I deferred to the State Department agents who were standing by.

Mr. Hello was escorted to an interview room where he was asked extensively about his status as a diplomat. He was adamant that he was a diplomat and seemed offended by the State Department agent's persistent questioning. Finally, Mr. Hello admitted he was a fraud. He was not a diplomat, and he acquired his A-2 visa fraudulently by paying a large sum of money to a yet-to-be determined individual. Although he admitted that he was a fraud, there were still many holes in his story. Mr. Hello had approximately $500 on him, and he said he was going to look for a job and stay at a local hotel. He claimed to know no one here in America and was on his own. We found this preposterous but couldn't get the truth out of him. Mr. Hello seemed extremely remorseful and talked constantly of his wife and child back home. He said he owned a machine shop back home and sold it to get the money to buy the visa. Once he was established here, he was going to try to bring his wife and child over. So many parts of his story seemed plausible and believable; however, there were still implausibility. Having no other choice, once we were done interviewing Mr. Hello, it was off to jail for him. We arrested him for visa fraud, and some time next week, he would be brought in front of an Immigration judge. The judge had many options to choose from: he could elect to prosecute Mr. Hello, he can admit him, or he can order him removed. We would have to wait till next week to see what happens.

In the meantime, we did what is called a post-seizure analysis. Our subject was not an isolated case. We identified at least twelve more individuals that had already come to the United States or were due shortly. They all had A-2 visas and all had travel arrangements that we could link together. Mr. Hello turned out to be part of a huge smuggling ring. I believe he was coming here to America to seek a better life for himself and his family, but others appeared to fit the drug smuggling scenario and possibly even had terrorist-related interests. Because this smuggling ring had national implications, we contacted the National Targeting Center (NTC) in Washington, D.C., so they could disseminate the information throughout the country. With any luck, maybe we could catch some of these guys before they get into the country.

TWENTY EIGHT

Hong Kong Heroin

The call came into the CET (Contraband Enforcement Team) office at the airport late in the afternoon. It was a Customs supervisor on the seaport calling. He had some kind of information that he was relaying to CET from Red, a detective with the Massachusetts State Police. The information was vague, but it was something about a suspicious cargo shipment coming from Los Angeles. The supervisor suggested that we call the detective ourselves in order to get all the particulars. After hanging up with the supervisor, I put a call into the detective at his Troop F office. He answered the phone on the first ring and thanked me for calling him right back. He told me that he had received a weird phone call earlier in the afternoon. It was from a lawyer who explained to him that a client of his had received a letter in the mail from China. Inside the letter was a piece of paper from a cargo company, and it described some kind of machinery that was being sent to America from China via sea transportation. The lawyer's client was completely confused because he never ordered anything from China. The lawyer went on to say that as his client was looking at this piece of paper and trying to figure out what he should do with it, he heard a sharp knock at his door. When he opened the door to see who was knocking, he gasped when he saw who it was; it was a couple of the local Chinese wise guys who he knew were involved in just about everything that was illegal in Chinatown. He asked them politely what they wanted. In a short, tense conversation, these wise guys told him that the letter that was just delivered—and that he was still holding in his hand—contained a bill of lading for a piece of freight coming from China. They wanted him to clear this freight through U.S. Customs and then go down to Chelsea and pick it up. He started to stammer a protest when the wise guys interrupted him. They told him it was a real simple procedure and not to even think of protesting. Just do what they told him to do, and everything would be OK. If not, everything would not be OK. With this said, they issued a few more instructions and then were off.

The lawyer's client slowly closed the door. He was perplexed, confused, and scared as hell. He wasn't sure what to do and could only think of calling his lawyer for some advice. When he explained the whole story to the lawyer, the lawyer told him to do exactly what the wise guys told him to do. Otherwise, he would probably be killed. Besides, all they wanted him to do is pick up a piece of cargo. There's nothing illegal in that. And that ended the initial conversation between the lawyer and his client.

After hanging up the phone, the lawyer reflected on the advice he gave to his client. It was true, all they wanted his client to do was pick up a piece of freight; but deep down inside of him, he knew something was amiss, and he wasn't feeling any too comfortable with the advice he gave to his client. Therefore, he called his client back and told him to stand by, he was going to make a couple of phone calls and he would get back to him. This is when the lawyer called the State Police, and fortunately, the phone call was directed to Red. I say fortunately because Red is a real heads-up type of guy; and as soon as he heard the lawyer's story, he knew he was going to call Customs for help because Red wasn't even sure what a bill of lading was, but he knew something coming from China had to have Customs involvement.

As Red finished his story to me, I knew we had something good. The intrigue excited me, and I was looking forward to pursuing this case. Red told me he was going to meet the lawyer that night to obtain the bill of lading and if we could meet somewhere in the morning. I told him absolutely, and we decided to meet at Berth 14 on Conley Terminal at nine in the morning. I could hardly wait.

Joe, my partner on CET, and I met Red that morning as planned. The first thing we did was to look at the bill of lading. Sure enough, the shipment was a "bean sprout washing machine" coming from China to Boston via Los Angeles. This "via Los Angeles" was the part we didn't like. Obviously something was up with this shipment, and we couldn't wait until it got to

Boston so we could inspect it, but it would be in Los Angeles first. Even though we didn't want to, we had to call Los Angeles Customs and give them the heads-up. If they could examine this shipment when it was first off-loaded in Los Angeles, that would be the best procedure, whether we liked it or not. Since LA was three hours behind us, it would still be a couple of hours before we could call them. In the meantime, Joe and Red were going to drive up to the Topsfield State Police barracks where a meeting had been arranged with the lawyer and his client. I would stay behind and attempt to call Customs in Los Angeles as soon as they opened.

Shortly after 11:00 AM our time, I placed the call to the U.S. Cargo Operations in Los Angeles. I talked with a cargo supervisor and told him the whole story about the bean sprout washing machine. I strongly suggested that they inspect this shipment as soon as possible and wished them luck. The cargo supervisor wanted to check on the status of the shipment and asked if he could put me on hold. He came back in a few minutes and told me he was sorry but no can do; the shipment had already passed through Los Angeles and was en route to Boston via truck. I was ecstatic with this news. We did what we were supposed to do by contacting Los Angeles, but it wasn't our fault the cargo had already left. Now we would have the opportunity of inspecting this shipment and hopefully finding something. I immediately called Joe on the phone and gave him the news.

The next day, we had an all-hands meeting at the CET office. Customs agents from the Office of Investigations (OI), DEA, State Police, and CET were all present. We had to work out a game plan for the anticipated arrival of this shipment of a bean sprout washing machine. We knew the arrival date was still several days away, so we had ample time to develop a good plan. CET was responsible for keeping track of the shipment and to inform everyone when the actual date and time of arrival was ascertained. We were able to accomplish this by keeping in touch with the trucking company that was transporting the shipment from Los Angeles to Boston. Every night the trucker called into dispatch and gave them an update on his status. This was a normal business practice that we were able to tap into, and thus we were able to plan accordingly. OI, DEA, and the State Police were involved in a lot of background investigation. They were attempting to find out who was behind this shipment without showing our hand. Remember, nothing illegal had transpired up to this point, and maybe nothing illegal would happen; so we had to proceed carefully. Everything we did would be based on the results we found during the inspection. However, we all knew something was about to happen; and by the look of it, it was going to be big.

We checked with the trucking company every night, and finally we received word; the truck carrying the bean sprout washing machine was due to arrive the next day about lunchtime. With this information, our plan began to be implemented. We would have troops at the cargo facility beginning at eight in the morning just in case the truck arrived early. We would also have people stationed at strategic locations all around the area. We wanted to make sure we detected any counter surveillance that the bad guys might set up. After all, they knew when the shipment was due to arrive just like us, and they wanted to be around to see if there was any unusual law enforcement activity in the area that would tip them off to the fact that we were wise to their shipment. Basically, it was a big cat-and-mouse game, and whoever was the best player would win.

Around noontime the next day, everyone was anxious, anticipating the arrival of the truck. However, noontime came and went and still no truck. I was in a car with Jim, a special agent, in an adjacent parking lot. The clock was fast approaching 4:00 PM, and both Jim and I were getting worried. But as they say, it is the darkest just before dawn. As Jim and I were discussing what possibly could have gone wrong, we saw the truck turn into the parking lot. The trucker left the truck running in the middle of the yard and jumped out to go into the office to see what bay they wanted him to back into. Unbeknown to this trucker, at least a dozen pair of eyes were monitoring his every move. After only a couple of minutes, the trucker returned to his truck and backed it into his designated bay. Once he was in place, he shut down the truck, and the loud hiss of the air brakes shattered the air. We already had people inside the warehouse, and the plan was that once the truck was unloaded and the trucker drove away, the rest of us designated to be part of the inspection team would slowly enter the warehouse as if we were customers entering to pick up our freight. While we were doing this, the guys already in the warehouse would be making arrangements to have our shipment transferred to a part of the warehouse where it was quiet, and we could have some privacy.

Jim and I entered the warehouse together and met up with a couple of the other guys. They brought us way down to another part of the warehouse where the shipment was. They were still trying to turn the lights on in this part of the building, and the owner himself was assisting them. We had already briefed the owner that something hinky might be going on in a couple of days, and he was more than helpful. Anything we needed, he said, he would provide; and he did. We wished that all warehouse proprietors were as helpful.

My first glimpse of the shipment revealed a large wooden crate about eight feet long, four feet wide, and four feet high. There was black stenciling on the crate indicating the country of origin (China), what end was up; and in black marker, the bill of lading (B/L) was scribbled. I checked that number with the one I had on a piece of paper, and they matched; sure enough, this was the correct shipment. Billy, Joe, and I began to use a couple of flat bars and hammers to disassemble the crate. We worked with extreme care and deliberation because we didn't want to damage the crate and make it obvious someone had been in it in case we found something and were going to attempt a controlled delivery (a controlled delivery is when we attempt to deliver something to its rightful owner with the goal to arrest this individual). Slowly we pried the top off the crate and had our first glimpse of the shipment. It was nothing but a big stainless steel tub that had five rollers, approximately four feet in length that run side to side the entire length of the tub. There was also a length of what looked like bicycle chain and some belting sitting on the bottom of the tub, but that was it. There wasn't anything obvious in sight. We continued to work on the sides of the crate; and after a lot of work, we eventually had all the sides off, and the entire shipment was exposed. We carefully examined the now-fully-exposed tub, and we were all in concurrence that there wasn't anything there. But inside the tub, the five rollers were begging to be inspected. That is the only place left that anything could be hidden. We had to unbolt the rollers in order to remove them from the tub, and this took more time. We were becoming impatient and started to wonder if this whole thing was nothing but a wild-goose chase. Once we removed the first roller, Joe attempted to drill into the end of it. After breaking a couple of drill bits, we decided to drill right in the middle of the roller. The bit took to the metal like a hot knife to butter, and almost immediately we were through. I wasn't anticipating such an easy job and was pushing hard on the drill, consequently the bit went deep into the roller. As I pulled the bit out, a cloud of white powder appeared. Everyone looked on in utter amazement. This is it, once again we found something. Before we all became too excited, Joe tested some of the white powder that was around the edge of the drilled hole. Immediately the drug test kit reacted positively to the presence of an opium substance—heroin. We didn't bother drilling any of the other rollers. By tapping on them, we could tell they weren't hollow. There was something in all five rollers, and we could only assume the other four had heroin in them also. If this was the case, we had some serious weight here. The rollers were four feet long and between six and ten inches in diameter, enough space to hold a lot of dope.

We decided we had to take these five rollers to a machine shop to have them professionally opened so we could see what was inside. One of the guys said his uncle owned a machine shop in Hyde Park, and maybe he could help us. We told him to get on the phone and see what he could do. Within minutes, he was back and said everything was all set, but it couldn't be done until the morning because his uncle was already shut down for the night. No problem, we thought. We still had to get the other four rollers out of the tub, and the delay would also give us some time to organize and catch our breath. For the next couple of hours, we worked on freeing the other rollers from the tub. Eventually, we had all five rollers lying on the ground side by side all set for delivery. In the morning, we would find out how much weight we actually had, but we all knew it was significant. In the meantime, we set up a guard schedule for the night. We wanted to have plenty of people babysitting this shipment. Obviously, the State Police was in concurrence, indicated by the fact that they brought in a fresh contingent of troops for the night—all wielding machine guns.

The next morning, as planned, we reconvened to transport the rollers to the machine shop. As I said before, the management at the cargo facility went out of their way to be helpful, and this morning was no exception. Counter surveillance by the bad guys was of utmost concern to us, and we attempted to do everything as inconspicuously as possible. We were able to pull our vehicles inside and load all the rollers into our Jeep Wagoneer without being seen by anyone. Once we were all set to go, we opened the bay door, and a caravan of three vehicles took off for the Hyde Park machine shop.

When we arrived at our destination, there were people standing by to assist us. We talked with the boss, and he fully examined the rollers. He said he felt comfortable putting the rollers on lathes and cutting open one end so we could gain access to whatever was inside. To be on the safe side, we would experiment with the roller that we had already drilled. If this test went OK, we would perform the same procedure on the other four rollers.

A couple of the workers from the machine shop placed the roller on a huge lathe and made a bunch of adjustments. After a while, they turned on a switch, and the roller began to spin rapidly. A worker wearing goggles started to turn a lever that caused a sharp bit to cut into the side of the roller. It was not long before the entire end of the roller was cut free. They shut off the lathe, and the roller slowly spun to a halt. They removed the roller from the lathe and placed it on the floor for our inspection. When we looked in, we saw countless small rectangular brown boxes. Jimmy Scotch, the agent in charge, began to remove the boxes. In preparation for this, we had laid out on the floor five pieces of heavy brown paper—one piece for each roller. Jimmy slowly began to remove the cardboard boxes and placed them on the paper. About halfway through, Jimmy opened one of the boxes and reached inside and pulled out a plastic bag that contained a pure white powder. We weighed the package, and its weight came to just about eight hundred grams. Jimmy continued to remove the boxes until the roller was completely empty. As Jimmy was doing this, everyone else was busy doing something. We were taking pictures continuously throughout this process, people were outside keeping guard, and others were on the phone calling their bosses to keep them abreast on what was going on. Jimmy was on the phone the most because this whole operation was basically his. Once we discovered the heroin by drilling the roller the previous night, the scenario evolved from an inspectional stage to an investigative stage, and Jimmy was the head investigator.

Most of Jim's conversations were with the U.S. Attorney's Office because this case was definitely going to be prosecuted on the federal level. Jim wanted to coordinate every move we made with them because we didn't want to make any mistakes and jeopardize the case. After one of Jim's lengthy conversations on the phone, he called everyone together for a briefing and a meeting of the minds. According to the U.S. Attorney's Office, we could attempt to make a controlled delivery, but we had to remove the heroin from hopefully all five rollers and replace it with an equal amount of sand in terms of weight. The reason for doing this is because of how the law is written. We can seize the dope and replace it with a like amount of sand with a representative amount of the original heroin and still prosecute for the entire amount of the dope. If we removed the dope and only left a representative amount, we could only prosecute on that representative amount. Thus, the placing of the sand was imperative.

After the successful removal of the heroin from the first roller, the green light was given to attack the other four rollers in the same fashion. Meanwhile, a couple of us ran out to get some sand. All morning and into the afternoon we worked. Every roller was loaded in exactly the same fashion as the first. We were keeping meticulous records and taking chronological pictures as the events unfolded. Finally, after all the heroin was removed and laid out on its designated piece of brown paper, we tallied up the total weight. It was an unbelievable 187 pounds of pure heroin! Not only was this a significant seizure, but it was also almost unbelievable. The dope weighed more than the average man. This seizure would be memorable for all concerned and would probably be the biggest in all our careers. We had to keep our emotions in check however because we still had plenty of work to do, and the clock was ticking.

In a reverse process, we placed in each roller an identical amount of sand as the heroin removed. Once this was done, the machine shop personnel welded the end that was cut off back on. To the human eye, you couldn't tell the end was cut off. We continued this process until we reached the first roller that was cut open—the one we had drilled the day before. We had to treat this one a little differently. First, we had to resolder the hole we drilled, and then we filled the roller with the same amount of sand as the heroin removed, minus eight hundred grams. To comply with the law, we had to place a representative amount of the heroin back in one of the rollers. The law didn't distinguish between smuggling 187 pounds of almost pure heroin to 187 pounds of maybe 1 percent heroin. Thank gosh, because this way, if we were able to pull off a successful controlled delivery, we could prosecute for attempting to smuggle 187 pounds of heroin that carried a more stiff sentence, much more than eight hundred grams. More importantly, we weren't jeopardizing losing the heroin like we would if we had to leave it in the rollers.

Once all the rollers were resealed, we had to transport them back to Chelsea and get them back into the tub and reseal the crate. Time was of the utmost concern because we knew the bad guys were looking for their shipment, and if there were any unusual delays, they would get suspicious and might not attempt to make the pick up. Besides, it was getting late. We had been working on these rollers all day, and we were tired. We drove back to Chelsea, stopping quickly to gobble down a sub, and went right to work reassembling the machine. Once this was done, we reassembled the crate and put it back into exactly the same condition as it arrived, with one exception; we installed a motion-detection device under the lid. Once the bad guys picked up the crate and started to open it, we would know immediately. By the time all this was done, it was approaching midnight. We made sure we had a sufficient amount of people for guard duty for the night, and then we went home. We had to be back bright and early in the morning for the anticipated pickup.

We were all in place by 7:00 AM. To say that we were a tired bunch would be a gross understatement. The only thing keeping us going was adrenaline. We anticipated the bad guys were going to pick up their bean sprout washing machine today because we knew they cleared the shipment with U.S. Customs yesterday, and they had inquired about what time they could come down and pick up their shipment. Therefore, we were all on our toes. We had people not only in the warehouse but also in cars all around the area. Our plan was simple. We were going to let the bad guys pick up their freight; and then, if everything went well, we were going to follow them and let them lead us to the brains behind this operation. The easiest thing we could do is arrest whoever came to pick up the shipment; but if we did this, more than likely, he wouldn't talk, and that would be the end of it. However, if we let them pick up the shipment, maybe we could get some more bodies. Anyhow, it was worth a try. All we could lose was eight hundred grams of heroin, sounds like a lot but not when compared to 187 pounds.

We waited all morning and nothing happened. What the hell was going on, we all thought. But shortly after 1:00 PM, a rental truck pulled into the parking lot with two Asians in the cab. This could be it! Sure enough, one of our guys who was working in the office posing as an employee gave us the alert on the radio. The yellow Hertz rental truck that was backed up to the platform was our target. We were all excited. Finally this whole deal was going to go down. It had been about a week since this whole thing started with Red's phone call, and we all were anxious to see it come to a successful end. In this pursuit, we made sure we had all the surrounding streets covered. Whatever direction the Hertz truck left in, we would have a car there to follow him. This initial car would constantly call out his location in order for all the other cars to follow. Frequently, the point car would break off and let someone else pick up the chase in order that we weren't recognized and spooked the bad guys.

The Hertz truck wasn't backed up to the platform for more than fifteen minutes before the two Asians reappeared from inside the warehouse and jumped in the cab of the truck. Moments later, they were maneuvering their way out of the parking lot and onto Eastern Avenue. There was constant but controlled chatter on our radio (mind you, this was before the days when everyone had a cell phone). calling out the position of the Hertz truck. Every once in a while, someone would come on the air and make a wisecrack or snide remark. Jim Scotch came on the air and told everyone to shut up in a not so pleasant manner and said the point car should be the only one talking unless someone had something urgent to say. After Jim's stern admonition, there was much less talk on the radio, and things became a lot less confusing.

Everyone was trying to figure out where the truck was headed for. It appeared to be going toward Boston but was taking quite a circuitous routing. Eventually it appeared we were headed for Chinatown. This was not the best scenario for us because it is such a heavily congested area. We could lose the truck easily in all the traffic, and if we tried to prevent this from happening by remaining too close, we could be made by the bad guys. Shortly, we were indeed on the busy and heavily traveled streets of Chinatown. We were keeping a good eye on the truck from a safe distance, and everything appeared to be going well—thank goodness, Hertz's trucks were a bright yellow. Suddenly, the truck pulled over to the side of the street opposite a gas station and parked

by a meter. The two Asians jumped out of the cab and began to walk up
the street. After a short walk, they turned the corner and were out of sight.
Jim Scotch yelled out over the radio to ignore the guys, keep our eyes on the
truck. And this is exactly what we did for almost the next twenty-four hours.
The truck just sat there, and no one came near it. We were able to park our
surveillance van across the street in the gas station, which helped immensely
with the surveillance. All night the truck just sat there unmolested. We thought
something would happen under the cover of darkness, but we were wrong.
The sun came up the next morning, and in the light of day, the truck was
still sitting there. *What are these guys up to?* We knew one thing, these guys
were professionals—and they were real cool. They knew the truck was hot,
and they were intentionally leaving it there in the open sort of as bait. They
wanted to see if anyone else was watching the truck, like the feds; and if so,
they would stay away.

Well, I guessed we fooled them because late that afternoon, a third Asian
male jumped into the truck, started it up, and began to drive away. We all
received the call from the surveillance van that the truck was on the move,
and we jumped into action. We had cars coming from all directions, but
most importantly, we had a car pull out from the gas station and was right
on the tail of the truck. Unbelievably, the driver of the Hertz truck drove
around the corner and proceeded up the street less than one hundred feet
and then pulled over and parked the truck once again. The driver jumped
out of the cab and walked away. These guys were messing with us big-time
now. They were being careful by making erratic moves in an attempt to flush
out any surveillance. Luckily, we weren't burnt, but once again, we were back
to the waiting game. Only this time, the surveillance van in the gas station
couldn't be used because we couldn't find a new location where we could
inconspicuously hide it.

On the third day of surveillance, things began to heat up; thankfully,
because we were using up a lot of man-hours and everyone was getting pretty
tired. Once again, two Asian males climbed in the cab of the truck and began
to aimlessly drive around Chinatown. We maintained a loose surveillance,
and everything was going well. Gradually, the truck left Chinatown and
drifted over to the South End. Again it appeared they were aimlessly driving
around until we noticed they kept driving around the same block time and
time again. Quickly, we figured out what they were doing. They must have
spotters on each corner, and as the Hertz truck goes by, they are looking to
see if there are any cars following the truck around the block. We called out
to all of our cars not to go around the block more than once; otherwise, we

might be made. New units would have to jump in and replace them. Tim, an agent out of Boston, and I had just joined the parade around the block when all of a sudden, instead of taking an anticipated right, the truck sped up appreciably and headed straight ahead. We were lucky to be where we were; otherwise, we might have missed this unexpected move. Tim called out the status of the truck to all the other units and told everyone it appeared they were headed for the expressway—north or south, we didn't know. Now the truck was really moving, and they even ran a couple of red lights. These guys were really good. They purposely blew the red lights to see if anyone else behind them did the same. If so, they would know that they were being followed. We had to be real careful with these guys. At a real safe distance, we watched the truck drive up the on-ramp of the expressway and head north. All the while, we were calling out to all the other units what was going on. They were scrambling to get behind the truck, and some were even attempting to get on the expressway ahead of them. We continued driving north on the expressway, driving through the city and then continuing on I-93 headed toward New Hampshire. However, when we approached the Stoneham exit, the truck suddenly changed lanes and drove down the exit ramp. This caught us off guard a bit, but we were able to follow. About a quarter of a mile off the highway, the truck pulled into a McDonald's restaurant. The guys must have been hungry, we thought, but later we would find out what really happened here that night. We stayed outside on the street and kept an eye out on the exit for the departing truck. Five minutes later out it came, and once again they headed north on I-93. We must have had at least fifteen units following the truck at this time. Some were ahead, some behind, and others were pulling off at exits so they wouldn't be made. About this time, one of the DEA (Drug Enforcement Administration) agents who were monitoring the motion-detector device that we had installed on the crate called out that he was receiving a signal from the device indicating that the crate was being tampered with. This was impossible, we thought, because the truck was rumbling up I-93 at about sixty-five miles per hour. The vibration of the truck bouncing over the road must be setting the motion detector off. We conversed on the radio about this probability, and we all agreed it had to be a false signal. Little did we know!

We continued our voyage north until we crossed the New Hampshire border. *Where the hell are we going?* Finally, the truck took an exit and got off the highway only to turn around and get right back on, only this time headed in the other direction, south back toward Boston. We followed the Hertz truck all the way back to Boston, specifically back to the South End. What this wild-goose chase was all about, we had no idea, but we would learn later on what was going on. The truck pulled into a courtyard of what appeared to be an elderly housing complex. It was impossible for us to follow, so Tim pulled into a public alley, and we got out of the car and attempted to get into a position to see what they were doing. Before we were able to do this, the truck was coming back out of the courtyard. We called over the radio and asked anyone if they saw anything. One of the units said that they weren't sure, but they might have seen the back sliding door open for a second, and possibly something was removed from the back. They didn't have a good visual, and the lighting was bad so they weren't sure what happened, but what could have been removed anyhow? The only thing in the back was the big crate, and they definitely didn't have enough time to remove that. Again, we were in for a huge surprise.

When the Hertz truck left the courtyard, it proceeded directly to a side street off Broadway Station in South Boston. The two Asians parked the vehicle and then entered a brick building opposite the MBTA yard. For the third night in a row, we were saddled with babysitting not only the truck but also the apartment building. Thankfully, the State Police was actively involved in this operation from the beginning. The amount of manpower they supplied was so crucial to the successful completion of this operation. They actually set up their command center in an empty lot behind a building close to Broadway Station. From here, they could coordinate the guard duty for the night, and the guys could actually return to the command center and get some shut-eye in one of the many racks that they had inside. Once again, it was a quiet night; and as day broke, absolutely nothing was happening. All day the yellow Hertz truck just sat by the curb, absolutely nothing was going on. I had a chance to run up to the Tip O'Neill Building to brief my port director and the assistant port director on the latest developments. Needless to say, they were both pleased on what was going on and were completely supportive of our efforts. The port director was concerned for our safety, but we told him not to worry, we were big boys. Somehow I don't think he was completely convinced. As we were talking, Jim, a Boston agent who I came up to the Tip O'Neill Building with, called me on the phone from his office. The bad guys were moving, and we had to get back down to South Boston in a hurry. I ran out of the office and met Jim in the lobby. As we were driving back to South Boston, we monitored all the traffic on the radio. A Chinese guy, who we thought might be the ringleader of this whole operation, had pulled up to the apartment building where the two Asian males had entered the night before. He went inside, and shortly, all three came out.

The ringleader got into his car, and the two Asian males got into the truck, and they all drove off together. We knew that this was the final act because the suspected ringleader had exposed himself, and we knew he wouldn't do something like this unless he thought everything was OK and that they had successfully pulled off this deal.

Jim Scotch orchestrated the final act like no one else could. He assigned units to follow the truck and car wherever they were going. The rest of the units were to remain behind to keep the residence under surveillance. We weren't sure what was going to happen, but we knew we weren't going to let this Chinese guy, who we thought was the brains behind all of this, out of our sight. Now that we had him, we planned on keeping him. Before the day was over, we were hoping that this whole deal would be complete.

A familiar voice crackled over the radio. It was Andy's, a State Police detective. Andy was informing Jim Scotch that they had followed the car and truck over to a junkyard in the South End. It appeared to Andy that they were trying to sell the tub of the bean sprout washing machine to the proprietors; but unbelievably, they were haggling over the price. Andy recommended that they grab these guys right now and terminate the surveillance. Jim Scotch concurred and advised Andy that the units remaining back at the house would commit themselves also. Simultaneously, we were committing all units to hopefully administer the coup de grâce to this entire smuggling operation.

Things went into high gear within seconds. Jim Scotch ordered all units to move into their preassigned positions. Some of us were to cover the rear of the building, others the side, and the rest were to meet up in front of the building in preparation to raid the house. It was an unbelievable sight that rapidly unfolded. Speeding cars with flashing blue lights on their dashboards or rooftops were coming from all different directions. A Boston Police officer on a construction detail at the corner of the street looked on with amazement. To add to all this excitement, a Customs chopper swooped over the building and hovered less than one hundred feet above our heads. People were running in all directions and shotguns and machine guns were brandished by just about everyone.

Within minutes, we had the entire building surrounded, and the raiding party was at the front of the building. We were preassigned different floors to search, and when Jim gave the word, we all moved in. What we were doing was way beyond being dangerous and crazy, but honestly I don't think anyone of us were scared because we were too busy and too concentrated on the mission. Besides, the adrenaline was pumping, and I think we could have run through a wall without knowing it at this point. An entire search of the building was conducted with negative results. All we found was a woman and what appeared to be her two young children. A team was set up to question her to see if she was implicated in this operation, but on the surface, it did not appear that she was. The two Asian males were living on another floor and didn't appear to have a connection with her. Regardless, we conducted a slow, methodical search of the building after our initial sweep and found absolutely nothing—no bad guys and no rollers.

In the meantime, things were happening in the South End with Andy's group. They had three arrests—the two Asian males in the rental truck and the Chinese guy who we were thinking more and more was the boss. More importantly, a search of the car trunk revealed three rollers from the bean sprout washing machine. We had them cold. We had the hard physical evidence that linked them to the heroin.

Jim Scotch was going crazy coordinating everything, but everyone was doing their best to help out. Slowly, things began to calm down, and we began to talk among ourselves about what just happened. A couple of the guys walked over to the Boston policeman who was still on his detail at the corner and apologized to him for all the raucous, and they explained to him what was going on. We called the chopper off and told them their services were no longer needed. As they departed, the scene became so quiet and peaceful. The guys in the back of the building were still snooping around, and they found the crate that the bean sprout washing machine was shipped in stuffed in a Dumpster at the rear of the building. *How the hell did this get in the Dumpster?* we all thought. We supposedly had the building and the truck under surveillance all night long, and nobody saw any movement whatsoever. We were puzzled. Slowly events began to unwind not only at the apartment building in South Boston but also at the junkyard in the South End. We were going to keep a couple of guys at the apartment for evidentiary purposes, but the rest of us could clear the area. In the South End, we had three bodies in custody along with a car, a truck, and three rollers. They were leaving the South End at the same time we were clearing out of South Boston. The bodies were going to jail, and the evidence was being transported to a secured Customs facility. After over a week of intense planning, coordinating, and dedication, it appeared our efforts were culminating in success; but we still had a lot of unanswered questions. Most notably, how did the rollers get from the truck to the trunk of the car when we had constant surveillance on the truck, and where were the other two rollers?

I will now attempt to explain to the reader what really happened during those last few days that even we were totally ignorant of until well after these events unfolded. Remember when the truck was headed north on I-93 and pulled off the exit in Stoneham and went into a McDonald's parking lot? We thought they were hungry and were getting some burgers. Actually, they had two co-conspirators waiting for them in the parking lot. As the truck pulled in, one of the guys jumped out of the cab of the truck and opened the back rolling door. The two co-conspirators jumped into the back with the intention of dismantling the machine as the truck rolled down the highway. This explains the alert that the DEA agent received that the motion detector was going off. We thought the vibration of the truck caused it as it bounced along down the highway. In reality, it was set off when these two co-conspirators were dismantling the crate and machine.

How did they get the rollers out of the truck without us seeing them? Remember when the truck was returning to Boston from their trip north and they pulled into the courtyard of the building in the South End? We couldn't see the back of the truck for only a short time because we would have exposed ourselves. In this short period of time, perhaps one minute, they, along with the two co-conspirators from McDonalds, were able to remove all five rollers and move them into an apartment of the housing complex. The apartment turned out to be the Chinese guy's who we later arrested in the South End with the three rollers in his trunk.

We had three rollers, where were the other two? The Chinese boss had intentions of driving to New York with the three rollers in his trunk that he thought were full of heroin. But before he did this, he wanted to get rid of the truck and the bean sprout washing machine. That is why he was at the junkyard, getting rid of the evidence. The other two rollers were still in his apartment in the South End. When he returned from New York, he would sell and distribute the contents of these two rollers. Thankfully, we didn't afford him the chance to do this. Once we figured everything out, we obtained a search warrant and retrieved the other two rollers from the apartment.

How did the crate wind up in the Dumpster at the rear of the apartment building? No idea. Sometimes it is best to leave certain things alone. The only possibility we could think of was that someone had let their guard down when they were supposed to be guarding the truck in South Boston. The two Asians were told by the Chinese boss to get rid of the crate that night and the next day they would get rid of the remnants of the machine at the junkyard. Therefore, they could return the rental truck nice and clean (no evidence) before their anticipated trip to New York.

Hopefully, I have fully explained the events that occurred during this heroin seizure. Believe me, we were in the dark ourselves for quite a while.

The next days *Globe* came out with a big picture on the front page of us standing in front of the building in South Boston. We were pleased to receive the recognition. My brother Bill, who worked for the *Globe* at the time, told me he knew the photographer who took the pictures. He told me that the photographer was originally going to print a different picture that had me prominently in the foreground. Knowing that I wouldn't want to be recognized, he asked the photographer to print a different picture, which he did. I thanked my brother, but told him next time to mind his own business.

Many months after these events occurred, all participants got together at a well-known restaurant in Charlestown and celebrated. The Hong Kong heroin caper was officially over.

Bean sprout washing machine

Heroin-filled rollers in bean sprout machine

TWENTY NINE

International Love Affair

I t was a Friday afternoon many years ago. I was working at the passenger terminal at Logan Airport, processing international travelers coming to visit America. As I was standing in my booth, a beautiful, immaculately dressed young lady in her late twenties or early thirties approached me with Declaration in hand. Not only was I overwhelmed with her beauty, but also when I made eye contact with her, I realized she was one of the most attractive women I have ever seen in my entire life. This is saying a lot because at the airport, there are some real beauties. After I regained my composure, I began to ask her the rudimentary Customs questions—that is, why she is coming to America, who she will be visiting, for how long, etc. Well, to put it bluntly, she failed the test. She told me she was coming to Boston to do some clothes shopping and would be here until Sunday. When I asked her how much money she had with her, she told me she had about one hundred French francs. When I asked her if she had any credit cards, she replied in the negative. I am not the most intelligent person in Customs, but everybody knows you can't buy clothes without cash or credit cards. When I asked her how she was going to buy clothes without cash or credit cards, she stared at me with a blank expression on her face. *Uh-oh*, I thought, *something is up with this young lady.* I continued to pursue this line of questioning, and her responses became quite feeble. She told me she wasn't sure how she would pay for the clothes, but she would find a way. *Huh?* I thought. As I continued to seek an explanation from her, she became less responsive and turned ashen. Her beauty was fading fast. I repeated my question on how would she pay for the clothes, and she just stared at me. Her eyes glazed over, and she just stared ahead. At this time, I suspected her to be an internal carrier of drugs. I asked her again when all of a sudden her whole body went limp, and she fainted.

I jumped over the counter and knelt down beside her. She was out cold but didn't appear injured from the fall. I yelled to a nearby inspector to call for the medics and redirected my attention to her. She was still passed out, but she was moaning slightly. I couldn't believe such a beautiful young lady could be a swallower, but it was looking that way to me. As I was checking her breathing, her eyes opened, and she became responsive once again. After a few minutes, she was sitting up and sipping some water that we offered her. Soon the medics showed up, and they examined her and gave her a clean bill of health. They said she was probably dehydrated from the long flight and she should be fine.

Good, I thought, but the question remained, what the heck she was really up to? I no longer felt she was a swallower because she wouldn't have regained consciousness if a balloon had burst inside of her, but I was still confused. I decided the best way to get to the truth was by a frontal assault. I told her I didn't know what she was up to, but if I didn't get some answers pretty quick, we were going to put her on the next plane back to Paris. When she heard this, she went berserk. No, she couldn't go back, she said. She had to come to Boston. She began sobbing and told me she just had to come to Boston. Fine, I told her, but she had to tell me the truth. Finally she did.

She told us that she had met an American in Paris when he was on a business trip. They had fallen in love and wanted to be together for the rest of their lives. One problem however, he was married. Well, the next best thing to being together for the rest of their lives was weekend visits. And this is exactly what she was up to, visiting this guy for the weekend. She didn't want to tell me the truth in the beginning because this guy was a well-known businessman from the area, and she didn't want to cause an embarrassing situation for him. I was totally satisfied with her story but told her I wanted to go out into the lobby to see if this guy was really out there. She pleaded with me not to, but I was insistent. She told me what he looked like, and one other inspector and I trekked out into the lobby looking for this expectant lover. Sure enough, there he was holding a dozen of roses with an expectant look on his face. When I approached him and asked him if he was waiting for a young lady, he confirmed that fact and gave me the young lady's name. He thought something had happened to her, but I quickly told him everything was all right and she would be exiting the Customs Hall shortly. He was relieved. The other inspector and I returned to where the young lady was waiting and helped her repack her bags and suggested to her that she might want to freshen up before she left the Customs Hall. She readily agreed and was most appreciative of our suggestion. Within a few minutes, she was on her way, and everybody was happy. We knew she wasn't doing anything illegal (at least she wasn't violating any Customs laws), and she was finally going to be reunited with her friend from Boston.

THIRTY

Sybil

As unbelievable as it seems, thirty-one years ago today, April 30, 1975, the North Vietnamese entered the capital of South Vietnam, Saigon, and had the city in their grasp. The next day, the last choppers would take off from the rooftop of the American embassy; and for the Americans, the long and costly war was over. North Vietnamese troops stormed through the main gates of the embassy and raised their flag for all to see. The unimaginable just a few years previous became the reality. The United States of America was defeated and humbled by a far less powerful force than ours. Like what Napoleon said, "The morale is to the materiel as three is to one." We should have listened to him. It would have saved a lot of suffering and dying.

Thirty-seven years ago, I met a nineteen-year-old from Cleveland, Ohio, who would have an impact on the rest of my life. Bernie Kozak joined the ranks of the 503rd MP Company of the Third Armored Division that was stationed at Drake Kaserne in Frankfurt, Germany, in the spring of 1970. A fellow Vietnam veteran, Bernie and I became close and lasting friends upon first sight.

Now, the obvious question that the reader should have is, "What the hell does this have to do with U.S. Customs?" My simple answer to you is this, *everything*. Bernie and I went through a lot while serving in the army, and when we got out, we leaned on each other and relied on each other for years after. In fact, we still do. Frequently we visit each other, and virtually every day, we talk with each other on the phone—and I don't even like the guy.

Bernie had an influence on me and impacted my life dramatically. Probably for the worse, some will say. But they don't know what they are talking about. The person who wrote all these stories and participated in all the events contained within—me—was fundamentally structured, developed, and molded by the same events and experiences that affected Bernie. Luckily, we have been there for each other over all these years. Without him, maybe I wouldn't have made it. This is why I felt compelled to include him in this book because I owe him a huge debt of gratitude—besides, he told me I had to include him.

As all the characters in this book have done, Bernie has given much of his heart and soul to this country. "Unappreciated," "disowned," "neglected," "rejected" are a few adjectives that describe Bernie's homecoming. Instead of going into a shell, Bernie developed numerous different personalities that he could lean on when confronted with one of the many obstacles in life. Although his core personality remained intact and steadfast, these superficial, self-imposed personalities helped get him through some of the more severe obstacles in life.

Always when I called upon him for a little piece of advice or just plain uplifting, Bernie answered the call above and beyond all normal expectations. If the world had a few more Bernie Kozaks in it, it would be a much safer, warmer, and happier place to live in. So that is why I mentioned Bernie in this book. Simply because he deserved to be in it as much as anyone else because if it wasn't for him, I wouldn't have been in it either.

THIRTY ONE

M/T *Orion*

The following story is fiction, but based closely on an actual seizure. One night as Dave and I were conducting surveillance on a Peruvian tanker, we seized forty pounds of cocaine off five Peruvian sailors. They were wearing modified vests that had enlarged pockets sewn into it. A brick of cocaine fit nicely into these pockets. Massachusetts State Police and Boston Police responded to our call for help, and without their assistance, I am not so sure the outcome would have been the same. All five crewmen were successfully prosecuted, and after a weeklong trial, they were all convicted and sentenced to seven years in jail. The ship was fined over a million dollars, and the last I heard, they were appealing; but the U.S. government was not being too receptive to their remonstrations.

A Hopeless Mission

The sun had risen only a few short hours ago, yet it was already stifling hot. The village that Carlos lived in with his mother and two brothers and one sister was typical of most of the small towns on the outskirts of Bogota. The population hovered around the 2,500 figure, although no one was sure exactly, and it also depended on whether there was recent activity in the area

by one of the many army units that constantly patrolled the countryside
around Orocue. The army's usual reign of terror always accounted for much
death and destruction. The homes were all alike, walls of clay piled six feet
high and left to be hardened by the sun. A window on each wall was common;
the eternal hope of a breeze to alleviate the repressive, ubiquitous heat was
paramount in everyone's minds. The roofs were constructed of tin, cardboard,
grass, or anything else that they could get their hands on. The homes needn't
be constructed with permanence in mind; one of the frequent mudslides that
the area suffered would frustrate all their efforts at an attempt to have a nice
home. The lack of food and the deplorable state of the little that they did
own only made their plight all the bleaker. In the homes of Orocue, death
by starvation was commonplace—as frequent a visitor as the "common cold"
in a typical Boston household. Carlos had already lost a little brother by this
injustice of life. Work was virtually nonexistent. Many townspeople had
wandered into the streets of Bogota looking for some kind of employment,
only to find thousands of people just like themselves with the same thought
in their minds. Most left Bogota to return to their villages frustrated and
worse off than when they arrived. The few that remained would turn to a life
of crime. They had no choice. Prostitution, pimping, and stealing was the
only way out. Usually their life in Bogota was swift and violent. Either they
wound up dead and left on the streets, or they wound up in jail, the key all
but thrown away. For those who had ventured onto the streets of Bogota and
were fortunate enough to return to their villages, nothing had changed. They
made continuous, feeble attempts at farming, but ignorance and thievery
usually prevailed. For Carlos, his husbandless mother, and fatherless brothers
and sister, the only thing that remained was hope; and that was disappearing
faster than the final rays of sunshine of a hot tropical sunset.

   Then Juan came into Carlos's life and answered all his prayers. Juan offered
Carlos money, food for his family, and even a job. Juan was Carlos's savior.
All his prayers and hopes and desires had finally been fulfilled; no longer
would his family suffer from starvation, no longer would he see his mother
cry herself to sleep. Carlos would now be able to provide for his family like
the head of a household should. Carlos attributed Juan's sudden appearance
into his life as a message from God. He had finally answered all of Carlos's
prayers and was now finally rewarding him for his years of hard work taking
care of his mother and brothers and sister. Where did Juan come from, and
why was he being so kind to Carlos's family? Carlos really had no idea, unless
it was providential. He didn't care, and why should he? All he knew was that
Juan was providing for his family, and he would be eternally grateful for his

generosity and kindness. The thought that Juan had ulterior motives didn't ever cross Carlos's mind. His only concern was the welfare of his family, and he knew deep in his mind he would do just about anything to continue the good fortune of the past few months. Carlos saw how happy his family had finally become. When he tucked his brothers and sister into bed at night and saw how happy and content they were, when he said good-night to his mother and saw the joy sparkling in her eyes as bright as the equatorial stars, he made a firm commitment to himself. Whatever he had to do, whatever danger and obstacles he might have to overcome, he would. No way was he going to allow his family to slip back to the level of poverty of just a few months ago. His commitment was sincere and final.

It was late in the afternoon when Juan arrived at Carlos's home. They were just about to have dinner, and of course, Carlos asked Juan to join them. He readily accepted the offer, sat down, and excitedly started to tell Carlos that he had good news to tell him. Carlos's family patiently and politely listened to every word out of Juan's mouth. What more could this wonderful man do for them? Then Juan told them. Through his influence with one of the shipping lines in Bogota, he was able to obtain a position as a seaman on a big oil tanker for Carlos. The pay to start was over $250 a month. Upon receipt of this news, Carlos jumped from his seat and ran over and gave Juan a big hug, tears streaming down his face. Carlos's whole family began to cry for joy. Their family hadn't earned $250 in the past five years, never mind in one solitary month. As Juan explained the details of Carlos's new job, Carlos and his family sat mesmerized by each word that flowed ever so eloquently from Juan's mouth. The ship that Carlos was going to work on was named the Motor Tanker *Orion* and was the same ship that Juan was the boatswain mate on. They were going to sail the following Monday from Cartegena, and Carlos and Juan had to be onboard by Sunday. Carlos had two days to pack his belongings and to make sure that everything was in order at home. Juan said that he was going to have to be off because he had other matters to attend to, but he'd be back Sunday at noon to pick up Carlos and bring him to the ship. As Juan left, everyone walked him to the yard and kissed and hugged him before he bid adieu. Juan walked down the path out of the village of Orocue, Carlos's whole family out in the yard graciously waving good-bye.

As promised, noontime on Sunday, Juan arrived to pick up Carlos. Although Carlos's family was sad to see him go, they knew it was for the best. He now had an excellent-paying job, which would keep them out of poverty forever. He would be back within two months, and the loneliness of his absence would be tempered by the fact that he would be returning as the provider and the head of his household, of major importance to this still-proud Colombian family. After much kissing, hugging, and crying, Carlos and Juan said their last good-byes and set out for the Motor Tanker *Orion*. Along with his baggage, Carlos carried an air of excitement and adventure with him. Juan's baggage consisted of nothing but treachery, deceit, and death.

Suburban Weston is a small town west of Boston with a population of twenty thousand people with a mean income of $150,000. Not too many people want for anything in this town, least of all David Harwood. David's life history is typical of just about every other twenty-two-year-old young man from Weston. He never wanted for anything, always went to the best schools (in fact he went to quite a few of the best schools because he kept getting himself kicked out of them for what they called adjustment problems). In the urban schools of Boston, they would have called him a spoiled brat, and someone would have rang his bell for him the first day of school; but in suburbia, he only had adjustment problems. I have never been able to figure out how the English language can take on such different meanings in the space of such a short distance such as between Boston and Weston. Or is it the long distance between the Weston rich and the Boston inner-city poor? Whenever David found himself going to school, he always went with a full belly and nice clothes on his back. The maids that the Harwoods employed would always see that David had a nutritional breakfast before he left to pursue his academic endeavors. They would also lay out his clothes for him so he wouldn't have to tax his feeble mind so early in the morning. David somehow struggled through the first twenty years of his life in this fashion. He somehow overcame all the burdens and tribulations of his youth and proceeded on to Boston University, hopefully to eventually study law. But in order to attend Boston University, poor David would need to be provided with transportation since he had no intention of traveling on public transportation; and he didn't have enough money to buy a bicycle, never mind a car. So old Daddy came through for David once again. The agreement between David and his father was that if David maintained a 2.5 GPA, a brand-new Iroc would be bought for him, and a full tank of gas would be assured because his father was giving him a credit card. To make the deal even sweeter, David's father would provide him with a weekly stipend of $100. David had it made in the shade.

For the first year at BU, David struggled along maintaining a 2.6 GPA without it having too much of a detrimental effect on his social life. However, during the summer between his freshman and sophomore year, a major transformation in David's lifestyle occurred. This is when he was first exposed and then personally introduced to cocaine. From that point on, it was all over. David was at a fraternity party with his on-again, off-again girlfriend, Susan. They were all having a good time drinking a little beer, blowing a few joints, and grooving on the music. Then Paul (David didn't even know his last name, all he knew was that he was a real rich kid from Philly and was in his English Lit class) offered David a little coke. Naturally, David refused, afraid of the unknown. Then he decided the hell with it. He wasn't having that great a time at the party, his girl Susan was dancing with another guy, why not! Paul took David to one of the upstairs bathrooms of the fraternity house and showed David how to snort a line of coke. An instantaneous and lasting relationship between David and cocaine was formed that night. David became obsessed with cocaine. There wasn't a moment that David wasn't involved in buying and snorting cocaine or else working on different methods to get the cash to fund his habit. David at first found it easy to get the money. He would explain to his parents how there were some unexpected costs at school and could they just give him the money, and he'd see to it that the bills were paid. This went on for six months before his parents started to question David about the "unexpected costs." Then David would give them some lame excuse about a girl in trouble and pregnancy, and the parents didn't want to hear anymore. They continued feeding him money. Life went on for David in this fashion for close to two years. Obviously his studies suffered, and then he eventually dropped out of school. He told his father that once he got his life straightened out, he was going to return to BU to complete his studies. With that stipulation and not knowing fully about David's "girl in trouble," David's father agreed to continue financing him over this rocky road in his life. The only problem was, that rocky road that David was traveling on was fast coming to a dead end, and at the end of the dead end was a sheer cliff with a hundred-foot drop.

The M/T *Orion* had been to sea for three days now. She was somewhere in the Atlantic Ocean off the Bahamas headed north—destination: Holton Oil Terminal, Boston, Massachusetts. The estimated time of arrival (ETA) was 0400 hours on the fourteenth of February 1985. Three days sailing, that's if all went well. The past twenty-four hours, the wind and the seas have been picking up out of the northeast, and conditions were worsening by the hour. The printout from the weather machine up on the bridge didn't have anything encouraging showing. There was an intense low pressure forming off the coast of the United States, somewhere near Cape Hatteras; and if the low formed as predicted, the M/T *Orion* was going to be in for some heavy, nasty weather. Just what Carlos didn't need.

As planned, Carlos and Juan joined the ship on Sunday, the seventh of February. Juan introduced Carlos to the captain, and he officially signed onboard. Carlos's first impressions of the ship and her crew were quite favorable. All the officers were Spaniards, and the crew was Colombians. Therefore, everyone spoke Spanish, and Carlos wouldn't have any problems understanding orders. He had visions of being onboard with a bunch of "foreigners," and he was fearful that he wouldn't be able to understand the language. After Carlos signed onboard with the captain, Juan brought him down to the mess deck in time for the evening meal. Once again, Carlos was extremely impressed. He hadn't seen so much food in his whole life. And it was free. After he and Juan had satisfied their appetites, they went below to their stateroom to stow their gear. Carlos was literally speechless. The accommodations were beyond his wildest expectations. He had a bed with a thick mattress, a closet to store his clothes, and a bathroom all to himself. Carlos wasn't sure what to expect when he and Juan were traveling to the ship earlier in the day. He didn't want to ask Juan too many questions, fearful that Juan might think that he was unappreciative of all that he was doing for him. Now that he saw the ship and all her luxurious accommodations and knowing that he was getting paid $250 a month to enjoy all these luxuries, Carlos knew that he had made the right decision. Juan showed him where to stow all his gear and then suggested that he get to bed because they were sailing at 0500 hours and Juan would be waking him two hours prior to sailing time. They said good-night, and Carlos immediately jumped into bed so he could get a good night's sleep. As he pulled the thick warm covers up around his neck, Carlos was a satisfied man. He looked forward to returning to the village of Orocue so he could tell his family all about his good fortune.

Juan was knocking on his door at 0300 as expected. The rest of the crew was already on deck bustling about handling the mooring lines and securing the gangway. As the boatswain mate, Juan was in charge of the deck gang and all the work that was performed on deck. This is where Carlos was assigned, and Juan told him that he would show Carlos exactly what he was to do. Carlos, never being on a ship before, was thankful for this. The M/T *Orion* sailed on time, and as soon as she cleared the sea buoy and discharged her pilot, the captain rang up the engine room and ordered sea speed, fifteen knots. They were off. It was an uneventful, though for Carlos interesting, transit of the Caribbean Sea. The *Orion* entered the Windward Passage, and as they sailed northward, Carlos could see Haiti far off on the eastern horizon. As soon as they transited the Windward Passage, the captain ordered a course change with the intention of leaving the Bahamas off to port. After three days sailing, they cleared the Bahamas and set a new course, direct for the northern Port of Boston.

Luckily, the low that appeared to be forming off the eastern coast of the United States never developed. It fizzled out to nothing but a few showers and light winds. Carlos was quickly getting into the routine of shipboard life. With the close supervision of Juan, he was fast learning a completely new and different way to live. Juan arranged the watch list that they were both on watch at the same time, eight in the morning to noontime and then eight at night to midnight with eight hours off in between. Carlos was learning how to tie knots, scrape and paint the ship, run and upkeep all the deck winches, and what he loved the most, steer the ship. He was fascinated when Juan had him get behind the wheel on the bridge and steer a course. Initially, Carlos couldn't keep the ship within twenty degrees of the proper heading. Eventually, after numerous attempts, Carlos lessened the error to five degrees. Everyone on the bridge gave Carlos a hard time on how poorly he steered the huge tanker. It was all in good fun, and Carlos still couldn't believe how such a small steering wheel could make such a huge ship go this way and that way.

Midmorning on Saturday the thirteenth of February, the M/T *Orion* entered the Boston Traffic Separation Zone southeast of Chatham, Massachusetts. They were on their final approach to Boston Harbor, and their original ETA of 0400 on Sunday the fourteenth looked good. Plans were made via the VHF radio to have a Boston Pilot meet them at the Boston sea buoy at 0200. Once the pilot was onboard, they were going to sail into Boston Harbor and should be tied up at the Holton Oil Terminal by 0400 as planned. Everything onboard was going well, and Carlos was fitting in fine with his new shipmates.

At 1200 hours, Carlos and Juan were relieved, and they went below to the mess deck for noon chow. They had a pleasant meal together, and when they were finished, Juan asked Carlos if he would come back to his stateroom because he wanted to talk with him. When they arrived at Juan's stateroom, Juan pulled out of his refrigerator a couple of beers and started to talk to Carlos, asking him if everything was going OK. Carlos explained to him how everything was fine and how he really appreciated all that Juan had done for him. Then Juan dropped the bombshell. He reached under his bed and pulled out a heavy gym bag and threw it onto his bed. He told Carlos to open the bag and look inside. When Carlos did, all he saw was a whole bunch of small packages with a shiny brown tape around them wrapped in the shape of thin bricks. Juan asked Carlos if he knew what was inside the packages; and Carlos, being honestly ignorant, said no. Then Juan went into detail. He explained to Carlos that what he was looking at was forty pounds of almost pure cocaine. With Carlos's assistance, he was planning on taking the forty pounds of cocaine ashore once they arrived in Boston and deliver it to a man that was going to be waiting for them in a car at a predetermined location. Once they delivered the cocaine, the man was going to give Juan $5,000 in U.S. money. Juan would give Carlos $2,000, and he would keep $3,000 for himself. He was taking the extra $1,000 because, after all, he was the chief courier, and he was the one that had made all the arrangements. The truth was, Juan was going to receive $10,000 from the man in the car, but he didn't see any reason why Carlos should get more than $2,000. Juan reached into his drawer and pulled out two specially designed vests and showed Carlos how they would do it. All they did was put on the vests over their shirts, slide the packages of cocaine in the specially designed pockets, put on their heavy winter coats, and then go ashore. Once they met the man in the car, they would give him the coke; he would count the packages and then give Juan the $5,000. Simple as that. He asked Carlos if he would help him. Carlos was completely dumbfounded. He didn't know what to say or what to do. He knew Juan was a real good friend of his and had taken real good care of both him and his family. Also, the plan that Juan had just told him seemed foolproof. Anyhow, how could he say no to this man? After all that he had done for him. The thought of the $2,000 was also extremely enticing. Carlos looked into Juan's eyes and said, "Yes, I am with you." Juan let out a yelp, and both he and Carlos embraced. Juan told Carlos that when the time came to off-load the cocaine, he would tell him but in the meantime, not to mention their plan to anyone. He told Carlos that you couldn't trust anyone else on the ship. Carlos swore to secrecy, and then both he and Juan proceeded to get good and drunk celebrating their newly formed partnership.

The M/T *Orion* docked at the Holton Oil Terminal early Sunday morning; and after all the port formalities were concluded (Customs, Immigration, and Agriculture clearance), she began to pump her cargo of number 6 heavy fuel oil ashore. If everything went well, the captain anticipated sailing early the next afternoon. During the day, the majority of the crew members went ashore to go shopping, to have a beer, or to just plain get off the ship and take a walk. When Juan's watch was over at 1200 hours, he took a quick shower and jumped into some clean clothes and went ashore like everyone else. Only Juan's reasons were quite different, he was going ashore to call his contact and make arrangements for the pickup.

The phone hadn't rung twice when a low, gruff voice on the other end answered hello. This was Juan's point of contact, and the owner of the low, gruff voice was to tell Juan exactly where the delivery was to be made. After a five-minute exchange in rapid and curt Spanish, the arrangements were finalized between Juan and this unknown figure with the gruff voice. They decided that since the ship was sailing the following afternoon, the delivery would have to be tonight. They didn't want to conduct their business during daylight, and since the ship was only going to be in port for one night, they didn't have any choice. Tonight had to be the time. Actually, the exact time of the meeting was to be 0200 on Monday the fifteenth of February. The place for the meeting was at the intersection of Salem and Willow streets in the South Boston section of Boston. Juan, having sailed to Boston on other ships, was familiar with the area and knew exactly where the intersection was. The man with the gruff voice said he would be driving a brand-new black Toyota. When Juan hung up the phone and stepped out of the phone booth into the clear, crisp New England wintry air, he felt content. Everything went exactly as he had anticipated. All the proper code words were exchanged between him and the voice on the other end of the line. The deal was set.

During the rest of the day, Juan and Carlos left the ship several times. A couple of times, all they did was walk around the streets adjacent to the oil terminal that they were tied up to. Mostly they just wanted to walk around and shake off their anxiety and nervousness, but they also wanted to check out the area. They wanted to make sure that there wasn't any police in the vicinity that might have their ship under surveillance. When it became dark, they went ashore again to walk by the intersection of Salem and Willow streets. Juan wanted to make sure that he knew exactly where it was, and he also wanted to check out the area one last time. Although Juan wasn't nervous or suspicious, he felt more comfortable making sure the area was free from any police. Juan had made several previous successful off-loads in the Port of Boston, and he always followed these same steps. He figured that if they worked before, why change them now? Who can argue with success? When Carlos and Juan felt comfortable with the area, they returned directly to the ship in order to stand their eight-to-midnight watches. As Juan walked up the gangway to the ship, he felt happy about everything. In a little over six hours, the deal would have been made and they'd be back aboard ship counting their money. As he stepped from the gangway onto the cold, hard steel of the main deck of the *Orion*, a smile came to his face. Once again, he was going to pull off a successful off-load. In a few weeks, he'd be back in sunny Colombia spending his money on wine, women, and song.

The time was 0100 hours on the fifteenth of February. In exactly one hour, Carlos and Juan would be making the exchange. They were in Juan's room putting the final packages of cocaine in their specially made vests. Once all the packages were secured, they put on their heavy overcoats, and Carlos decided to put on a thick wool stocking cap and gloves. He wasn't used to this cold and wanted to do everything he could to protect himself from its cold bite. Once Carlos was all set, they left Juan's stateroom and proceeded to leave the ship. This time it was the real thing. All forty pounds of cocaine was with them, strapped to their chests. When they stepped off the gangway and started to walk up the street, the time was 0130, a half hour to their meeting.

At 0130, Tom and Jack were on their fifth cup of black coffee. Tom decided that he wasn't going to drink any more after this cup. All he was doing was going to the bathroom. Tom and Jack were United States Customs inspectors. Earlier in the day, their boss called them at home and changed their shift for them. He said a ship was coming into Holton Oil Terminal from Colombia, and he wanted them to pull surveillance on her the whole night. *Great*, they thought, *another surveillance.* They were constantly conducting surveillances, stopping crew members off ships, and patting them down, looking for drugs and constantly coming up with nothing. They weren't sure why their boss kept giving them all the surveillances. Why didn't anyone else from the drug team do them? Oh well, no sense complaining. He wouldn't listen to them anyway. They were talking about the Red Sox and the recent trades when they saw a couple of people walking out of the main gate of the Holton Oil Terminal. *Probably a couple of workers from the terminal going home*, Jack thought as he reached for the binoculars on the seat next to him. He focused the binoculars on the two people and realized, nope not workers, they were crew members off the ship. They both looked at each other and asked the same question. *Where the hell are two crew members going at this hour of the night?* All the bars and strip joints were closed, and it sure as hell was too cold for a walk. Interesting, they thought. The two crew members left the oil terminal facility and began to walk up West Fifth Street in the direction of downtown. Tom and Jack decided to watch them walk a few hundred yards up the street, seeing what they might be up to. Even though Tom and Jack had done this numerous times in the past, this was different. These guys were up to no good. They could sense it. Their hearts began to pump a little faster; Tom wiped his sweaty hands on his pants. After watching the two crew members walk up the street a couple hundred yards, Tom and Jack decided they better stop them before they got out of sight. Jack started up the car and took off. As he got alongside the two crew members, Jack pulled over the car, and he and Tom jumped out. They both pulled out their badges and identified themselves as United States Customs inspectors.

Before they could get these words out of their mouths, Juan took off with Jack right on his tail. Tom pulled out his .357 Magnum revolver and pointed it at Carlos and told him to lie down on the sidewalk. Carlos couldn't understand what Tom was saying but understood his gestures. Carlos fell to the ground face-first. After a brief chase, Jack returned with Juan in tow. He had Juan lie down on the ground next to Carlos. With Tom standing in the gutter covering him, Jack began to pat down Juan. Immediately he let out a yelp and said, "Bingo." Both Tom and Jack looked at each other with big grins on their faces. No kidding! Well, it's about time. After all these surveillances and all the pat-downs they've done, they finally made a hit. Quickly, Tom and Jack became nervous again. If they had these two guys packing cocaine, they knew someone else was out there on the streets waiting for the delivery. They were going to have to be real careful. Tom took a couple of steps backward and reached into the window of the car and picked up the mike to the radio. He called the local Customs dispatcher and asked him to get them some backup. And quick! Tom kept his gun out, covering Jack as he continued to pat down Carlos and Juan. However, he kept looking around, making sure there weren't any other bad guys sneaking up on them. After about a five-minute wait, the first backup car arrived. Thank God! It was Tom, a state trooper who patrolled the waterfront. Shortly thereafter, three Boston cruisers arrived with their lights flashing and sirens blaring. Tom and Jack felt relieved. For a while there, they knew they were in a real shaky situation. With the arrival of all the reinforcements, Tom and Jack could relax and see exactly what they had. They were both shocked. In front of them were twenty packages of cocaine, each weighing approximately two pounds for a total weight of forty pounds. This was unbelievable. Initially they thought each crew member had one or two packages, but never in their wildest dreams did they think that they were going to have forty pounds. After they finished the pat-downs, Tom and Jack handcuffed the crew members, put them in the car, and along with the Boston Police units, drove off to jail. Tom couldn't wait until they got there; he had to go to the bathroom again.

Monday the fifteenth of February wasn't the best day in David's life. He had spent the majority of the day at the Boston Municipal Courthouse accounting for his actions of the past weekend. A weekend that started out bad and proceeded to rapidly go downhill. David's problems started when Susan broke the date they had for Friday night. She told David that she wasn't feeling good and thought she was coming down with the flu. Actually, she had a date with another guy from one of her classes at Boston University. She didn't want to tell David the truth, not that she was concerned about hurting his feelings. Susan knew David had an explosive personality, and if she told him the truth, he'd drive over to her house and create a big scene. David didn't need to be told however. He had sensed Susan's unfaithfulness for quite a few months. He was slowly weaning himself from his reliance on her and was more and more relying on cocaine as his security blanket. Friday night was to be no different. After Susan cancelled their date, David stormed out of his house and jumped into his now well-abused Iroc-Z and headed into town. He knew his coke friends wouldn't shun him like Susan had. His intentions were to solve all his problems and rejections by snorting them away. And that is exactly how he spent his whole weekend, in a coke-induced stupor. He never went home, changed his clothes, ate, or washed. All he did was keep his mind clouded with the dust of cocaine. Sometime Sunday night, while driving to his home in Weston and suffering severely from depression, David was involved in a major traffic accident with many injuries. The police were still investigating who was at fault, with the preliminary findings indicating it was David. But that was the least of his problems. When the police arrived at the accident scene, they found David slumped over the steering wheel of his wrecked Iroc. On the seat beside him was a plastic bag containing at least an ounce of white powder that tested positive for cocaine. David was arrested and, except for a brief visit to the hospital for the treatment of a severe laceration to his head, spent the rest of the night in jail. In the morning, he was arraigned at the Boston Municipal Courthouse, and his father had to post a $25,000 cash bond for his release. The trial was set for the second of March.

David was home now, sitting in his bedroom. He was nursing his head wound and reflecting on the past weekend. His mental state was one of severe confusion and depression. As usual, his solution to this state of mind was to snort some more coke. He went into his closet to gain access to his reserve stash of coke that he always hid there. He prepared himself a couple of lines and then anticipated snorting himself into a euphoric state. Only this time it was different. Immediately after inhaling the white powder, David's body began to quiver. His head felt like it was going to explode, and he couldn't catch his breath. He stood up to walk to the bathroom and didn't make it five feet. He tripped over the corner of his bed and fell face first to the floor. This is how his mother found him. She immediately called the fire department; the ambulance and the EMTs arrived within minutes. They valiantly fought to revive David all the way to the hospital. The doctors and the nurses were waiting when the ambulance pulled up to the emergency room door. They applied every piece of modern technology at their disposal. The doctors called upon every last piece of training they had received at medical school. For well over an hour, they sweated and cursed and fought. Finally, reluctantly, sadly, the doctors stepped back and said it was no use. David was dead.

There is absolutely no happiness in this story. It contains only misery, suffering, and death. The United States attorney in Boston successfully prosecuted Carlos and Juan. They both received sentences of seven years in jail. They are presently serving their sentences in a federal penitentiary; and even with the benefit of a parole, they have many more years to serve. Carlos's family has once again slipped back into the hands of poverty. His brothers and sister are once again suffering from the ravages of hunger and disease, worse now than ever. Now they don't have their older brother to look after them. Tom and Jack are still out there working a lot of nights, still trying to hold back the tide of drugs that is washing up on the shores of America.

THIRTY TWO

Our Heroes

A little over a week ago, on the ninth, we participated in an exercise with folks from the U.S. Army. Specifically, these folks are agents with United States Army Counterintelligence. The purpose of the exercise was to conduct mock interviews of agents-in-training who were, for role purposes, coming from America and attempting to clandestinely enter a third world Mideastern country. For the purpose of the exercise, this third world country was called Bostonia, and we were playing the role of Bostonian Customs inspectors.

To make the situation as realistic as possible, we met the Delta Connection flight coming from Washington, D.C., (America) and introduced ourselves to our targeted passengers as they exited the aircraft and identified ourselves as Bostonian inspectors. We had been provided pictures of these two individuals beforehand that made positive identification a possibility. As soon as we verified we had in our custody the correct two individuals, the fun began. To play a mind game with them, we immediately separated the two and went in different directions. They were both escorted to the Customs and Border Protection facility in Terminal E by different routes. Upon arrival, we escorted them into separate interrogation rooms and began processing them into our country—Bostonia. However, before we would admit them, they had to prove to us that they were bonafide visitors. To say the least, we purposely made this almost impossible. We badgered, insulted, intimidated, and harangued them for over an hour. We gave them no quarter. To their credit and to the high caliber of training that they had received to this point, none of them revealed to us the real reason for why they were coming to visit Bostonia.

After over an hour of being hauled over the coals by us (Bostonian Customs inspectors), we released them and allowed them to enter the country. These two had little to look forward to because on their agenda was a week of more intense exercises involving units from the Boston Police SWAT and the local FBI office. All this training was realistic, and the stress level on these two individuals was unimaginable. However, we all wanted this training to be as intense as possible in order to toughen up these two guys in order to better prepare them for the real thing.

I only mention the above to reveal to the reader what is going on in today's world in the fight against terrorism. So much is happening, and so many people are giving so much of themselves that the rest of the world is ignorant of. These people that I have mentioned in the above story are truly exceptional individuals. They are full-time army soldiers that have committed their lives to their country. They are constantly deployed either stateside or overseas and suffer long periods of separation from their families. In fact, these two individuals will be deployed to Iraq at the end of the month for at least a four-month deployment. While we are home enjoying the companionship of our families in the warmth and luxuries of our homes, these guys will be out on some lonely, dangerous, isolated assignment in far-off Iraq.

So I say this to the reader: take some time out of your hectic life, and sit back and reflect on what these guys and many other thousands of men and women in uniform are doing for us on a daily basis. Remember them in your prayers, and when you see a soldier on the street, stop him or her and shake their hand and thank them. Because of them, this world is a bit safer. And regardless of your political views, remember the age-old adage—hate the war but love the warrior.

THIRTY THREE

Letter Drop

O ne morning many years ago, a bunch of us from Boston CET were examining the international mails at the Customs Mail Division at the South Postal Annex in South Boston. The volume of mail that is processed here is staggering and goes on twenty-four hours a day, every day of the year. While one of the guys was inspecting a stack of letters from the Netherlands, he became suspicious of a letter that was going to a mailbox in Hingham, Massachusetts. Upon opening the letter, his suspicions were confirmed by the presence of a fine brownish powder that field-tested positive for heroin. There wasn't that much powder, perhaps forty grams, and we were sure federal prosecution would be declined; but we still had to make the obligatory call to the United States attorney's office and run the facts of the seizure by them. As expected, they immediately declined and suggested that we call the state and see if they were interested. Our next phone call was to the State Police, and surprisingly, they told us they thought they might be interested but would have to call us back. We gave them the name and address of the person that was on the envelope, and they told us they needed to make some checks and would get back to us as soon as they were finished. Within fifteen minutes, Bill, a State Police detective assigned to the Plymouth County Drug Task Force, called and said they were indeed interested in pursuing this case. Their checks revealed that the consignee of this letter had prior problems with law enforcement regarding drugs and there actually might be an outstanding warrant out on the guy. Since this was a Friday, nothing would be done until the following Monday. We made tentative plans to meet at 8:00 AM Monday at the Hingham Police Station where we would formulate plans on how and when we would deliver this letter to our unsuspecting friend.

Monday dawned bright and beautiful. Joe and I met in South Boston and, in possession of the heroin filled letter, drove down to Hingham together. Customs agents, Hingham detectives, and Bill of the State Police met us there. After we all introduced ourselves, we sat down and worked out our game plan. The letter was actually going somewhere called a letter drop. I never heard of one of these, but I was quickly educated by some of the others in the group. A "letter drop" is actually a storefront business that rents out mailboxes to people who want mail delivered to them at a place other than their homes. This is done for a multitude of reasons, most of them being rather seedy and secretive. (A mailbox address at a letter drop will say "Box 123" compared to a mailbox at a post office that will say "P.O. Box 123.") The letter drop that this letter was going to coincidentally was right down the street from where we sat in the Hingham Police Station. The plan that we formulated was as simple as it could be. A couple of us were going to pay the proprietor of this letter drop a visit and seek his cooperation. If all went well, we wanted to put the letter in the assigned box and clandestinely sit on the box and wait for the guy to come and claim it. Joe was assigned as the inside man, and the rest of us would hang outside. When the guy showed up for his letter, Joe would give us a shout over the radio and give us a description of the car he was driving. The rest would be up to us. We all liked the plan because it was simple and to the point.

We sat on the site of the letter drop all day Monday with negative results. No one went near the box containing the letter with the heroin. When the store closed at 6:00 PM, we all regrouped at the Hingham Police Station to make plans for the next day. The Customs agents told us they had other commitments and would not be able to participate anymore. Bill and the Hingham Police wanted to continue the surveillance, and we on CET wanted to also, but I had to make a quick phone call and get the clearance from my boss. He readily agreed that we should stay if the State Police wanted to continue, and he told me to do whatever we had to do to make a controlled delivery possible. Having a boss like this made the job so much easier. He fully supported us and made sure we had whatever we needed to professionally complete our job.

All day Tuesday, Wednesday, and Thursday, we sat on the store; but nothing at all happened. Joe remained on the inside; and Bill, a couple of Hingham detectives, and I remained in our cars outside. As time progressed, I began to ride with Billy in his unmarked State Police cruiser—a bright green Ford Mustang that was all souped up. The time dragged by, and we were all wondering if the guy was ever going to show up to claim his letter. Although there wasn't anything to do but wait, Billy and I did a lot of talking and got to know each other pretty well. On Thursday evening when the store closed, we met in the parking lot of a car dealership along Route 3A. We decided to continue on for one more day, and if nothing happened by the end of Friday, we would call it quits. We were wasting a lot of money and resources, and eventually, we had to cut our losses whether we liked it or not.

It was about 11:00 AM Friday, and as usual, all was quiet. The potential for a pickup was getting bleaker by the hour. Someone or something must have tipped the guy off that everything wasn't hunky-dory. Bill asked me if I was hungry, and I told him that I was starved. Bill was glad to hear this because he was hungry also, and he knew a great seafood takeout restaurant just down the street. *Great*, I thought, *let's go*. If something happened like the guy coming to pick up the letter, well, we were just down the street. I ordered a huge seafood platter with plenty of french fries and coleslaw. I forget what Bill bought, but I know we we're both anxious to get back to our position across the street from the letter drop so we could dig into our food. As soon as we parked the vehicle, we began to chow down. I placed my soda and bowl of coleslaw on the dashboard to give me some maneuvering room, and then I used my plastic fork to dig into the scallops and fish. It was simply delicious, and my mouth is watering as I recall how good the food was. We weren't even halfway done when we heard Joe's voice come over the radio. "He's leaving the store right now and is pulling out onto Route 3A headed north toward Boston. He is driving a—" *What the hell*, we thought. We looked up, and sure enough, the car Joe just described went speeding by us. Why didn't Joe give us some heads-up? Well, now was not the time to be asking questions; we had to catch this guy. Without hesitating, both Billy and I threw all our food out the window. We were off in high pursuit. Billy didn't even bother leaving the parking lot by the exit; he just flew right over the curb. Once the tires hit the street pavement, they let out a squeal, and we were off.

As Billy was weaving between cars in an attempt to regain visual sight of our target, he was also reaching behind him and searching for something in the backseat. Finally, I asked him what the heck he was looking for. He told me, "My gun! My gun!" I was shocked. Here we were speeding down the highway, coming within inches of hitting other cars, and Billy was looking for his gun. I yelled at him to forget about the gun and pay attention to the road. He was going to get both of us killed the way he was driving, with or without his gun. Eventually, we regained sight of our target and began to follow him, always keeping a couple of cars between us. After following him for a couple of miles, we decided to make a stop as soon as it was advantageous. We did not have to wait long for an opportune moment. Our target had to stop at a red light, and thankfully we had a Hingham police cruiser pulling out of a side street at the same time. We radioed the cruiser and asked him if he could pull in front of the cars at the red light and stop all the traffic. All the Hingham Police knew we were in the area and were asked to be available if we called for help, so this request was not all that unexpected. The officer in the cruiser immediately turned on his blue lights and siren and pulled right across the traffic lanes, effectively stopping all movement.

Billy and I jumped out of the car and approached the target's vehicle. Billy went to the driver's side, and I remained at the right rear quarter of the vehicle. Billy identified himself to the driver as a state trooper and ordered him out of the car. The driver immediately complied with Billy's command and was cooperative and docile throughout the entire encounter. Billy explained to the gentleman that he was under arrest for the possession and distribution of a Class 1 substance, heroin, and we escorted him to the Hingham cruiser for transportation back to the Hingham Police Station. Billy and I stood by at the car waiting for a tow truck. As things began to settle down, I began to harass Billy about not knowing where his gun was. I told him I was going to tell everyone what had happened. Here he was, a big strapping state trooper; and when the chips were down, he was completely unreliable. He could have got someone—me—hurt because he wasn't properly armed. This was all in fun, but Billy was a little concerned. He asked me if I was serious about telling everyone what had happened, and I told him yes. Billy asked me not to say anything, but I kept harassing him. Finally the tow truck arrived to pick up the car, and we followed it back to the Hingham Police Station where we planned to conduct a thorough search of the interior. As we pulled into the parking lot at the rear of the station, Billy once again asked me if I was going to tell everyone how he couldn't find his gun. When I said yes, Billy looked at me and said, "Well, I guess you don't want this back." I looked down to see what he was holding in his hand and saw my wallet containing my badge and credentials. *How the hell did he get my wallet,* I thought. After a bunch of bantering and laughing and assuring Billy that I was only kidding the entire time, he reluctantly gave me back my wallet. Billy turned my joke around and made me eat my words. What had happened was when I jumped out of the car, my wallet fell out of my rear pants pocket onto Route 3A. In the excitement, I didn't even notice. Billy noticed it on the ground afterward and picked it up for me but didn't tell me. He was planning on holding my credentials and badge as ransom against my idle threats to inform on him to all the other guys. His plan worked!

When we entered the Hingham Police Station, the desk sergeant told us they had the prisoner sitting in the conference room. While Billy, one of the Hingham detectives, and I interviewed our prisoner (he was fully Mirandized and wanted to talk), Joe and others conducted a thorough search of the vehicle. Joe's search came up with negative results, and we weren't having much luck either. According to this guy, he had a menial job working in some kind of a stationery store. He became involved with some pretty bad guys, and over the course of time, he built up a huge gambling debt. The only way out of his predicament, or so he thought, was to sell heroin at a huge profit. He had a buddy overseas in Holland going to school, and his friend could get him as much stuff as he wanted, and cheap. This plan worked for a while until we stumbled upon the letter at the Customs Mail Division. Now he was in a lot of hot water. The ironic thing is that this guy came from money. He was from Colorado, and his parents still lived there. I forget what his father did, but I remember it was a real good job and he had a few bucks. When we asked our prisoner why he didn't go to his father for the money to get him out of the jam with the gambling debt, he told us he couldn't. It seems that he had previous transactions with his father, and even his father was fed up with him. Basically, this guy was a spoiled brat and became a loser who couldn't even get help from his own family. Well, it was too late now. He stepped over the line big-time, and now he was going to have to face the music; only I don't think he was going to enjoy the songs that they were going to play.

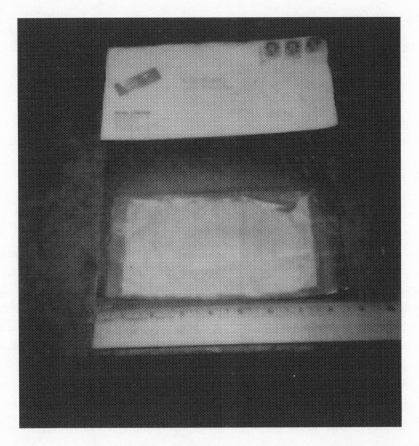

Letter Containing Heroin

THIRTY FOUR

Boston Pilots

From the fall of 1977 through all of 1978, the period just before my joining the United States Customs Service, I was a boat keeper with the Boston Pilots. The primary responsibility of a boat keeper was to put a harbor pilot onboard an incoming ship and to take the harbor pilot off an outbound vessel. Usually this evolution transpired somewhere between the BG buoy and the B buoy some fifteen miles offshore from the dock that we tied up to at Long Wharf in Boston. Two boat keepers would man one of the pilot boats for a period of usually five days at a time, and we would pull shifts that consisted of six hours on and six hours off. Needless to say, after five days "in the bay," we were quite tired and beat-up, especially in the winter months when the weather was the roughest. My regular partner was a pleasant young man who lived down Cape Cod by the name of David Krocker. Although young in years, he was an exceptional boat handler and was pleasant company throughout every trip that we made. We had two pilot boats, the *Boston Pilot* and the *Thomas Knox*. The *Boston Pilot* was a seventy-foot steel hull boat and was quite seaworthy. She burned a lot of fuel, and consequently, we would only run her during the winter months when the need for a good sea boat was the greatest. During the summer months, we would run the *Thomas Knox* because of fuel efficiency. She was a lot smaller and not as comfortable as the *Boston Pilot*, but the smaller fuel consumption necessitated this move.

On a normal trip, we would leave the dock at Long Wharf in the early morning hours and not return until five full days had elapsed. We would steam out to the Pilot Station—somewhere between the BG and B buoy—and either drift around or steam at an extremely slow speed, waiting for either an outbound or inbound ship to loom over the horizon. Oftentimes, we would have hours to kill between ships and not much to do; so we had to find some kind of activity to take up this time besides eating, sleeping, and reading. Usually we resorted to fishing, at least when the weather was good.

Where did we fish, and what did we fish for? Well, an old tugboat captain with many, many years of sea-going time under his belt took care of this problem for us. His name was Captain Jack Lang, and he was one of those guys that you only met once in a lifetime. He knew more about ships and the sea than almost anyone. If we had a problem with one of our engines or with the radar or with anything else, Jack would be there to show us what we were doing wrong. Shortly after Jack appeared on scene, the problem would be solved. This was exactly the case with our fishing. Jack came with us on one of our trips to spend a couple of days to show us where the good fishing holes were. And did he know them! The most memorable spot Jack showed us was called the Eye of the Whale—at least this is what Jack called it. When we asked Jack how this spot got its name, Jack pulled out a chart of the area and began to explain. He showed us the contour lines on the chart indicating the depth of the water. A line often forming funny-looking shapes would connect similar depths. In this one area, the line formed the shape of a whale; and exactly where the eye of the whale should be, the water was the shallowest, causing it to be a great spot to fish. Why? Well, as best as I can explain, the water on the incoming tide would flow past this high spot, sweeping plankton and algae along with it. Small fish would be on the lee side of the hill, swimming against the tide and eating the plankton and algae as it flowed by. Made sense, and one other thing that Jack said made sense also. Where small fish are, bigger fish come to eat them. Therefore, that is where we should be. If it is an outgoing tide, the process is simply reversed. Well, Jack had us convinced, and we were at least willing to put his theory to the test. God help us for even thinking of questioning Jack's knowledge of saltwater fishing.

As soon as we lowered our jig to the bottom of the ocean floor, a fish would strike. We would reel the fish in, land him on deck, take the hook out, and lower the jig back in the water. Once again, as soon as the jig hit bottom, we would have another strike. This went on for a solid half hour, and our arms were actually getting sore from all the work. We had mostly cod on deck with a couple of flounder and several sand sharks. This was the best fishing that David or I ever experienced, and we weren't exactly novice fishermen. Now, however, we had a problem. What the heck were we going to do with all the fish? We solved part of the problem immediately by filleting some of the cod and pan-frying them. However, we had too much on deck to eat, and we didn't feel like filleting and freezing them. Then David had a bright idea—"Let's give the fish away." I thought David was going crazy and looked at him rather skeptically until he explained to me what he meant. David said that we had a ship due in about an hour, and once we hear from them on the radio, we can ask them if they want any freshly caught fish. Surely they would because they probably didn't have any fresh fish in weeks if not longer.

Sure enough, within fifteen minutes, we received the anticipated call from the *Columbus Australia*, a huge German container ship. The radio conversation was of the regular routine—they gave us their ETA (estimated time of arrival) to the B buoy and told us what their deep draft was, and we returned with asking them to have their Jacob's ladder on the starboard side of the vessel about four feet above the water and to maintain a speed of five knots. Once all this pertinent information was exchanged, we asked them if they were interested in having some fresh fish. In a thick German accent, whoever was on the radio responded by saying he didn't understand what we were talking about. I then went on and told them that while we were waiting for their arrival, we were fishing and had some pretty good success. We had at least a half-dozen fish on deck that they could have if they so desired. The radio operator of the *Columbus Australia* excitedly responded in the affirmative. He said they would love to have the fish. I told them that once we came alongside to put the pilot onboard, they should have a heaving line handy to throw down to us. We would tie the heaving line off to the fish, and they could haul them onboard.

As I maneuvered the pilot boat alongside the *Columbus Australia*, the pilot going onboard and David were standing by on deck. In anticipation of receiving the heaving line, David had already put a line through all the gills of the fish that we had on deck. Once he received the heaving line, all he had to do is tie it off to this line. I put the pilot boat alongside the ship right where the Jacob's ladder was dangling over the side. *Good job*, I thought as I watched the pilot scramble up the ladder. Then I heard the heaving line hit the deck. David grabbed the line, tied it off to the fish, and then the crew from the ship hauled away. We waved good-bye and broke away from the vessel.

No sooner had I done this than we heard the crew from the ship yelling at us. When we looked up, they were waving at us to come back in. David and I started to mutter to each other. "This is the last time we try to be nice to someone," David said. "They probably don't like the size and type of fish," I said. Whatever, we were upset and were ready to tell the ship to go to hell. After some tricky maneuvering, I brought the pilot boat back alongside the vessel. We looked up the side of the vessel and saw the crew lowering some kind of box. We were perplexed but stood by to receive whatever they were lowering to us. Once the box reached the deck, our eyes bulged out of our heads. It was a case of German beer. David and I, both being dedicated beer drinkers, were ecstatic. We once again waved to the crew and broke away from the ship. Only this time, we both had huge smiles on our faces.

Our next sailing wasn't for a few hours, so David and I shut the boat's engines down and drifted around in the bay. We continued fishing and enjoyed a couple of German beers. The rest we saved for the other guys. Shortly thereafter, I was hired by U.S. Customs as a file clerk at the Customs House in Boston. My illustrious career in the U.S. Customs Service was about to begin.

I would like to add one little footnote to this German beer adventure. As I gained experience in Customs and learned all the Customs laws, I realized we shouldn't have taken this beer because we never paid the applicable duties. Thus—unbeknown to me at the time—this was my first exposure to international smuggling, and I was the perpetrator.

Oil tanker inbound Boston Harbor transiting North Channel

Pilot boat *Boston Pilot*—great sea boat

THIRTY FIVE

Donna Corazon

The weather off the New England coast in January is usually inclement at best. January of 1978 was no exception. Because of the severity of the weather, we used the seventy-foot *Boston Pilot* exclusively to take the pilots into the bay to meet arriving vessels. The seas were continuously in a confused state and beat us up pretty good. Every chance we had, we tried to duck in behind the headland of Nahant and tie up to a mooring buoy that we had anchored there. Even if we could get a couple of hours of rest in the lee of Nahant, the respite was most welcome for a weary boat crew.

One such night, we had Captain Jim "Skip" Drye onboard with us. He was scheduled to pilot an arriving bulk ship, the *Donna Corazon*, into Boston Harbor and anchor her in Anchorage #2. Since we had a couple of hours before the arrival of the *Corazon*, we took advantage of the free time and cooked ourselves up a little meal. It was simple, macaroni and cheese with some fish cakes, but it really hit the spot. Skip had been a harbor pilot for years and exuded confidence as he plied his trade. Like all the other pilots, Skip knew the harbor and approaching waters like the back of his hand. He served his twelve-year apprenticeship on the old schooners and was an old salt. In spite of being overweight and a constant smoker, Skip still could climb up the side of ships with the best of them. Having him onboard the boat with us was always pleasant and entertaining, and we always welcomed his advice and tutelage.

Since the *Donna Corazon* was due in less than two hours at the pilot station, we decided we had best cast off from the mooring buoy and head out to where we belonged. Reluctantly we came on course and headed out to open sea. As soon as we came out from behind the lee of Nahant, the seas attacked us off our port bow. Solid water enveloped the boat, and we felt more like a submarine than a pilot boat. As much as we detested these sea conditions, we knew that once we put Skip on the ship, we could return to the mooring buoy because the next arrival wasn't until the following morning. With the way the weather was kicking up, this time could also be significantly pushed back.

Slowly and inexorably, we reached a point midway between the B buoy and the BG buoy where we anticipated meeting the *Donna Corazon* and putting Skip onboard. Thankfully, upon our arrival, we could distinctly see the hulk of the vessel looming in the near distance. We could wait for the ship to reach us, all the while the seas would beat us up, or we could jog out to the vessel and get Skip onboard. Skip directed us to avail ourselves of the second option.

As we came close aboard the ship, we called them on the radio and requested that they make a lee, reduce speed a bit, and stand by the Jacob's ladder. They immediately complied with our request, and I brought the *Boston Pilot* alongside the vessel. Thankfully, she was in ballast and riding high in the water. This made a good lee for me and really calmed down the water. However, because she was so high out of the water, Skip would have an exceptionally high climb to get onboard. Everything went as planned, and as soon as Skip went up and away, David (my crewmate) and I went under the stern of the vessel and headed back to the Nahant mooring. We were looking forward to an anticipated long, quiet, and calm night.

Even though we were safely tied up to the mooring, David and I still had to maintain our watches—six hours on and six hours off. You never knew when someone might be calling on the radio looking for a pilot, but more importantly, the watches were maintained for safety purposes. If we both fell asleep and didn't maintain due diligence, the boat and us could be put in jeopardy. It was not unheard of hearing about a line parting and a boat being set adrift—or worse.

David relieved me at 0100 hours, and I went off watch. I was exhausted and was looking forward to a good night's sleep. At about 0645 hours, David was rousing me out of bed to relieve him. Like me the night before, he couldn't wait to get to bed. Six hours on and six hours off for days on end was a grueling pace to maintain. I grabbed a cup of coffee in the galley and proceeded up to the wheelhouse to have a look-see. I didn't even reach my destination before I heard a distraught voice booming over the VHF (very high frequency radio). "*Boston Pilot, Boston Pilot,* this is the *Donna Corazon.*" Immediately thereafter, he repeated himself, "*Boston Pilot, Boston Pilot,* this is the *Donna Corazon.*" As soon as I reached the radio, I placed my mug of coffee down and grabbed the microphone and responded to this voice booming over the speaker. "*Donna Corazon,* this is the *Boston Pilot* on Channel 16," I said as I wiped the sleep out of my eyes. This unknown voice responded with a plea for help that was palpable through the airwaves. "*Boston Pilot,* I need a tug. I need a tug. I am hard aground."

It is an understatement to say that I was shocked. How could he be aground? The night before, Skip had safely anchored him in Anchorage 2, and now he was aground! I was confused. Through a whole bunch of radio transmissions, we ascertained that somehow during the night, the *Donna Corazon* had dragged her anchor at least a mile and had run up on the beach—Spectacle Island to be exact. For a huge ship like the *Donna Corazon* to drag her anchor for a mile is a virtual impossibility unless something else was going on. As the story unfolded, we found out that indeed there was something amiss; but before I explain, I will tell you how we responded.

I yelled down to David and told him what was going on. Reluctantly, he climbed out of his bunk and came up to the wheelhouse. Through a series of calls to the pilot office, it was determined that David and I should bring the *Boston Pilot* into the inner harbor and determine exactly where the ship was grounded. In the meantime, the office was calling Boston Tow to see if they could get some tugs out to the *Donna Corazon* to assist. Fortunately, four tugs were returning to their dock in East Boston from a job that they just finished on the Fore River in Braintree. They were asked to respond to assist, which they readily agreed to do.

It took David and me about forty-five minutes to steam back into the harbor to look for the *Donna Corazon.* As we transited Anchorage 2, it was funny not to find the ship there where she belonged. After another ten minutes of groping around in the snowy conditions, we found the *Donna Corazon* exactly where she said she was—on the rocks of Spectacle Island. Already there was a Boston Tow tug alongside of her, and they were attempting to pass a towline to her. The ship had grounded herself starboard side to with her bow pointing out to sea. She had a pronounced port list on her and was totally helpless. The only fortunate thing going for her was that when she went up on the rocks, it was low tide. Hopefully, she could be refloated when the tide came in, if the tugs could keep her from going further up on the rocks. In a matter of twenty minutes, three more tugs arrived on scene. Now there were four tugs alongside the ship, and they were all making fast towlines that would keep her in one place. Too much movement of the ship would only worsen her plight. The steel plates of her hull would grind and twist and eventually would start opening to the sea. Instead of having a simple grounding, we would have a potential sinking with the risk of bodily harm, not to mention the pollution concerns. Since it would be several hours before the tugs would attempt to pull her off the island and not serving any useful purpose on site, we were instructed by the office to return to our dock on Long Wharf. The weather was worsening by the hour, and the next ship arrival was delayed, so we could tie up and relax for a while. This was sweet news for me but especially for David. He hadn't been to bed yet, and he was really dragging.

So what happened to the *Donna Corazon* that made her go up on the rocks? The best that we could ascertain after hearing all the facts was one simple answer—human error. After Skip had anchored the vessel in Anchorage 2, the crew relaxed and involved themselves in some serious libations. It was the end of a sea passage, and they thought that they were safely anchored and let their guard down. Instead of maintaining a bridge watch like what the Rule of Good Seamanship dictates, they all got drunk and went to sleep. This is totally inexcusable behavior, and ultimately the master has to take responsibility for the consequences. Especially in light of Skip's warnings to the captain to be ever vigilant, the conduct and behavior of the crew is vexing. Skip knew it would be blowing hard all night. He told the captain to keep his engines on standby. If the vessel appeared to be dragging her anchor, Skip told them to let out more anchor chain. If that didn't prevent the dragging, Skip told them to drop the other anchor. If this still didn't help, Skip told the captain to steam into the seas on a slow bell and to call the pilot office. We would get a pilot out to them and get underway and steam out of danger. In spite of all these warnings, the captain allowed his ship to drag anchor for a mile and eventually run up on the rocks.

At a little before high tide, the tugs in unison took a strain on their towlines and successfully pulled the *Donna Corazon* off the rocks. They immediately shepherded her to a dock and safely tied her up. Divers were standing by to go into the water to inspect her hull. If there was any damage, the ship would have to be dry-docked and the necessary repairs made. Thankfully, the dives confirmed that there was only minimal damage. A few hull plates were dented and scraped, but that was it. This was real good news for the captain—and crew—but their behavior was still contemptible. I am not sure what the company that owned the *Donna Corazon* was going to do with the captain, but I am sure the Coast Guard was going to have a chat with him.

The *Donna Corazon* was a "slack ship." She sailed the seven seas on a whim and a prayer. She appeared to be an accident waiting to happen. These were our feelings at the time, but it was none of our business. They were only our gut feelings. However, believe it or not, an incident happened several years later that only confirmed our gut feelings.

One day as I was reading the *New York Times*, there on the front page was a picture of a ship in distress on the high seas. The name of the vessel? Yup, you have it—the *Donna Corazon II*. They renamed her, but it was the same vessel. The attached story told how the *Donna Corazon* was en route to New York and encountered heavy weather. In fact, the seas were so big that they broke the back of the vessel. In the ensuing rescue of the crew before the ship sunk, a couple of lives were lost. How is this possible? Many ships run into trouble at sea for a multitude of reasons. However, many more encounter the same dangers and challenges and escape unscathed. I wasn't familiar with the details of this incident, but deep down inside of me, I wasn't surprised. The sloppy handling of the vessel finally caught up with them and cost a couple of seamen their lives. The fate of the *Donna Corazon* was sad but not unexpected. The sea is unforgiving and challenging, and when you are on it, you must always remember that you are only a guest. The sea will always remain the master. Obviously, the crew and officers of the *Donna Corazon II* forgot this age-old adage of the sea—to their misfortune.

Donna Corazon aground on Spectacle Island, Boston Harbor

THIRTY SIX

No Fly List

I t was early Saturday afternoon, and I was enjoying a day off by visiting my son, daughter-in-law, and grandchildren who lived in Ellsworth, Maine. My son was stationed with the Coast Guard at Southwest Harbor, so my being temporarily assigned to Bangor was indeed fortuitous. As I was talking with Anna, my daughter-in-law, my omnipresent cell phone began ringing on my hip. I immediately answered the call, and lo and behold, it was the boss in Boston. As soon as I answered, he began to talk rapidly in a concerned voice. He told me something was going on with a flight coming from Paris and destined for Washington, D.C. There was an individual onboard that appeared to be on the No Fly List, and Headquarters was figuring out what to do about it. One option that they were considering was diverting the plane to Bangor. (Although I didn't mention it, I agreed with this thought process. If it was indeed true that we had a guy on this aircraft that was on the No Fly List, we surely didn't want him onboard an aircraft flying over Washington, D.C. Whatever he was possibly up to, it would be best to at a minimum rearrange his plans.) My boss asked me where I was and if I could get up to Bangor as soon as possible. Ellsworth was about fifty miles east of Bangor and about an hour drive, but I told him I was on the way and would get there as soon as possible. While I was driving, I would use the cell phone to coordinate our activities with the state and other federal agencies that surely would be involved with a situation such as this.

When I arrived at the airport at Bangor, I parked directly in front of our office and went inside. I was met by a flurry of activity and found myself immediately immersed in the unfolding events. I was told that the flight was indeed being diverted to Bangor and the ETA was in an hour and fifteen minutes. No problem, I thought. We had plenty of time to coordinate our activities and make plans how we were going to handle the situation. Between working with the FAA (Federal Aviation Administration), TSA (Transportation Security Administration), FBI (Federal Bureau of Investigation), ICE (Immigration and Customs Enforcement), and the Bangor Police Department, we settled on a hastily developed plan. Originally, FAA wanted to park the plane remote, which means on the tarmac. I nixed this idea and requested that the plane pull up to a finger of the terminal. I wanted complete and unfettered access to the aircraft that would only be possible if the plane was alongside the terminal. As soon as the plane opened the cabin door, I had a team of four individuals assigned to board the aircraft and escort the two individuals in question off the plane. (Although we only had one name on the No Fly List, further research of the ticket reservation indicated he was traveling with another person.) We had two search rooms designated to put these two guys in where they could be inspected and interviewed. The FBI would stand by until CBP ascertained their status and determined if they truly deserved to be on the No Fly List. If they were, we would turn them over to the FBI once we were done with our processing. All seemed in order, and all that was left to do was the waiting. Since I was satisfied that everything was covered, I decided to go up to the ground control tower and await the arrival of the aircraft. From this vantage point, I could monitor all radio communications between the tower and the aircraft, and I could also have a visual of the aircraft as soon as it came in sight.

Within twenty minutes, the incoming flight was on final approach. She glided majestically out of the sky and smoothly and effortlessly landed on the runway right in front of the control tower. After the aircraft dramatically slowed down, the pilot maneuvered the well-lit blue-and-white plane to the Jetway that was attached to the main terminal. As planned, as soon as the cabin door was opened, the assigned inspectors boarded the aircraft and were escorted by two flight attendants to the assigned seats of our passengers of interest. One individual appeared to be in his early fifties while the other gentleman was considerably older—maybe in his midseventies. Both gentlemen were extremely cooperative and cordial as we escorted them off the plane. The younger gentleman spoke fluent English while the elderly man only spoke French. As we were escorting the gentlemen to the CBP inspection area, other inspectors were climbing into the baggage hold with airline personnel looking for their checked baggage.

A long, detailed interview ensued that confirmed the findings of Headquarters. The young gentleman was on the No Fly List and should never have been allowed on the plane. We were going to take him into custody, incarcerate him for the night; and in the morning, we would transport him to Boston to be put on an outbound flight to Paris. From whence he originated he would return. His traveling companion came up negative in all our checks, and therefore, he could reboard the waiting plane and fly on to Washington, D.C. However, when we told him he could leave, he wanted nothing of it. He wanted to stay with his friend no matter what. Considering his age and state of health, we decided to let the older gentleman accompany his friend. In the morning, they would both be returned to France via Boston. The plane continued onto Washington, D.C., minus these two passengers after a two-hour delay.

This is how the events in Bangor evolved that night, a couple of years after the attack on the World Trade Center. The challenge that we confront is that we must identify these "no fly" passengers *before* they board the aircraft. This might cause a slight delay in the departure of the aircraft; but if the airlines require all passengers to check in earlier than what is required now, this should address the problem. This way we will have enough time to vet the passenger list and take any necessary action. Therefore, the situation that arose in Bangor will never be repeated again, and inconvenience to the traveling public will be kept to a minimum while security will be enhanced. Obviously, it will take some time to work all the bugs out; but as usual, working together we will make it happen, and inconveniences to the traveler will be a thing of the past, and their safety and security will be assured.

In fact, these bugs were worked out shortly after this incident. The current system addresses any previous concerns and has further improved air travel security.

THIRTY SEVEN

A Fishy Tale

H appy 230th birthday, America.

For at least the past twenty-five to thirty years, small coastal freighters with containers of frozen fish have arrived in the Port of Boston from Iceland. These ships tie up at a pier in Everett and are usually in port for a couple of days discharging their cargo. Back in the seventies when I was a boat handler with the Boston Pilots, we used to call these ships "secret ships" because the owners of the vessel were attempting to keep their notice of arrival a secret from the longshoremen. It seems the owners wanted to use less-expensive, independent labor (usually off-duty firefighters) to off-load their vessels and were attempting to avoid using the longshoremen, thus their desire for secrecy. The steamship line involved used three ships that were almost identical in design. All three vessels were extremely shipshape and were manned by a crew of approximately twelve native Icelanders. Customs and Border Protection never had a problem with any of these ships over all the years that they called on the Port of Boston—except for one night.

Boston CET was conducting outbound currency checks in Terminal E at Logan Airport. In fact, we had luck this night and made a significant currency seizure off a gentleman who attempted to smuggle money out of the country by strapping it to his calves and thighs. We were suspicious of this guy's story and decided to conduct a routine pat-down. Pursuant to this search, the money was found. Because it was a significant amount of money, we escorted the gentleman back to the CET office to conduct an interview and begin a preliminary investigation. While we were interviewing the subject in the CET office, the phone rang, and one of the guys answered it. After a few seconds on the phone, the inspector who originally answered waved at me and pointed to the phone and made gestures as if he wanted me to pick up the phone. *What now,* I thought as I reached for the handset. The voice on the other end was real low and raspy, but I could distinctly make out what he was saying. He wanted us to know that there were at least several suspicious people lurking around a sea container that was grounded on the pier at a particular waterfront facility in Everett. He didn't want to give me his name or anything else and told me he just wanted us to know about this suspicious activity. With that said, he abruptly hung up the phone. As I put the handset back in its cradle, I stared at the phone and wondered what that call was all about. Was it a hoax, or was it for real? Was someone attempting to lure us down to the docks in the middle of the night to do us harm, or was this call for real? Well, I didn't have a choice but to send some people down there to check out the story. I yelled for the guys that were in the other room to come and see me. Immediately, Pat, George, and Brendan walked into my office. I explained to them the contents of the telephone conversation that I just had, and I told them I wanted them to get down to the Everett dock and check out the situation. All three readily agreed to go and were on their feet, ready to walk out the door. I stopped them and reinforced in their minds to be careful. I told them to stick together and not to get separated. If anything was going on when they arrived, I told them to call me on the radio, and I would respond. They all shook their heads in concurrence, and before I could say another word, they were out the door. With them gone, I could redirect my attention to processing the money seizure that we had just made.

We were just finishing up doing all the paperwork pertaining to the money seizure when the radio began to blare. I could distinctly make out Pat's familiar voice, but this time, I heard something in his voice that I had never heard before. There was an edge to his voice mixed with a tinge of excitement and anticipation. I pressed the button on the office radio and told Patrick to go ahead with his message. Patrick answered immediately, and his message was brief and to the point. He requested my presence ASAP to the dock at the Everett facility. Without hesitation, I answered Patrick and told him I was on my way. I wasn't sure what was going on, but when the usually unflappable

Patrick is calling for my presence ASAP, I figured I better hurry. I had to leave a couple of guys behind to finish the money seizure, so one other inspector and I rushed out the door and headed for the seaport.

It was only a fifteen-minute drive from Logan Airport to the facility, but the drive tonight seemed to take an eternity. As we turned left off the main road and onto the side street that led to the dock, I could see the headlights of our car attempting to penetrate the total darkness that enveloped us. When we got closer to the terminal, figures began to appear out of the darkness. I first noticed a group of about seven people, and my peripheral vision told me that there were others all about. The closer we got, the more distinguishable the whole scene became. The group that we initially saw consisted of five unknown individuals with two of our guys keeping an eye on them. We pulled up to this group, and I exited our vehicle in anticipation of receiving an explanation of what was going on. George and Brendan immediately began to brief me. They told me that when they first arrived, they found three guys inside of a sea container that was alongside the docked ship. Along with these three unknown individuals, Brendan and George saw cases and cases of liquor stacked in neat piles. Immediately, they thought they had a case of theft of booze out of an international sea container. Then they noticed more people carrying cases of booze from a van in the adjacent parking lot toward their direction. Now they were confused and weren't sure what was going on. To their credit, they quickly brought the situation under control and called me on the radio. As I was responding, they secured the area by handcuffing the five suspected individuals and posting a guard on the container.

After being properly briefed, I walked into the container to see what we had. All I saw was case after case of booze. I pulled a bottle out of one of the boxes and noticed that there wasn't any state tax labels affixed to the bottle. I checked many more bottles, and none of them had this tax label on them. I was trying to figure out what was going on, but honestly, I was confused. Finally, I used the age-old trick in law enforcement—I asked the bad guys what they were up to. Their answer simply floored me. They responded to my question with honesty and clarity that totally explained everything. Because booze is so expensive in Iceland, these five individuals who we had handcuffed on the dock and happened to be crewmen on the ship floating next to us decided to test the waters as entrepreneurs. They pooled their money—it turned out to be over $17,000—and drove to a liquor store on Route 1 in the borrowed van that was sitting in the parking lot. They intended buying $17,000 worth of booze and smuggling it back into Iceland aboard their ship. They said they could probably sell the booze in Iceland for at least five times their initial investment. And this is exactly what they were in the middle of when we came on scene. They were unloading the van of the booze and loading it into the sea container. They had already made several trips to Kappy's, a local liquor store, and this happened to be the last run. Somewhere in the process is when we received the anonymous phone call about suspicious people on the docks. After they loaded the container with all the booze, they were going to use the ship's crane to hoist the container onboard the ship. Once the container was onboard, they were going to unload the booze and hide it in strategic places around the ship to avoid detection by Icelandic Customs if they decided to come onboard and search once they arrived home. Once the authorities safely cleared them, they intended to smuggle the booze ashore and make a huge profit.

Well, their plans went awry because of our intervention, and they were none too happy. At the minimum, they were out $17,000 and could even face smuggling charges. I instructed one of our inspectors to go onboard the ship, find the captain, and bring him down to where we were. I wanted to bring him into the picture and to see what he had to say for himself. One of the crew who was involved in this enterprise objected to my requesting the presence of the captain. He told me the captain was asleep and we were not to wake him. I nodded to the inspector, and he took off to get the captain. After a lengthy wait, the captain finally arrived. He wasn't in a pleasant mood and didn't hesitate to tell me that he didn't appreciate being woken up in the middle of the night. I let the captain ramble on for quite a while, and when he finally ran out of steam, I addressed him. I told him that I couldn't care less about what he thought or if he was inconvenienced or not. His crew was involved in a major international booze smuggling scheme, and his ship was directly involved in the entire operation. His ship was subject to seizure, and the entire crew could possibly wind up in jail. I was stretching it a bit, but I wanted to humble him and to do it in front of his crew. The captain eventually saw the light and dramatically changed his attitude.

After countless phone calls to the Custom's lawyers; Fines, Penalties, and Forfeitures; and the port director, the decision was made to release the five crew members into the custody of the captain. The container with the booze would be sealed and babysat by us through the night. In the morning, a truck was scheduled to arrive to transport the booze to a Customs warehouse. As usual, it would be months before a final decision was made regarding this matter. For now, the booze would be safely stored away and, in all likely, would be destroyed. The ship would be held responsible for the crew members' actions and would be hit with a hefty fine. As regards to the crew, they would lose their seaman's visas and would never be able to sail in American waters again. All in all, it was a good seizure, but it would never had happened if we didn't receive that anonymous phone call.

As we drove back to the office, we reflected on the night's activities. We had a pretty successful night—a money seizure and a booze seizure. The money seizure was pretty standard, but the booze seizure was unique. As usual, everyone did an exemplary job, and we were all quite pleased with the results.

THIRTY EIGHT

A Man of Honor

One of the primary duties of the shift supervisor in the passenger processing area of Customs and Border Protection at Terminal E at Logan Airport is to constantly walk the floor and watch the officers do their job. Usually, everything runs pretty smoothly; but when things go awry, you are right there to assist. One day as I was walking around, I noticed an inspector filling out a seizure form. *That's funny*, I thought, because I didn't authorize any seizure, but maybe another supervisor did. I walked over to the inspector and asked him what was up. He looked at me with an incredulous look and said, "I'm seizing this box of Cuban cigars from this guy." *Oh yeah!* I thought. "Who authorized the seizure?" I inquired of the inspector. With this, the inspector began to stammer out a feeble explanation. He told me he thought it was OK, and after he was done with the paperwork, he was going to find me and ask permission to make the seizure. I upbraided the inspector and explained to him that he should seek permission to make a seizure before the fact and not afterward. He wasn't too appreciative of what I said, but I really didn't care. It has been a policy in effect for years that before anything is seized, a supervisor must approve of the action. This inspector was well versed in the policy but chose to disregard it. I didn't want to make a scene in front of the passenger; so I told the inspector we would talk later, and for now, I asked him to tell me the facts of the case.

The inspector told me it was pretty straightforward. The passenger, a U.S. citizen, was returning to America from overseas and was attempting to bring in a box of Cuban cigars. Since we had a total embargo on products from Cuba, this was verboten, and that is why he was attempting to seize the cigars. Everything the inspector said was true, but I decided to chat with the passenger to see what he had to say for himself.

This was a classic case of what you thought was going on was totally different from what really was happening. The guy that the inspector previously referred to was actually a major in the United States Marine Corps. He was stationed in Kuwait and was coming home to Illinois for a week to visit his elderly mother. As he was transiting through the airport in Zurich, he noticed some Cuban cigars for sale at one of the local shops. Being a lover of cigars and since the price was right, the major decided to buy the cigars. He was looking forward to doling out the cigars to his military friends in Kuwait and sitting back and enjoying a nice smoke with them once he returned from his visit to the States. Therefore, since the major wasn't really importing the cigars into the States but rather was only transiting the States with the cigars, I told him to repack the cigars into his bag and to be on his way. As the major was leaving, I shook his hand and thanked him for all that he was doing for our country. He thanked me for interceding on his behalf and assured me that the Cuban cigars would not be touched while he was in the States.

Well, the inspector that was hoping to seize the cigars went berserk. He couldn't believe I was doing what I was doing. Not only was I breaking the law—at least according to him—but I was also taking a seizure away from him. I tried to explain to this inspector that there was a difference between the letter of the law and the spirit of the law. Could we have seized these cigars? Absolutely! But why? Here was a guy that was a major in the United States Marine Corps and was serving his country overseas and had been for quite a few years. Yes, he was bringing Cuban cigars into the States, which is technically a violation of U.S. law; but he wasn't going to consume these cigars here and in fact would be exporting them when he left. "Couldn't we make an exception?" I asked this inspector. He retorted to my reasoning by sarcastically saying, "How do you know he will keep his word and not smoke the cigars here in America?" Well, with this, I couldn't hold back my emotions any longer. I told the inspector that unlike so many people of today, the major's word meant something to him; and unlike many people, the major would fight and even die to make sure his honor and integrity remained intact and unblemished. I really forget everything I said to this inspector, but I remember unloading a lot of venom and fire on his lowly soul; and I meant it then, and I mean it now. Here we have troops serving this country overseas, and all we want to do is bust their chops? Hell no, I say. We should be doing everything in our power to do just the opposite. We should be welcoming these guys and girls and do anything possible to make their homecoming as pleasant and seamless as possible. As for this inspector—the hell with him. I could talk to him all night, and he still wouldn't understand what I was talking about. He never had his face shoved in a pile of dung to know how sweet roses really do smell.

Bottom line, the major came in with his cigars, and I am sure he left with them in the exact same condition. I was glad to help the major out, and I was glad that I bit off a chunk of the inspector's backside. It should have been done a long time ago. I hope the major and his buddies back in Kuwait enjoyed the smoke, and I only have one regret regarding this entire incident—I wish I were with them to enjoy a fine smoke.

THIRTY NINE

A Woman's Wrath

T he weather today was exceptionally warm for the beginning of October. The temperature actually reached the low eighties in some places.

Last week, we had a woman come to see us at Terminal E at Logan Airport to tell us all about her ex-husband who, according to her, was scheduled to arrive on an international flight from Beirut via Paris in a couple of days. She told us her husband had threatened her life, had many illegal weapons in his house, and that he was somehow connected with Hezbollah in Lebanon. Frankly, the woman seemed credible and appeared to be genuinely in fear, but we also had it in the back of our minds that this woman could be a jilted lover and would do and say anything to give her ex a hard time. This wasn't the first time we received information from an ex, and nine times out of ten, it was all nonsense. However, something was different with this one. The woman seemed too sincere, too honest, and too reputable to be a fraud. Also, she actually came in person to make the report. Usually we receive information over the phone from an ex, and when we attempt to identify the caller, they insist on anonymity and hang up the phone.

Whatever, we thought, we would follow the lead to wherever it took us. A quick check of our airline databases did reveal that a man with the exact name that the woman gave us was arriving into Boston this weekend, and he was coming from Beirut. In fact, a woman who appeared to be his fiancée was accompanying him. She carried a Lebanese passport with a visa issued by the State Department indicating she was coming to America to be married. We thought, now we saw what was going on. This woman was probably incensed with her ex for dumping her and picking up a new wife overseas. Well, part of her story checked out. Now all we had to do was wait for this weekend to see if the information was credible or not.

Saturday morning dawned clear and crisp. It was a beautiful day to go fishing or simply a nice walk in the woods with the dog. No such luck for us. We were destined to spend the vast majority of the day within the confines of Terminal E. A check of the passenger manifest for the flight indicated that our subject and his fiancée were on the flight, and their ETA (estimated time of arrival) was in a little more than three hours away. While we were discussing the possibilities of this woman's information leading to anything of significance, a trooper from Troop F, the State Police troop located at Logan, walked into our office. A genial chap that we had worked with numerous times in the past, this visit was far from a social call. The trooper told us that they had received word from a local police department that they had an outstanding warrant for this guy that we were waiting for. It seems that this woman that came to us with the information also went to this local police department and gave them the same information. This local department was in the same town that the woman and her ex still lived in. Because of the severity of the woman's allegations, the local police department went to court and sought to obtain a search warrant from the local magistrate. Their attempt was successful, and a search of the ex's apartment revealed numerous handguns and shotguns that were in the ex's possession illegally. Based on the results of their search and on the woman's statements, the police obtained an arrest warrant for weapons charges and domestic abuse from the courts. Things were beginning to heat up.

About an hour before the flight arrived, three detectives from the local police department showed up at our office in Terminal E accompanied by a State Police detective. They had the warrant for this guy's arrest in hand and were anxious to snap him up. However, before they did, we had a few minor issues to address with this guy—like what was his connection with Hezbollah and what was the immigration status of his female companion. About fifteen minutes before the arrival of the flight, two other inspectors and I walked up to Gate 7A, the scheduled gate of arrival. We wanted to observe the passengers as they deplaned in order to identify our targets so we could keep a close eye on them. We knew what he looked like from the picture on the warrant, and we could also assume his companion would be by his side. Sure enough, after about half the passengers were off the plane, our targets exited the aircraft and began walking down the corridor to be processed into the country. We kept a constant, loose surveillance on them and never let them get out of our sight. He was a solidly built guy, about five feet and ten inches tall, weighed at least 250 pounds, about in his early forties and looked to be a tough guy. I could see how he could intimidate someone, especially his ex-wife. His lady friend was a diminutive, rather attractive (but surely not beautiful) young lady and appeared to be a lot younger than him. I remember thinking to myself, *I wonder if she really knows whom she is getting involved with?*

We waited patiently and let matters evolve in a routine manner. Once our targets were admitted into the country, they were directed down below to the baggage claim area. We were close on their heels. Once they claimed their baggage and began walking toward the exit, we committed ourselves. I stayed back and watched the two inspectors make the initial stop. They introduced themselves to our two passengers and then directed them over to one of the many baggage inspection belts that we have in the secondary inspection area. Now the fun would begin.

We had three areas of concern: the outstanding warrant, the Hezbollah connection, and the possible marriage fraud. The warrant was a simple matter to deal with. He was going to jail after we completed our inspection. The Hezbollah matter had to be developed. We thoroughly searched their bags and found "incriminating evidence relating to Hezbollah." The Hezbollah matter was addressed. The next issue was the potential marriage fraud. We found documents that verified that both of our passengers were legally divorced from their previous spouses. However, we also found some incriminating evidence to suggest that these two were already married: they had in their possession pictures showing the two of them exchanging marriage vows and posing with what looked like their parents; brand-new, shiny wedding bands on their fingers; him referring to her as "my wife" and then immediately correcting himself; and lastly, one of the inspectors who is fluent in Arabic overheard him telling her to "stick to our story and tell them we are not married." Based on these facts, we deemed the female passenger to be inadmissible. Remember, she was granted a visa so she could be married in America, but she was already married. Therefore, she was out of status and was inadmissible.

As the inspection began to wind down, our male passenger began to get pretty feisty. He demanded to know what was going on and why were we delaying them. His true disposition began to emerge from the shallow façade that he had maintained up to this point. He was real intimidating, and I could see how his ex-wife could be in real fear of him. Without further delay, I explained the facts to both of them. As I was talking, the local and State Police detectives came walking out of our office. The look on our passenger's face was one of incredulity. Up to this point, he didn't know the local police were on-site. When he saw them, he must have put everything together and realized he was in trouble. I explained to them that he was being put under arrest for weapons violations and domestic abuse and would be immediately escorted off to jail. We were detaining the "incriminating evidence" we found in the bags. The female was being ordered out of the country forthwith and would be put on an outbound plane within the hour. He became quite agitated when he realized his world was falling apart all around him. His fiancée/wife was going in one direction—Lebanon—and he was going in the other direction—jail. All of a sudden, he began to complain of chest pains. This is an often-used ruse whenever someone knows they are about to be carted off to jail, but you must take each incident as if it were for real. We immediately called for the airport EMTs and put everything on temporary hold. Well, at least six EMTs showed up, and they began to conduct all sorts of tests on our passenger. After at least forty-five minutes, the EMTs said he was fine; but if he wanted to go to the hospital, they would transport him. I think he realized he was postponing the inevitable and declined the EMTs' offer. He said he was feeling better and that he thought he would be OK. We allowed both passengers a couple of minutes to talk with each other—with us standing close by—and then told them it was time to go. He went with the local detectives to jail, and she went back on a plane to Lebanon

As of this writing, he is out on bail, but is facing some pretty severe charges. If the evidence we detained proves to be something, he will really be in some hot water. The fiancée/wife is back in Lebanon, and it hasn't been determined yet whether she will ever be allowed back into this country. This story can be seen as sad on one hand but heartwarming on the other. It is sad because we ripped the two apart from one another and caused a lot of angst. However, it is heartwarming because we took a threatening, intimidating individual off the street; and in so doing, maybe we protected at least a couple of women from bodily harm. The ex-wife surely knows he is dangerous, and perhaps our actions prevented his new wife from suffering the same fate as his first one. We hope so. All because of the courage and fortitude of one brave woman who had the guts to step up and demand that justice be done.

FORTY

The Bogus Baseballs

Perhaps one of the funniest stories to come out of the annals of Boston Customs involved Donald, a supervisory Customs inspector. Before I tell the story, I must give a brief background on Donald. He was in his late fifties at the time of this story and had over thirty years of government service. During this thirty years, Donald had learned every trick in the book, and he used every one of these tricks to his advantage whenever possible. Donald was one of the nicest guys around, and it sure was a pleasure working with him. Like I said, Donald knew how to take advantage of every situation; and he always, always benefited from the encounter—except once.

We were working the twelve-to-eight shift at Logan Airport. It was about five in the afternoon when we received word that the Boston Red Sox were scheduled to arrive in Boston from Toronto after tonight's game between the two teams. The time of arrival was of course only tentative, but midnight was a pretty good guess. Since we didn't have an overnight shift at that time, we had to assign an inspector to cover the arrival. As luck would have it, one of the newest inspectors, Billy, drew the plum assignment. He was going to have the opportunity to see the entire Red Sox team face-to-face. Billy was quite excited about the opportunity, and he was the envy of all the other inspectors.

The reader must be saying about now, "What does this have to do with Donald?" Well, my response to the reader is simple—everything. Donald, as usual, was figuring out how he could exploit this situation of the Red Sox arriving in Boston. And it wasn't long before Donald worked out his game plan. Donald walked up to the second level of Terminal E to the gift store. Once there, Donald bought himself two baseballs. With baseballs in hand, Donald returned to the Customs Hall and approached Billy. Donald told Billy in a rather stern tone that he expected Billy to have each Red Sox player sign both balls before they exited the Customs Hall. If not, Donald told Billy that it would be in his best interests not to show up for work the next day. In fact, Billy might as well find himself another job if he didn't comply with Donald's request. Billy, being a relatively new inspector, was intimidated by Donald. One of the older inspectors would have told Donald what he could do with the baseballs, but not Billy. Billy assured Donald that he would comply with his request, and all would go well. Donald told Billy that that was what he expected and left it at that.

Well, Billy was traumatized. He had no idea what to do. He asked everyone for help, and as expected, not too much was at hand. In fact just the opposite was happening. Everyone was giving Billy a hard time. They told him that if he didn't do exactly what Donald told him to do, Donald would probably have him fired. Of course, this was nonsense; but Billy, being a father of two little kids, couldn't take the chance. As the evening progressed, Billy realized that the only thing he could do was comply with Donald's request. He had no other alternative if he wanted to keep his job.

Shortly after midnight, the Red Sox arrived at Terminal E to be cleared by U.S. Customs. As they deplaned and entered the Customs Hall, Billy was standing by to clear them into the country. He was spellbound when he saw all the players. Sure, he had seen them on TV before, but not up close and personal like this. Simply put, Billy was intimidated by the situation. As the players approached Billy with their Baggage Declaration in hand, he totally forgot about the baseballs that Donald wanted signed. He was so awestruck and overwhelmed by the mere presence of the players that he had everything he could do just to process the team. Before Billy knew it, the entire team was cleared, and all the players had exited the hall. Once again, Billy was alone in the Customs Hall. This is when it struck him. *Holy cockeyed Marie!* Billy thought, *I forgot to have the players sign Donald's balls.* Billy was devastated. All he could think of was what Donald was going to do to him in the morning. He might not even have a job if it was up to Donald. Billy was scared, confused, and despondent as he left the Customs Hall to go home. He wasn't sure what was going to happen in the morning, but he knew he was in a lot of trouble. Needless to say, Billy spent a restless night in bed constantly bouncing about and thinking what was in store for him. *Why didn't I get the balls signed?* Billy kept asking himself.

Come the next morning as the inspectors arrived for the morning shift, a few of them noticed that Billy seemed quite aloof and standoffish. Kevin, a seasoned inspector of many years, asked Billy if anything was the matter. Initially, Billy said everything was OK; but shortly thereafter, he spilled his guts. He told Kevin how Donald had ordered him to have the two balls signed by all the Red Sox players. But because he was confused, intimidated, overwhelmed, or whatever, he didn't have either ball signed by any of the players. At first, Kevin gave Billy a hard time and told him that Donald would skin him alive. However, after Kevin saw how distraught Billy was, he let up on him. He told Billy to calm down and to relax because they would figure something out. Billy was beside himself. *What the hell could they figure out?* he thought. He was supposed to have the stupid baseballs signed, and he didn't do it—plain and simple. Suddenly Kevin's head jerked up, and he asked Billy if he had the morning Herald. *Sure,* Billy thought, *I am in a world of trouble, and all Kevin wants to do is read the morning newspaper.*

Eventually they found a copy of the Herald, and Kevin revealed his plan to Billy. Kevin turned to the sports page and showed Billy a copy of the Red Sox roster. "All these names were supposed to be on the balls, right?" he asked Billy. Billy grudgingly concurred but was confused about Kevin's intentions. Then Kevin dropped the bombshell. He told Billy that all they had to do is get a whole bunch of different pens, and the two of them could write the names of all the players on both balls themselves. There was no way that Donald would ever know that the players really didn't sign them. Billy's eyes lit up, but then he thought, *What if Donald found out what they did?* Kevin explained to Billy that it was up to the two of them to make sure Donald never did find out. Slowly Billy warmed to Kevin's devious plan, and the two of them began signing both balls. After less than one half hour, their task was complete. They were sure that Donald would be ecstatic when he came in for work.

Sure enough, as soon as Donald reported to work, he sought out Billy and asked him where the balls were. Billy reached into his bag and produced two well-signed balls. Well, you should have seen the look on Donald's face. He had an ear-to-ear smile and was giggling like a teenager. From seeing Donald's reaction, Billy took a deep breath and began to relax a bit. Donald gave Billy a perfunctory thank-you and walked away with his balls in his hands. He was much satisfied.

And that is how the story stands to this day. Donald has retired to sunny Florida where on his mantle he has prominently displayed two glass-encased balls signed by all the "Red Sox players." He loves to show them to guests and regales them with stories how he has personally met and talked with all the old Red Sox players. His guests are usually awestruck and ask Donald to tell them stories about his encounters with the players. Donald, a natural-born storyteller, immediately complies with some off-the-cuff story. We all hope that Donald enjoys these baseballs to his final days and only hope that he never shows them to someone who recognizes the autographs to be forgeries. If that day ever comes, God help Billy.

FORTY ONE

Youran's Flight to Freedom

Saturday, February 10, was a long day for me. I had driven up to my son's house in Sanford, Maine, from my house in Norwood, Massachusetts, the night before. I wanted to go to my grandson Liam's basketball game early Saturday morning. Because I had to drive back to Boston's Logan Airport to go to work that afternoon, I wanted to split up the driving between the two days. But sleeping on the couch was the price I had to pay, and it didn't help my disposition any when I awoke in the morning. Before the game, Liam, Mike, and I went down to the Home Plate for breakfast. Then we enjoyed a basketball game between the kids in town; Liam's team even won. After the game, I immediately headed out. It was at least a two-hour drive to Logan, and I didn't want to be late.

My shift, four to midnight, was turning out to be quite uneventful; but what do they say about the quiet before the storm? It was almost midnight, and we were processing the last remaining passengers from the last flight arrival. Then I heard Craig's voice calling my name over the radio. Craig, a rather new supervisor but quite competent, asked me if I could meet him at the bottom of the escalator on the main floor of the CBP (Customs and Border Protection) hall. I answered in the affirmative and proceeded down below. When I arrived, I was met by Craig and Anthony. Craig began to fill me in on what was going on. At the E&C window (the area where the public comes to transact business with CBP at Logan), there were four Asians with a serious problem. According to them, they were concerned about a Chinese girl that was on a school trip here in America. They feared she was kidnapped. When Craig told me this, I know I rolled my eyes and thought to myself that we were in for a long night. After Craig gave me the generalities of their story, I suggested that we go talk with them face-to-face. Upon the first encounter, I was quite impressed by the demeanor of the entire group. They were well-spoken, sincere, and quite articulate. Lana, the unofficial spokesperson of the group, introduced herself to me and told me she was an attorney for a human rights group. She introduced a Mr. Erping and told me he was a spokesperson for the same human rights group. Then she introduced me to Xiufen, the aunt of the girl that might have been kidnapped. Lastly, Lana introduced Kangang, a friend of the aunt. Everyone spoke fluent English except for the aunt. In fact, everyone was a U.S. citizen except for the aunt. She held a permanent residence card (green card). After talking with the group and getting a general feel of the situation, I decided we had best adjourn to the conference room where we could talk in private. Just in the first few minutes of talk, I realized this situation could be serious and could have international and human rights implications, not to mention the life and safety of a fourteen-year-old girl.

Once we arrived at the conference room, Craig and I offered everyone bottles of water and showed them where the facilities were located. I remember looking into their eyes and saw their desperation and concern. I still wasn't completely aware of the totality of the situation, but even then, I knew that I was going to do everything humanly possible to help these folks.

As we settled in, I pulled out a pad of paper and grabbed a pen. Once everyone appeared to be comfortable, I suggested that they start from the beginning and tell me the entire story about this "kidnapped fourteen-year-old Chinese girl." Over the next hour, the entire story unfolded before us.

Back on January 30, a group of Chinese kids left China for a tour of schools in America. There were thirty-eight kids in the group, and they were accompanied by several chaperones. The plan was to tour the West Coast first and then come east. Princeton, West Point, MIT, Harvard, and Yale were on their itinerary. The girl in question, Youran, was a member of this group; but her plans were not quite like all the others. According to the attorney, Lana, Youran, and her parents were members of Fulan Gong. I was only vaguely aware of this name, but Lana and Erping explained that it was somewhat like a religious organization that was frowned upon by the

YOURAN'S FLIGHT TO FREEDOM

Chinese Communist Party. In fact, in China, the members of Fulan Gong were imprisoned, tortured, killed; and their body parts were sold on the international market. Supposedly, while Youran and her schoolmates were on this tour, the Communist authorities found out that Youran and her parents were members of this prohibited society. When Youran went home, the Communists would be waiting for her at the airport and planned on arresting her. This is where the aunt comes into the picture. Youran's parents contacted the aunt at her home in New Jersey and told her that she had to intercept Youran on her tour and tell her not to come home. They advised the aunt to tell her to claim political asylum. To facilitate this process, the parents of Youran e-mailed power of attorney over her to the aunt.

Armed with this information, the aunt and her male friend who spoke fluent English reviewed the itinerary of the group and decided that West Point would be the best place to make contact with Youran.

On the afternoon of Saturday the tenth of February, Youran's aunt and her friend were waiting at McDonald's in Highland Falls, New York, for her arrival. McDonald's was right outside of the gate to the only entrance to West Point; therefore, they were sure to meet Youran. After a few hours' wait, the aunt's dreams came true; she saw Youran walk down the steps of a big white bus. Immediately, the aunt went to Youran and took possession of her. This is when everything became confusing. Youran's aunt was attempting to put Youran into a car, and the chaperones were attempting to retrieve Youran and put her back on the bus. People on the street saw what was going on, and believing it was some kind of child abduction, they called the police. Shortly thereafter, a couple of Highland Falls police cruisers were on the scene. A few minutes after that, the chief of police arrived. The police attempted to sort out the confusion, but the aunt didn't do well in explaining. When the police asked her why they should allow Youran to be taken off the bus and put into the aunt's custody, the aunt said something like "that is the way it should be." Well, that wasn't good enough for the police. They couldn't see any reason to take Youran away from the group and in fact were reassured by the chaperones that everything was all right. If the aunt had shown the police her power of attorney letter, things might have been different, but she didn't. Consequently, Youran was put back on the bus, and the school group was allowed to proceed on their way. The aunt's efforts to free Youran had been thwarted, at least for now. As these events were being related to Craig and me, I glanced over at the aunt sitting at the table. Her head was down, but I could see that she was crestfallen. If she had only done things a little differently, maybe Youran would have been free. Trying to make the aunt feel a little better, I said something like, "Let's not worry about the past, and let's look to the future." This seemed to brighten the aunt's spirits a bit.

So that is how this group happened to be before us at the conference room at Logan airport at one o'clock Sunday morning. They failed to free Youran in New York, and they wanted to attempt another try at the school group's next stop—MIT and Harvard. As the aunt and her friend drove into the Boston area, they called Lana and Erping and asked for their help. They met somewhere in the Boston area, and not knowing really what to do, they came to the airport where they knew they could find some government officials. Craig and I were those government officials.

After hearing the whole story, I knew the implications of this story were big. Not only were there international political ramifications, but there were also possible human rights abuses. I have been in the government long enough to know when you should kick something up to your superiors, and this is exactly what Craig and I did. We called a chief inspector of the airport, the ICE duty agent through Sector, and NTC (National Targeting Center) for help and guidance. NTC was the most helpful. They agreed with us that probably the best thing to do was to post an outbound lookout for Youran. We knew from Lana that Youran and the rest of the group were scheduled to depart from New York on Tuesday, so we felt somewhat comfortable with this course of action.

However, when we told Lana and Erping our intentions, they vehemently disagreed. "Don't you understand?" they said. The itinerary of the group—at least for Youran—would not remain the same. The Chinese government knew there were people in America trying to grab her, and they would do everything in their power to prevent this. Lana told us that she was sure that Youran would be taken out of the country before Tuesday, and if this happened, Youran would definitely be arrested when she returned to China. After her arrest, she would be imprisoned, tortured, and maybe even killed. This is why everyone was so intent on finding Youran as soon as possible. This really struck home with me. We had the fate of a fourteen-year-old girl in our hands! It is funny what goes through your mind while under stress. All I could think of was the incident that happened over thirty years ago of a Lithuanian seaman, Simanas Kidurka, who jumped from a Russian trawler to a U.S. Coast Guard ship while the two vessels were moored up together off the island of Nantucket, Massachusetts, engaged in fishery talks. Because of a communications breakdown between the Coast Guard ship, Coast Guard Group Boston, the State Department, and Coast Guard Headquarters in Washington, the Russians were allowed to board the U.S. Coast Guard vessel on the high seas and forcibly removed Kidurka from the Coast Guard vessel and took him back to the Russian ship. Afterward, the Coast Guard admitted they acted unwisely; but it was too late, Kidurka was back in Russia. I was determined that this would not happen to Youran.

Then I had an idea. Why didn't Lana and her group go to the Cambridge Police Department and file a missing person report with them. We knew the next scheduled stop for the school group was supposed to be Harvard and MIT (both in the city of Cambridge), and maybe they could find the "big white bus" and determine where the students were. Then they could find out if Youran was indeed gone, or if we were all worrying for nothing. Everyone thought this was a good idea, and thinking of nothing else that we could do, we parted company about five in the morning. I actually prayed for Youran's safety and hoped for some good news. In this hope, I gave Lana and Erping my cell phone number and told them to call me with any news or if they needed any assistance.

I finally got home about six Sunday morning. I took a nice hot shower, jumped into bed (more like crawled), and was soon fast asleep. About nine in the morning, my wife was waking me to tell me someone was on the phone and was insisting that he talk to me. My wife said she couldn't really understand the guy, but it sounded urgent. Well, it was Erping, and he had some good news but also terrible news. The Cambridge Police found the bus and found out where the school group was staying. When they did a head count of all the students and chaperones, they realized that Youran was missing along with two chaperones. Our worst fears were realized. Between nine in the morning and noon, I was on and off the phone talking with everyone concerned with this matter. Finally, even though I didn't have to be at work until four in the afternoon, I decided to head in early. I wasn't really sure what I could do, but at least at work, I had a better chance of doing something. After all, a little girl's freedom, and maybe even her life, was at stake.

During the next couple of hours, not much materialized. However, at precisely 2:59 PM, Lana called me and told me that she had just received an anonymous phone call. The caller told Lana that Youran was on a China Airlines flight at JFK Airport that was due to depart at three-thirty in the afternoon—only half an hour away. The two missing chaperones were with Youran, and supposedly she had a lot of makeup on to disguise her real identity. The anonymous caller said that the Chinese consulate was orchestrating this whole thing. Lana kept talking, but I had enough information to act on and not much time. I told Lana I had to go and I would call her. Then I called JFK's Outbound Team. I got in touch with an officer named Meese and told him quickly what was going on. He immediately picked up on what I was telling him and promised me that they would get right down to the plane. I hung up the phone and could do nothing else but wait. Finally after about thirty minutes or so, Meese called me. *They found* Youran!

Immediately, tears started flowing down my cheeks. I was so, so happy I just unabashedly started to cry. Perhaps it was because I was so tired and the emotions of the past twelve hours just overwhelmed me. Anyway, I couldn't care. Youran was freed. After I regained my composure, Meese filled me in on what happened. CBP officers, led by a supervisor named Sal, boarded the China Airlines plane minutes before they were scheduled to depart. A search of the aircraft resulted in finding Youran and the two chaperones. All three were escorted off the aircraft under CBP custody and escorted to a CBP office in JFK.

Events unfolded rather quickly after that. A call to the U.S. Attorney's Office was made along with a lot of other calls. Lana was informed of the good news, and she said they were en route to JFK Airport. I guess they were already headed back to New Jersey where they lived and only had to divert a little from their initial course. Meese told me that once they arrived, power of attorney was substantiated, and the legal guardianship of the aunt was established. Therefore, Youran was released into the custody of the aunt. As for the chaperones, the FBI was looking into the possibility of prosecution if complicity could be established. If the chaperones were unwittingly being used, they would be let go. Meese also told me that Youran had been granted refugee status by the Department of State. All this was fine with me, but all I really cared about was that she was free and would be able to live a long and healthy life here in America. For the rest of the day, I received countless calls from Lana, Erping, and the aunt and even Youran thanking me for all that we had done. These calls were understandable but totally unnecessary. Youran's freedom was thanks enough. I went home that night one happy man, and I am still happy today.

When I returned to work the next day, there was a big flower arrangement waiting for me. Youran's aunt and uncle wanted to express their thanks for all that we had done. Also when I read my e-mail, Youran and her aunt and uncle sent me messages of thanks. These messages were so touching, and I will cherish them forever. Someday, I hope to meet Youran and give her a big hug. Until then, I only thank the Lord that we were able to do what we did.

Postscript

August 29, 2007

Today I was able to give Youran that big hug. In fact, I gave her a couple of big hugs. Youran and her uncle drove up from New York to visit me and my family this morning. They could only spend a few hours with us because Sam, the uncle, had to get back home; but we had a great time nonetheless. Two of my granddaughters, Shannon and Meghan, were at my house with us; and they got along famously with Youran. The three girls played Hula-hoop and Wiffle ball and swung on the swings in the backyard. My wife, Donna, made a big meal of chicken, rice, and salad that we all enjoyed eating while sitting out on the patio. Sam and Youran brought many presents for us, and we in return presented several gifts to Youran.

Youran is a bright young lady with a constant smile on her face. Her English is improving daily, and she radiates warmth and happiness. As I looked at her, all I could think of was what almost happened to her a mere few months ago. Sam is a diligent worker and spokesperson for Falun Dafa. He has dedicated his life to this cause and works seven days a week promoting the human rights movement. An extremely articulate speaker, he was a joy to converse with that afternoon. The only thing that dampened my spirits was the news about Youran's parents back home in Beijing. Youran's mother is missing from her home, and no one seems to know where she is. Obviously, it is suspected the Communist Party of China (CPC) has something to do with her disappearance. Youran's father is still at home, but it is reported that he is under constant surveillance.

12/02/2007

Dear Mr. Cunningham,

I want to say "Thank you very much" to you in person, but now I can only tell you it through the Internet so that you can hear from me instantly.

You have saved my life and I am so happy to be a free person and to be with my Aunt and Uncle finally. My Aunt told me about your hard work over the days and nights to make the rescue a success. I am very grateful to you for rescuing me from the kidnapping. If it were not for you, I would now end up somewhere in China and may never be found again.

I want to say you are the best officer in the United States of America and I want to see you soon in the future.

Lots of love

Youran
14 Year Old Student

2/12/2007

Michael H. Cunningham
Supervisory CBP Officer
U.S.Department of Homeland Security
Logan International AIRPORT

Dear Mr. Cunningham,

My wife and I would like to express our heartfelt gratitude to you for the all the immense help you extended to Youran, our niece who was kidnapped for as long as two days in the states of New Jersey, Massachusetts and New York. We are delighted to let you know Youran is now with our family safe and sound.

We are deeply moved by your big heart, your extraordinary effort, and your professionalism at work. Your support for human rights and Falun Gong practitioners will be kindly and long remembered by Youran, her parents, and us.

The family is looking forward to having an opportunity to meet with you in the nearest future to thank you in person and to share with you the happiness of our re-union. Please do let us know if you ever come to New York city. And we will be in touch soon.

Warmest regards,

Sam (Youran's Uncle)

Xiufen (Youran's Aunty)

E-mails of appreciation from Youran and her relatives

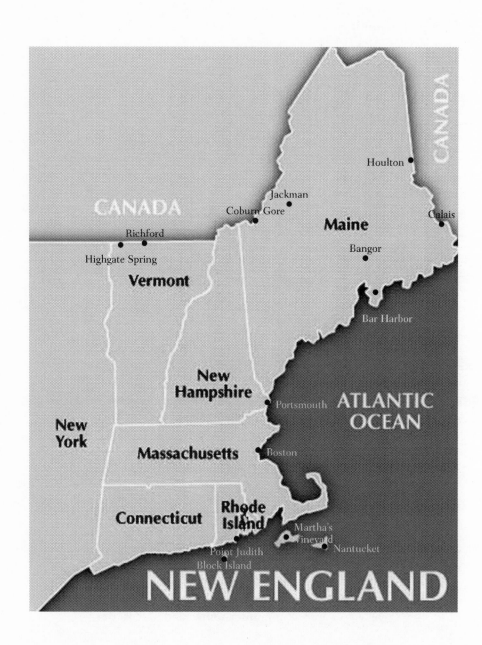